Dead for Good

Martyrdom and the Rise of the Suicide Bomber

Hugh Barlow

WITHDRAWN

Paradigm Publishers

Boulder • London

Copyright © 2007 by Paradigm Publishers.

Published in the United States by Paradigm Publishers, 3360 Mitchell Lane, Suite E, Boulder, CO 80301 USA.

Paradigm Publishers is the trade name of Birkenkamp & Company, LLC, Dean Birkenkamp, President and Publisher.

Library of Congress Cataloging-in-Publication Data

Barlow, Hugh D.
  Dead for good : martyrdom and the rise of the suicide bomber / Hugh Barlow.
    p. cm.
  Includes bibliographical references and index.
  ISBN-13: 978-1-59451-324-4 (hardcover : alk. paper)
  ISBN-10: 1-59451-324-4 (hardcover : alk. paper)
  ISBN-13: 978-1-59451-325-1 (pbk. : alk. paper)
  ISBN-10: 1-59451-325-2 (pbk. : alk. paper)
  1. Martyrdom—History.   2. Violence—Social aspects—History.   I. Title.
  BL626.5.B37 2007
  363.325'12—dc22

                    2006011991

Printed and bound in the United States of America on acid-free paper that meets the standards of the American National Standard for Permanence of Paper for Printed Library Materials.

Designed and typeset by Straight Creek Bookmakers.

11 10 09 08 07 1 2 3 4 5

To the memory of Karen Brown

Contents

Acknowledgments

I began research on this book in the fall of 2002, quite unaware that breast cancer would soon take the life of my wife, Karen Brown. She died on September 8, 2004. Karen had encouraged me to write this book and continued to do so during her illness, thinking as usual not of herself but of others. She read every page of the developing manuscript, and her insights were invaluable. There is no way I can adequately put in words all that she meant to me.

Many colleagues and friends read parts of the book, two the entire manuscript: Alice Hall Petry, professor of English language and literature, and Jerry Runkle, emeritus professor of philosophy. I am very grateful for their helpful suggestions, and I hope the end result contains none of the errors they uncovered. I am also thankful for the help and encouragement of John Farley, Steven Fulk, David Kauzlarich, Linda Markowitz, Mike Mikhayel, Danny O'Malley, Matt Petrocelli, Lisa Romanowski, Carl Springer, Stephen Tamari, Albert Thompson, and Reem Younis. Other friends I would like to thank for their support and encouragement are Steve and Suzie Castleberry, Doyle Featherston, John and Shirlee Gentles, and Eric Rhein.

It has been a pleasure to work with Dean Birkenkamp and Leslie Lomas of Paradigm Publishers. The copyediting of Julie Kirsch helped make this a much better book.

I owe Colette Biano a special debt for her love, understanding, and timely support as the final chapters took shape.

My children are an inspiration, and now that I am a grandpa, I appreciate all the more the contributions they make to my life. Thank you (in alphabetical order), Alison, Chelsea, Colin, Eric, Kelsey, and Melissa.

Introduction

At 8:46 on the morning of September 11, 2001, the world changed. Mohamed Atta had just flown an American Airlines Boeing 767 passenger jet into the North Tower of the World Trade Center in New York City. It was 7:46 where I live, and I had one eye on NBC's *Today Show* as I prepared to leave for work. Stunned by what I saw and heard, I fell into a chair and didn't leave it for hours.

As the months passed and cleanup continued in New York City and at the Pentagon outside Washington, D.C., my thoughts turned to Atta and the eighteen men who had executed the world's most daring and destructive suicide attack. It turned out that all were Muslims, and fifteen hailed from Saudi Arabia. The mastermind, however, was Kuwait-born Khalid Sheikh Mohammed, a senior al-Qaeda field commander whose nephew, Ramzi Yousef, had tried to blow up the World Trade Center with a truck bomb in 1993. Neither had participated in the actual attacks on 9/11, which al-Qaeda leaders called the "Planes Operation."

The suicide-hijackers were hailed as martyrs by some fellow Muslims but most condemned them as evildoers and betrayers of Islam. Around the world, people simply referred to them as terrorists, but with a difference. These al-Qaeda operatives had killed themselves in order to kill others. They died to kill—literally. And some people praised them for it. That was hard to understand.

1

This was not the first time al-Qaeda had used "suicide terrorists," nor would it be the last. And al-Qaeda wasn't the
only group to send killers to their deaths on behalf of a cause.
Militant Palestinian groups were using suicide bombers in
the conflict with Israel, and the tactic had been adopted by
the Tamil Tigers fighting for independence in Sri Lanka. Nor
was this the first time the United States had been attacked
by suicide terrorists. Back in 1983, the militant Islamic group
Hezbollah, "Party of God," had blown up the U.S. embassy in
Beirut, Lebanon, and soon afterward American and French
military barracks. Then, in August 1998, al-Qaeda used trucks
laden with explosives to blow up the U.S. embassies in Nairobi,
Kenya, and Dar es Salaam, Tanzania. These attacks killed 231
people, including twelve Americans, and wounded thousands.
Two years later, a boat filled with explosives rammed the USS
Cole off the coast of Yemen. Seventeen American sailors were
killed in this al-Qaeda suicide attack.

Even so, 9/11 stood out for a variety of reasons: the number killed—almost three thousand; the fact that most of the
dead were civilians; the method used—turning passenger
planes into bombs; the devastation left when the Twin Towers collapsed; the financial cost of the operation to al-Qaeda,
the United States, and ultimately, the world; the degree of
planning and preparation involved in these attacks, including
flight training in the United States and FAA certification of four
pilots; the time between origination and consummation of the
plan—well over two years; the fact that this was the first successful attack on U.S. soil by a foreign organization; and the
fact that it was the first destructive attack on the Pentagon.
Finally, and perhaps most significantly, the attack did not
come as a complete surprise to American intelligence services:
Osama bin Laden had declared war on America five years earlier, and he had already ordered suicide attacks against the
United States abroad. Intelligence agencies expected an attack
on U.S. soil but were uncertain as to where, when, and how.
Even so, in its 2004 report, the 9/11 Commission concluded
that the United States should have been much better prepared
for a devastating attack using suicide terrorists.

If al-Qaeda picked its targets on 9/11 for maximum effect, it
could not have done much better. In a taped conversation shortly
afterward, Osama bin Laden observed that the collapse of the

Twin Towers was unexpected icing on the cake. And pointing to a surge of interest in his religion and many reported conversions, he also said that the martyrs had done a great job for Islam.

The talk of martyrdom and religion in a terrorist context fascinated me. Although one person's terrorist is another's freedom fighter—it's all a matter of perspective—everyone I talked with and most of what I read did not consider the hijackers to be martyrs. Aren't martyrs people who voluntarily die for the Good? These guys looked more like psychotic fanatics. How could martyrdom be consistent with terrorism, I wondered? And how could either advance the interests of a religion? Even though Muslims were implicated in many of the suicide attacks, is religious extremism a necessary element in suicide terrorism? More to the point, is there something about Islam that promotes martyrdom in general and suicide terrorism in particular? And why did so many commentators speak of the "martyr's smile"? What is there to smile about when you are going to self-destruct and kill women and children in the process?

I decided to look more deeply into these questions. As I dug through scholarly literature, popular writings, newspaper and magazine articles, and myriad Web sites, I began to see that I needed to journey back into history, a long way back. People and events have biographies, but so do ideas and beliefs. Even though 9/11 had distinctive qualities and was certainly the most spectacular suicide attack yet carried out, I could see that it shared some qualities with other attacks while representing a type of martyrdom not seen before the 1980s. I call this latest type *predatory* martyrdom. But most important, 9/11 appeared to share a common history with less predatory forms of martyrdom.

The idea and practice of martyrdom began somewhere; I decided to work up from the beginning of written history to see if I could pinpoint the important developments and transitions that might have a bearing on our understanding of the 9/11 attacks. This book is the result of that effort. I have written it for people like me who are struggling to comprehend how the world got to a place like this.

I cover nearly three thousand years of human history, quite clumsily and superficially but I hope without undue distortion.

During the twentieth century, and especially in the past twenty years, the documentation of events became a living history, with participants' own words recorded on audiotape, computer disks, or film, the last two sometimes capturing their actions as well. For the distant past, and for many centuries in between, history is made up of stories and legends. What "really" happened is often a matter of speculation, but the stories people pass on become the truths for the next generation and influence what they think and do. I present these stories as evidence of emerging ideas in changing times, but I do not necessarily believe that they actually happened.

Readers may notice that in the next twelve chapters I only use the word *terrorist* or *terrorism* if I am quoting or paraphrasing someone else. In my research, it quickly became clear that martyrdom always occurs in the context of perceived persecution, exploitation, or oppression. Martyrs are people who sacrifice themselves for a cause that is highly valued but seen as threatened, denied, or exploited by others. "A death conceived as martyrdom turns what looks like defeat into victory," writes anthropologist Cynthia Mahmood. "The individual died, but in his or her bloody witness the truth lives on; the individual died, but the community to which he or she was linked continues."[1] The cause is sacred to the martyr even if it has no specific religious connotation. The cause is always the Good, even if others think it is bad, evil, or simply wrong. The Evil in the martyr's mind is the perceived source of the persecution, exploitation, or oppression that is experienced. In giving up their lives, martyrs make the ultimate sacrifice for Good, and this is recognized and rewarded as such by people who share in the cause.

The destructiveness of "suicide terrorism" might suggest that predatory martyrdom is different. It is not. The 9/11 hijackers gave their lives to their sacred cause, a cause they also served by attacking the perceived source of the Evil. In a sense, the expected value of their sacrifice is increased because Evil itself is targeted by their actions. While observers may wonder about the "benefit" or "instrumentality" of more passive forms of martyrdom (I will show that benefits are expected in *all* forms of martyrdom), they would surely not argue that the 9/11 hijackers saw their sacrifice as an end in itself. They expected something else to result from it—fear among the enemy, certainly, and eventually the restoration of their version of the Good. And they also expected personal rewards, among them eternal bliss in Paradise.

I acknowledge the aggression of predatory martyrs—those who die willingly for their cause through the indiscriminate killing of others—by using such words as *attack* and *murder.* Even though one of the motivations for and consequences of suicide attacks is to instill fear among the enemy, the word *terrorist* has such a negative connotation that it is impossible to associate it with anything good. Yet I believe it is crucial for Westerners, particularly Americans, to try to understand suicide attacks from the vantage point of those carrying them out. Solutions to the conflicts that give rise to predatory martyrdom will come only with that understanding. A few years ago my colleague Steve Tamari made the same point in an Op-Ed piece on the Israeli–Palestinian conflict he titled "Americans Need to Know Palestinian History."[2] And we cannot begin to appreciate the perceived experience of persecution and oppression, unless we step into the martyrs' shoes. I have tried to do that, even at the risk of offending some readers.

In order to convey something of the pain and suffering that are the backdrop if not the cause of martyrdom, I have largely taken a narrative approach to history, believing also that this would make for more interesting reading. My historical journey to understand better the idea and practice of martyrdom has led to this conclusion: While the suicide attacks of today share a common thread with all forms of martyrdom, they represent the latest, and perhaps last, iteration along a path that split off from the one originating in antiquity. The split happened with the birth of Islam nearly fifteen hundred years ago.

As we investigate the course of martyrdom in the chapters that follow, we will visit the Jews of antiquity, the early Christians and their Roman tormentors, the Prophet Muhammad and the rise of Islam, the warrior-martyrs of the Crusades, the Khalsa Sikhs of the Punjab in India, the kamikaze pilots of World War II, the Tamil Tigers of Sri Lanka, and, finally, the predatory martyrs spawned by the conflict between Israel and their Arab neighbors and by the actions of Western governments, represented most recently by the American-led invasion of Iraq.

Some readers may wonder why I do not include some of history's most famous martyrs. Joan of Arc comes to mind, or the elderly Buddhist monk Thich Quang Duc, who on June 2, 1963, calmly sat down on the main street of Saigon, poured gasoline over himself, and burned himself alive. His self-immolation was captured on film and caused an outcry around the world. It is one of the most powerful and unforgettable images of the U.S. era in Vietnam.

I do not discuss these cases partly because they *are* so famous—I thought it would be more interesting to share stories of martyrdom that would be less well-known—but more importantly because they didn't add anything to the overall picture taking shape. That picture shows an evolution in the idea and practice of martyrdom over the past three thousand years: The active submission of individuals to suffering and death as witness to a personal cause became eventually a group-supported act of witness and then diverged along two paths, one of which is primarily instrumental, organized, and policy-driven. That path led to 9/11. Along the way, ideas about the legitimacy and value of martyrdom were manipulated by religious and political developments and honed through the fearful experiences of persecution, exploitation, and war.

Of course once martyrdom becomes group-based, questions naturally arise about the role of leaders versus followers. Leaders sometimes promote their own martyrdom but more often they provide rank-and-file members with the intellectual and emotional incentives for self-sacrifice. In this way leaders encourage and corroborate suicidal decisions on behalf of the group. Sometimes this encouragement and corroboration give rise to a cult of martyrdom, as in the early Christian church and, some say, among radical Islamic groups today. Needless to say, the type of martyrdom promoted in this way will vary by its historical and evolutionary context. Yet leaders are amazingly consistent over time in their articulation of at least one potential group benefit from the martyrdom of their followers: "The blood of Christians is seed," wrote the North African theologian and Christian convert Tertullian around 200 CE.[3] This argument is reiterated time and again by leaders of campaigns where self-sacrifice is a dominant theme.

Our journey into the idea and practice of martyrdom begins on a relatively quiet and peaceful note: a brief visit with Socrates in the final moments of his life. Ancient Greece is an appropriate place to begin because the word *martyr* originates in the Greek *martur,* or "witness." I believe that Plato's account of Socrates' death gives important clues to the character of martyrdom at the beginning of its long journey through written history.

Part I

The Martyrs of Antiquity

The condemned man waved the women and children from the room. He asked the servant to fetch the jailer, who soon came in bearing a cup of hemlock. The man took the cup from the jailer's hand. The gathered friends protested and begged the old man to delay, but he would not. He cheerfully downed the poison and called on the gods to hasten his passage to the next world. Heeding the jailer's advice, the old man walked around to speed the poison's work. When his legs grew heavy he lay down, pulling the bedsheet about him. As death grew near, he pulled the sheet over his face.

So died Socrates, dignified and in charge. The place was Athens, Greece, in the year 399 BCE. Here was a man accused of corrupting young minds and showing irreverence to the gods, a crime punishable by death. A respectful and contrite demeanor might have saved him, but a defiant Socrates purposely chided and embarrassed the jury. He reminded them of their own ignorance and their misguided pursuit of wealth rather than truth. The jury pronounced Socrates guilty and sentenced him to death. Although Athenian law allowed the condemned to request exile, Socrates rejected that alternative. There was no dignity in it, and, besides, he had lived his life in Athens so Athens was where he would die. Even when his friend and disciple Crito offered to arrange his escape, Socrates refused to save himself. It was his time to die, or the gods would have given him a sign.

To many in the power elite of Athens, Socrates had long been an intellectual pest and a political liability, a thorn in the side of those favored by the status quo. The poet Meletus was among them, and it was Meletus who eventually authored the charges against Socrates. In the words of historian Lacey Baldwin Smith, all the props necessary for his arrest and conviction were there: personal animosity, civic paranoia, and political revenge.[1] A recent plague, costly wars, political intrigue, and growing social unrest had been sapping the strength of the great city and threatening its security. Its leaders found a convenient scapegoat in the annoying and blasphemous old philosopher.

Yet as Socrates himself admitted, he had made no attempt to appease his enemies; quite the contrary, in fact. As he had for forty years, he continued to challenge prevailing doctrine and scoffed at the intellectual abilities of its defenders. He likened himself to a pesky horsefly appointed by the gods to arouse, persuade, and reprove the citizens of Athens. During his defense he advised jurors to spare him, not for his sake but for their own: "If you put me to death, you will not easily find anyone to take my place."[2] Even though Socrates called the trial an "accident," he knew that sooner or later the law would be used against him. He did not expect the jury to heed his advice, and he told them so. As his final hours approached, Socrates was cool, a seventy-year-old sage ready for death and "the joys of the blessed" in the next world.

In Plato's writings about Socrates' life and death we see elements that will become defining features of martyrdom in antiquity. One theme is found in the seemingly contradictory idea that a martyr's death is both active and passive. Socrates had a direct hand in the events leading to his death, a result that he anticipated and accepted. He even shaped how death itself played out, manipulating the actions of adversaries and friends alike. At the end he chose a dignified, even contented, submission to the inevitable: no resistance, no flight. Socrates also suggested that the gods would have intervened if his death were not meant to be. They would not have let their servant die unless the time was right. So perhaps there was a divine hand and purpose in his death.

Active submission and notions of divine will and purpose were not the only themes elaborated by martyrdom in antiquity. Unlike the elderly Socrates, most martyrs of antiquity faced a terrifying death, usually preceded by torture. The martyrs were often young, as well, making their submission all the more extraordinary. To cap it off, the martyrs of antiquity were almost always given a last chance at life: They could renounce their allegiance or faith and live. They never did, of course, which underscores the voluntary nature of their deaths.

All this made martyrs newsworthy. Common people were awed by martyr stories because they were so extraordinary, so incomprehensible. They could not imagine doing it themselves, yet by passing on the stories they seemingly shared in the martyrdom itself. Perhaps the martyr was the hero they wanted to be, giving life selflessly to the cause. But heroes do not necessarily *want* to die, whereas martyrs seemingly choose death happily. If this was the aspect of martyrdom that most people found incomprehensible, the stories addressed it with this simple idea: There is a reward awaiting the martyr that is more valuable than anything found among the living. Socrates imagined an eternity discussing philosophy with history's greatest minds. The Jewish and Christian martyrs of antiquity, whose stories take up the next two chapters, imagined resurrection in the eternal glory of God.

Chapter 1

The Passionate Witness

Around the time Socrates was calling on fellow Greeks to forsake material wealth and join his divine quest for truth, the Jews of Palestine were slowly recovering from a string of tragedies. These had begun two centuries earlier with their exile to Babylon, in modern-day Iraq, following the destruction of Jerusalem and Solomon's great temple in 586 BCE. The covenant between God and His Chosen People set the Jews apart. The Jews believed in the One God, Yahweh. The faithful were required to obey His law as revealed to Moses and to follow strict rituals, including male circumcision and various dietary laws. Perhaps because the Babylonians had many gods—65,000 according to one count—the exiled Jews were allowed to practice their religion (what's one more god?), and many historical books of the Hebrew Bible, Christianity's Old Testament, were written during this time.

It is in a biblical story of the Jewish exile in Babylon that ideas about martyrdom as religious witness first took shape. The book of Daniel[1] recounts the adventures of the captive Jew Daniel and his three young friends, Shadrach, Meshach, and Abednego, in the court of King Nebuchadnezzar. Shadrach, Meshach, and Abednego had been given court appointments after Daniel cleverly deciphered the king's dreams. The story tells of the time the king built a golden idol ninety feet high and demanded his subjects worship it or be killed. True to their own God, the three young Jews refused to worship the idol, an affront that soon came to the king's attention. An angry Nebuchadnezzar ordered them to worship the idol or be thrown into a blazing furnace. He taunted them: "Then what god will be able to rescue you from my hand?"

The king had unwittingly put himself in a no-win situation, as the friends' response made clear. "If we are thrown into the blazing furnace, the God we serve is able to save us from it, and he will rescue us from your hand, O king. But even if he does not, we want you to know, O king, that we will not serve your gods or worship the image of gold you have set up" (Daniel 3:17–18). Astounded by this impertinence and determined to save face, the furious king ordered his soldiers to heat the furnace seven times hotter than usual. Shadrach, Meshach, and Abednego were then bound together and thrown in.

A few minutes later a stunned Nebuchadnezzar saw the three Jews emerge from the flames unharmed. Even their clothes were untouched. He was so impressed that he decreed death for anyone who spoke ill of the Hebrew God. Shadrach, Meshach, and Abednego were rewarded with promotions in the king's court. In one of the few clear biblical statements on martyrdom as religious witness, the author of Daniel then gives the point of the story: "They trusted in him [God] and defied the king's command and *were willing to give up their lives* rather than serve or worship any god except their own God" (Daniel 3:28; italics added).

The would-be martyrs had shown their mettle and their devotion to God. But in this story God was not ready for them to die; divine intervention saved Daniel's friends just as it had stayed the hand of Abraham centuries before. Despite their willingness to die for their beliefs, the sacrifice was not consummated.

The story of Shadrach, Meshach, and Abednego reasserted the long-standing biblical theme that God has a hand and purpose in the life and death of His servants. Although referring to pagan gods, Plato suggested the same idea in his story of Socrates' death. What better way to demonstrate the authority of any god than over life and death? Abraham submitted, as did Moses, Samson, Saul, and Jonah. Elijah was *taken away* by God. Some prominent biblical figures, Moses, Elijah, and Job among them, pleaded unsuccessfully with God to take them before it was their time, before He was ready. Daniel helped make divine will or compulsion a core theme of the martyr's story.

Four hundred years later, around the time the book of Daniel was actually written, another group of Jews showed their mettle and devotion to God. They, too, refused to obey the orders of a king. But the story of these Jews had a different ending—they died for their beliefs. These martyrs came to be known as the Holy Maccabees. Their story begins with the return of the Jews from exile.

Solomon, son of King David, had built his temple to God on Mount Moriah, a peak among a ridge of hills where God instructed Abraham to sacrifice his son Isaac (Genesis 22:1–2). Known as the Temple Mount, no place was (or is) more sacred to Jews. Rebuilding the temple in Jerusalem was thus their first priority when the Hebrews, led by Zerubbabel, returned to Palestine in 538 BCE following the conquest of Babylon by Persian king Cyrus the Great. Over the next two hundred years, the Jews fortified the city of Jerusalem, as well as their commitment to Yahweh and His law. No matter how dreadful the trials and punishments visited on them, faithful Jews believed that they would enjoy the final triumph of God's Chosen People—destruction of their enemies and their own collective resurrection.

But the Jews were not to be free of trials and tribulations anytime soon. The next great test began with the appearance of Alexander the Great, the Macedonian king, son of Philip II and Olympias. Upon his father's assassination by a jilted homosexual lover, Alexander inherited a full-time modernized army, the finest fighting machine the world had seen. The young warrior took a mere four years to wrest the Persian empire from King Darius III, which he finally accomplished in 331 BCE at the battle of Gaugamela, near the modern-day Kurdish capital of Irbil, Iraq. Eventually, Alexander's own empire would stretch from Macedonia and Greece south to Egypt, and east through Mesopotamia and Persia all the way to India. He built the great city of Alexandria at the mouth of the Nile and was declared pharaoh by the Egyptians. The region of Judah and its jewel, Jerusalem, now lay at the crossroads of Greek, Persian, and Egyptian influence.

Less than ten years later and still planning great exploits, the thirty-two-year-old king was enjoying himself at a drinking party when he became ill. Within days Alexander the Great was dead, probably poisoned, though nobody knows for sure. His vast empire was divided among his generals. Seleucus took control of Syria and the Asian territories taken from Persia; Ptolemy took Egypt, bringing Alexander's body back with him for burial in Alexandria. Antipater became king of Macedonia and conquered Greece, ending democracy there and the so-called Classical Greek era. After continuous warfare among Alexander's successors and their heirs over five generations, Judah eventually came under the rule of Antiochus III, a descendant of Seleucus.

This history is important because the Greek, or Hellenistic, influence on Egypt and the region we now call the Middle East was profound. As time passed, many Jews succumbed to its attractions, especially the emphasis on cultural integration and religious tolerance. Intermarriages increased among Jews, Persians, and Greeks. Some Jews even rejected circumcision and began eating forbidden foods. The Greeks, Thomas Cahill suggests, would have been pleased at this: "To the Greek mind, the unwillingness to compromise in religious matters—which were not all *that* important, anyway—was impious, unpatriotic, maybe even seditious."[2]

But compromise requires tolerance. In the unending battle for control of ideas and values, tolerance is often interpreted as a sign of weakness. Leaders worry that they will be taken advantage of, so they become less tolerant of differences and they take more active measures to ensure compliance with the doctrine they support. Antiochus IV Epiphanes ("the Illustrious"), who reigned from 175 to 163 BCE, is a case in point. Antiochus decided that the more or less voluntary embrace of Hellenism by many Jews was not enough. He sought absolute loyalty. To emphasize the point, Antiochus declared himself "God manifest" and abolished the Law of Moses, along with circumcision, observation of the Sabbath, and the prohibition against Jews eating pork. To prove their loyalty, citizens were ordered to sacrifice pigs to the god Zeus and then to eat the meat of the slaughtered pigs. Jews who refused to obey the new decrees faced torture and execution. In his monumental history of the Jewish people, *Antiquities of the Jews,* the Roman-Jewish author Flavius Josephus described how men were crucified alive, their wives put to the sword and children strangled. Circumcised boys were hanged from the necks of their crucified fathers, infants from the necks of their mothers. The rebuilt Temple, so precious to Jews, was turned into a pagan shrine.

History does not record the identities of all those tortured and killed under Antiochus IV, or how many there were. But fear must have run deep among Jews, and it is easy to imagine that many chose life for themselves and their families. Even some devout Jews would have wavered, there being no future in mass suicide. Yet out of persecution, legends arise over time that help to revitalize the flagging spirits and faith of people living under oppression. And so it was that stories emerged about this period in Jewish history that showed the triumph of faith over evil. But these stories also contained something new: They spoke explicitly of heavenly rewards for martyrs, even though the sacred Torah—the five books of Moses (Genesis, Exodus, Leviticus, Numbers, and Deuteronomy)—makes no mention of an afterlife. So the motivation and justification for any suicidal violation of Antiochus's decrees were difficult to reconcile with Jewish teachings. Unless, that is, ideas about martyrdom were modified to accommodate some notion of vindication through death. What greater vindication could there be than this: Death on God's behalf *leads to* immortality; death is *reversed* through resurrection in heavenly glory. It was no longer adequate simply to suggest that divine compulsion is at work in the martyr's act. Martyrdom now became a way to *acquire life.*

The legendary martyrdom of the Jewish Maccabees reflects this evolution in the idea of martyrdom. The stories were written over a period of nearly three hundred years as part of the books of Maccabees. These books were added to the Septuagint, the original Greek version of the Old Testament translated from Hebrew by Greek-speaking Jews living in Egypt. Many Jews, perhaps including Jesus, used the Septuagint side by side with the Hebrew version. It was later translated into Latin and used by the developing Christian church for nearly four hundred years. The martyrdom of the Holy Maccabees, as they came to be known, was as familiar to early Christians as it was to Jews. And the message was as powerful as it was simple: Salvation comes through suffering for God.

The story begins with Mattathias Maccabeus, a Jewish priest from the town of Modein, near Jerusalem. Mattathias refused to obey the laws of Antiochus IV. Outraged by the acquiescence and infidelity of many Israelites, Maccabeus killed a Jew who was taking part in a Greek sacrifice and also the royal officer responsible for enforcing the new decree. He then fled to the mountains outside Lydda with his five sons where he was joined by many other Hasidim—men who were strict adherents to Jewish law. The Hasidim waged a guerrilla war against the king. After his death, Mattathias's son, Judas Maccabeus, lead the Hasidim to victory over a Syrian army sent to destroy him; he occupied Jerusalem as high priest and ruler of Judah, and he reconsecrated the Temple in 165 BCE. The exploits of Judas Maccabeus have been celebrated by Jews and Christians for thousands of years; his story is the subject of an oratorio by eighteenth-century composer George F. Handel, better known today for his *Messiah,* and the reconsecration of the Temple is celebrated by Jews during Hanukkah. The Talmud, the immense written interpretation of the Torah, says that Maccabeus could find only enough oil in the Temple to keep a light burning for one day, but the light burned for eight.

At some point during the early days of the uprising against Antiochus, an elderly Jewish scribe named Eleazar and a devout mother (named Hannah centuries later) and her seven sons were arrested, probably at different times. They were tortured and executed. There are no eyewitness accounts, so the various versions in the books of Maccabees consist of stories written long after the events took place. They were passed down orally from generation to generation, undoubtedly embellished along the way.

Like Socrates two hundred years before them, the devout Maccabees stood firm in the face of death, sure of their beliefs and way of life. There was no turning back, no denial of the one true God. Given the choice of life or death, in the spirit of Shadrach, Meshach, and Abednego, they chose death rather than deny their faith. But unlike the quiet, almost gentle passing of Socrates, the Maccabees faced a brutal public execution. Eleazar was bent over a whipping drum, where he was beaten mercilessly, then burned and forced to swallow noxious liquid through the nose. The legend held that Eleazar repeated his love for Yahweh throughout the ordeal and died saying he was "glad to suffer"[3] the punishment. The second book of Maccabees says that Eleazar "welcomed death with honor rather than life with pollution" (2 Macc. 6:19).

Antiochus offered a way out if Hannah and her seven sons would "share in the Greek way." The offer was clear: renounce your faith and live. When the offer was contemptuously rejected, the killing ordeal began. The executioners first tore out the eldest son's tongue, then scalped him, severed his hands and feet, and threw him on a fire to burn. One by one the sons were tortured to death, with ever-increasing gore. When it came to the youngest son, said to be seven years old, Antiochus again offered life, power, and wealth for obeying the law and embracing Greek gods.

Did Hannah cover her eyes, weep, or scream out in pain for her sons? Did she beg the executioners to stop? Did she jump at that final offer and save one son at least? Wouldn't any mother have done the natural thing and fought for the lives of her children? Not this one. Hannah consummated the martyrdom. When her youngest son was offered life at a price, she implored him to greet death without fear, saying God would one day see them all resurrected. "Do not fear this executioner, but prove yourself worthy of your brothers and accept death, so that I may receive you back with them in the day of mercy."[4] Whether turned mad by the ordeal, martyred in turn, or dead at her own hand, the final plight of the mother is unclear. But her dramatic role is not: She faced the unimaginable with an unnatural public militancy that doubtless left Antiochus both amazed and furious.

According to Arthur Droge and James Tabor in *A Noble Death*,[5] an important shift occurred from the second to the fourth book of Maccabees. While in the earlier book the youngest son passively submitted to the executioner, in the later version he actively took his own life by flinging himself into the fire. The mother also committed suicide in this version. The writer of IV Maccabees clearly thought it important to emphasize the active role of the martyr in the death experience, not just in the events leading up to it.

Whatever actually happened to the Maccabees, and earlier to Socrates, matters less in the discourse on martyrdom than the meaning of the stories. The glory of suffering unimaginably for God became the core idea in the Judeo-Christian meaning of martyrdom, and the stories bind followers to the promise of a day of judgment and resurrection in which their faithful suffering will be vindicated. This is the ultimate reward of martyrdom. The gory stories of determined self-sacrifice explained *and justified* voluntary death. "The only time Judaism ever viewed suicide affirmatively was when it was committed as an act of martyrdom. Otherwise it was *never* sanctioned," writes Sydney Goldstein in *Suicide in Rabbinic Literature.*[6] The legend of the nine Maccabees is now regarded as the model for later Christian martyrs.

It is worth remembering here that a martyr's audience is always far larger than the one present at the time or place of death. Consistent images emerge in portrayals of the martyr experience that help convey the glory of suffering while unifying the events across time and space. One image from antiquity is a ritualistic declaration by the dying as they bore witness to their faith. During the Roman occupation of Palestine, Jewish martyrs recited the Shema: "Hear, O Israel, the Lord our God, the Lord is One." Christian martyrs declared, "I am a Christian." At times of oppression and persecution, later generations of Jews and Christians would rally around these declarations and reproduce them.

Another emerging theme in Judeo-Christian stories of martyrdom in antiquity was the near-erotic imagery contained in the account of death. Dying for God was increasingly portrayed through images of passion, love, beauty, and serenity. While Genesis (22:12) said that Abraham was willing to sacrifice his only son Isaac because he *feared* God, stories of martyrdom had the martyr dying *in love with* God. These passionate elements became more prominent as the literary artistry of the accounts improved and as the accounts themselves became more prevalent.

The Martyrdom of Rabbi Akiva

The legend of Rabbi Akiva (born Akiba) is told to Jewish children the world over and illustrates the glory of suffering and the martyr's passionate sacrifice. For the sake of appreciating the context of conflict and persecution in which martyrdom flourishes, the story is best told in a rather circuitous way.

Akiba ben Joseph was a poor, semiliterate Jewish shepherd who lived near Jerusalem a generation after the time of Jesus. He was pursued by Rachel, daughter of one of the richest men in the city, whom he eventually married. Having expected a scholar for a son-in-law, Rachel's father cut them off, leaving them penniless. Rachel encouraged Akiba to learn to read and then to attend religious school to study the Torah. Akiba must have been one of history's most contemplative students, for he began his Torah studies at age forty and continued for thirteen years before expressing any opinion in class! When eventually he did so, teachers and fellow students were amazed at his logic, insights, and memory. More years passed, during which he was ordained Rabbi Akiva and opened his own religious school. He attracted many students and emerged as one of the great scholars of the Mishnah, the earliest written form of the Oral Torah, the memorized interpretation of God's laws as they applied to everyday life.

Rabbi Akiva and the Jews of Palestine lived under Roman occupation. Three generations before the birth of Jesus, Pompey had brought Roman authority to the region by annexing Syria and Palestine. A rival of Julius Caesar, Pompey gained fame by helping crush the slave revolt led by Spartacus. In 63 BCE he arrived in Palestine and his legions seized Jerusalem. The area became the Roman province of Judea. Twenty years later, a family of Jews that had gained favor with the Romans was appointed to rule over Judea. Herod the Great is the most famous of these kings; he ruled from 37 to 4 BCE. He promoted Greco-Roman culture and was successful in suppressing the occasional rebellion by Jewish factions. He was the ideal ruler from Rome's point of view.

Herod rebuilt many fortresses across Judea and erected temples everywhere. He liked to call himself "King of the Jews," so the Senate in Rome obliged him with that title. Herod also rebuilt Jerusalem. In 20 BCE he began building a new temple using the same type of soft white stones found among the remnants of Solomon's Temple. Legend says that ten thousand workmen were used, a thousand of them carpenter-priests because Jewish law prohibited laymen from entering the inner temple. The task would eventually be completed in 63 CE, long after Herod's death.

Problems brewed among the Jews despite these signs of prosperity. The priesthood was corrupt, and many different factions arose vying for political power. Demonic activity and occult practices were common, and Jews continued to succumb to the influence of Greco-Roman culture—mostly, as Thomas Cahill puts it, to survive, to do business, and to fit in. The number remaining faithful to the one God of Abraham steadily declined. Many even abandoned Hebrew, their ancestral language, and spoke Aramaic.

Even so, chafing under foreign rule, the Jews periodically rebelled, led by various "messiahs." In response, Roman officials were increasingly cruel and violent. Things came to a head in 64 CE, when the Roman procurator Gessius Florus sent his troops on a mad rampage through Jerusalem, killing more than three thousand Jews. A group of nationalistic Jews known as the Zealots responded by seizing the fortress town of Masada and marching on Jerusalem. Open war ensued, culminating in a six-month siege of Jerusalem in 70 CE by the Roman general Titus. Some Jews committed suicide, while others starved to death; many hid in the city's sewers only to be killed when they emerged. Josephus estimated that more than a million people died before it was all over. Jerusalem was laid waste, and Titus ordered the Second Temple destroyed. Tradition holds that the temple was destroyed on the ninth day of Av in the Jewish calendar, the very same day that Solomon's Temple was destroyed in 586 BCE. Nine years later, Titus became emperor. Upon his death a mere twenty-six months after taking the throne, a great triumphal arch was erected in Rome to honor his victory over the Jews. It was set near the highest point of the "Sacred Way" leading to the Forum, and it still stands today. The spoils of war, stolen from the Temple and later paraded through the streets of Rome, are depicted on the arch's panels; clearly seen among them is the Jewish menorah, the candelabra used in Hanukkah celebrations.

It was during the revolt of the Zealots that a mass suicide by Jews took place. The only significant account of this is in the book *War of the Jews,* written two years after the event by Josephus, himself a veteran of the war. Mass suicides were not uncommon following defeat in war; Josephus had refused to participate in one after the Romans defeated his army. When captured by the Roman general Vespasian, Josephus had correctly prophesied that Vespasian would become emperor. Rewarded with an imperial pension and living comfortably in one of Vespasian's palaces, Josephus enjoyed a leisurely existence writing books, including his own autobiography. According to Josephus, Masada was the last fortress in Judea to be conquered by the Romans. It stood on top of a large rock with four-hundred-foot sheer cliffs running to the edge of the Dead Sea. Under command of the Roman governor Flavius Silva, soldiers of the Tenth Legion and thousands of Jewish prisoners of war built a wall around the base of the rock to prevent the rebels from escaping. They then built a long ramp to the top of the rock and prepared to breach the fortress walls.

Inside, rebel leader Eleazar ben Yair saw that defeat was imminent. He gathered his Jewish defenders and their families together and then gave a lengthy speech explaining why they should kill themselves: First, he said, it was a God-given opportunity to die in freedom; second, death "as executed by our own hands" would be a just punishment for "our manifold sins"; third, only through death would their wives and children escape the pain and dishonor of captivity. Some defenders apparently needed more convincing, so Eleazar spoke at length again, suggesting other important reasons for the mass suicide: Death, he said, "affords our souls their liberty, and sends them into their own place of purity." And then he added, "It is by the will of God, and by necessity, that we are to die."[7]

Still not finished, Eleazar once again reminded his followers of their horrible fate at the hands of the Romans if captured. But, Josephus writes, "they all cut him off short, and made haste to do the work." After burning all their possessions, they chose ten men by lot who then killed all the others. When these ten had finished the grisly work, they cast lots again "that he whose lot it was should first kill the other nine, and after all should kill himself." When it was all over, 960 Jews lay dead. Conveniently for Josephus the storyteller, an old woman, five children, and one of Eleazar's relatives survived, having hidden in caverns below the fortress. The next morning, instead of a battle, the Roman soldiers faced a bonfire and an eerie silence. When they learned from the survivors what had happened, their disbelief turned to wonder at the Jews' courage and "immovable contempt of death." The Masada story is revered today among Jews as one of the most dramatic and symbolic acts in Jewish history. The rock is a tourist attraction in Israel and a place of pilgrimage.

It is hard to imagine and more difficult to grasp what happened within those fortress walls. Josephus wrote that all were decapitated by sword, the men, women, and children in each other's arms. It must have taken a long time and a good deal of strength to kill nearly a thousand, some surely requiring more than one blow. Blood would have spattered everywhere. Were muffled sobs drowned out by screams in broken crescendos, or did families submit to the sword in quiet acquiescence? Did some children, older ones, perhaps, run from their parents, looking desperately for places to hide, only to be chased down by tireless executioners doing God's work? It all seems so fantastic, so incomprehensible.

Yet how well does the Masada incident fit the evolving portrait of martyrdom? Consider first the justifications for mass suicide offered in Eleazar's speech. These were varied and complex, packaged to appeal to a literate Greek and Roman audience familiar with philosophical debates over the meaning of death. Divine compulsion and the purity of paradise were mentioned, to be sure, but only as backup to the main reason—avoiding captivity—to which Eleazar returned at the end of the speech. Then can we believe that all wives, husbands, and children submitted voluntarily? Indeed, Josephus calls the incident a "calamitous slaughter," hardly the appropriate words to describe voluntary death inspired by faith and love of God.

On the other hand, the mass suicide did free the Zealots from persecution because of their faith. Read this way, the story meets a strict standard of rabbinic teachings on martyrdom. Droge and Tabor observe, "Those who have chosen death in the face of persecution are exalted and said to occupy the highest and best places in the world beyond."[8] This was the message of Masada that Jews have carried with them over the ages. As far as they are concerned, Eleazar and the other Zealots at Masada, reactionary though they were, qualify as martyrs.

After their defeat by the Romans under Vespasian and his son Titus, a period of second exile began for the Jews, who were scattered throughout the region. The aging Rabbi Akiva was among them. Any expectations of a Jewish revival in Jerusalem were dashed in 130 CE: The Roman emperor Hadrian decided to establish a new city, called Aelia Capitolina, on the ruins of Jerusalem. He built a new temple to honor the god Jupiter on the site of the ruined Hebrew temple.

Far from quelling the Jews, military defeat and desecration of their temple inspired new resistance. Taking lessons from the past, they embarked on guerrilla warfare. Hideouts were built in caves and weapons amassed. Surprise attacks were launched against the Roman legions. But life only got worse for the Jews. Hadrian brought in more troops and forbade the Jews to perform circumcisions. He appointed Tinneius Rufus governor of Judea. Rufus turned out to be a brutal ruler and a rapist; he particularly enjoyed assaulting Jewish women.

As the Romans began to level Jerusalem, word spread of the atrocity, and Jews in Caesaria and other cities rebelled. In response, Hadrian's army murdered thousands of Jews, provoking a larger rebellion in 132 CE led by Shimon Bar Kochba. Rabbi Akiva became the spiritual leader of the revolt. He even pronounced Bar Kochba the long-awaited Messiah, though he later retracted this claim. Nevertheless, thousands of Jews joined Bar Kochba largely because of Akiva.

Accounts of the Bar Kochba revolt are contained in the Talmud and also in the work of Roman historian Dio Cassius, born soon after the event. All agree that after an initial victory in which Bar Kochba liberated Jerusalem, Hadrian responded by sending in a huge army. Three years later the rebels were defeated and Bar Kochba killed.

Nobody knows exactly how many died in this war, but the highest estimates put the number of Jews killed at close to five hundred thousand, and Roman losses were staggering as well. After the war, many Jewish women and children were sold into the slave markets in Hebron and Azza. Hadrian renamed Judea "Palestino" after the Philistines who were living in the region when the Jews returned from Egypt. At first Jews were forbidden to come within sight of the city of Aelia Capitolina; after Hadrian's death they were allowed to enter the city on the anniversary of its destruction to mourn at a fragment of the old Temple wall, today known as the Wailing Wall, the holiest of Jewish places.

The aged Rabbi Akiva, spiritual leader of the revolt, continued his public teaching of the Torah in direct violation of Hadrian's decree. He was arrested by the Romans along with nine other rabbis. Talmudic legend says that all ten were tortured to death by Tinneius Rufus. According to the legend, Rabbi Akiva engaged in a dialogue with Rufus in which he expressed his love for God, which his own death would consummate. He recited the Shema and explained to those present that he now understood the true meaning of loving the Lord with all one's soul.

The students who witnessed their teacher's execution cried out for an explanation of his willingness to die. Rabbi Akiva is said to have replied, "All my life I was troubled by this verse, 'And thou shalt love the Lord with all thy soul'—even though he takes your soul, and I said, when will it come to my hand that I may fulfill it? Now it has come to my hand, shall I not fulfill it?"[9] Rabbi Akiva's recitation of the Shema was left incomplete, according to the legend, for his death came with the word "One." A voice came out of heaven at that moment, the Talmud says, crying, "Blessed are thou Rabbi Akiva, for you are already in the Next World!"

The memory of Rabbi Akiva was surely revered by his contemporaries, but probably as a defiant revolutionary rather than a martyr. Like many other Jews, Rabbi Akiva had knowingly committed a capital offense under Roman law and paid the price for it. It was only after the story of his death appeared in the Talmud a century later that Akiva's execution was elevated to martyrdom. For later generations of Christians and Jews, however, the lesson of Rabbi Akiva was that martyrdom as religious witness is an active, ecstatic death, rewarded by God at the moment of the soul's departure.

Chapter 2

"The Blood of Christians Is Seed"

To the Romans, Jews were a known quantity; Christians were not, and their emergence on the scene in Palestine was a complication the Romans didn't need. Here was a strange and possibly seditious sect that refused to participate in Roman life, held secret meetings, inflamed the Jewish leadership, and refused to serve in the army. The death of the Christians' leader had done nothing to quell their spirit, and the subsequent execution of key disciples, beginning with Stephen, merely made matters worse. The obstinate Christians turned the other cheek and continued their preaching and proselytizing, confident they would inherit the kingdom of God. The first full-fledged assault on Christians occurred under the emperor Nero in 67 CE. It was during this persecution that astute Romans began to appreciate the magnetic power of martyrdom, but the lesson did not take.

The story of the Passion, the suffering and death of Jesus of Nazareth, was crucial to the evolving idea of martyrdom. Could its authors have anticipated that thousands of Christians—rich and poor, masters and servants, male and female, young and old—would embrace martyrdom in imitation of the

Passion? The four evangelists—Matthew, Mark, Luke, and John—described the event sparsely and wrote their gospels sometime between 55 and 110 CE. They relied on a mixture of eyewitness accounts, oral tradition, and Judaism. They were Jews themselves, of course, as was Jesus.

Today, believers in the God of Abraham—Jews, Christians, and Muslims—have different ideas about who, or what, Jesus really was, although they agree that he lived in the service of God. Jews say Jesus was a prophet, not God; they also do not believe that Jesus was resurrected three days after death. Muslims also believe that Jesus was a prophet, but they say God would have raised him to heaven before he could be crucified if he was the biblical Messiah; they also believe that the revelations recited by the Prophet Muhammad in the seventh century supersede those of earlier prophets, including Jesus. Christians revere Jesus as the Messiah, the anointed one, the son of God, and God himself, whose coming, suffering, and resurrection fulfilled Old Testament prediction. These different beliefs about Jesus have haunted the three religions for centuries and have strained relations among the "Peoples of the Book" to the point of war, massacre, and genocide.

Whether a prophet or the Messiah, Jesus made decisions that virtually ensured his execution. Arguably the most critical among these was his decision to leave Galilee, where his teachings had mostly fallen on deaf ears, to preach in Jerusalem, the center of Jewish life. Though this decision was hardly suicidal in itself, other actions by Jesus helped make it so. He arrived in Jerusalem with a crowd of enthusiastic followers proclaiming him the Messiah; he openly challenged the council that governed Jewish affairs—the Sanhedrin, supported by Rome—by forcefully running the merchants and moneylenders out of the Temple and threatening their livelihoods; he claimed the power to forgive sin, which according to the Jews only Yahweh could do, and thus he blasphemed; worse, he refused to deny that he was the son of God. Less than a week after entering Jerusalem, Jesus was arrested, flogged, and crucified.

Crucifixion was a cruel and humiliating death. Victims were nailed to the cross through their palms or wrists and usually died of slow suffocation, a result of their inability to breathe properly. They were often left on the cross after death to be eaten by wild beasts or birds of prey. Crucifixion was used mainly as punishment for runaway slaves and common criminals. It was a cheap public execution that nevertheless could be spectacular, as when six thousand followers of Spartacus were crucified along the Appian Way as part of a Roman victory celebration in 71 BCE. By the time it was banned by Roman emperor Constantine in the fourth century CE, crucifixion had probably claimed more than a million lives during its eight-hundred-year Greco-Roman history.

Jesus did nothing to save himself from this painful and public humiliation. When arrested and interrogated he did not flee, as he certainly could have with help from his followers. Nor did he make any attempt to appease his Jewish interrogators, their high priest Caiaphas, or the Roman governor Pontius Pilate, whose initial reluctance to order Jesus's execution was quickly put aside in favor of stability and the status quo. Jesus broke the law, and Jesus would be punished. But Jesus had long before told his followers how to interpret these events: "The good shepherd lays down his life for the sheep," Jesus says in John 10:11. And to make sure they understood that his death would be *voluntary,* he said, "No one takes it [life] from me, but I lay it down of my own accord" (John 10:18). In John 12:27, Jesus predicts his death and says that he would not ask to be saved because "it was for this very reason I came to this hour."

In the recently released translation of the long-lost "Gospel of Judas,"[1] Jesus in effect *asks* his friend and apostle Judas to betray him and promises that he will be rewarded in heaven for doing so. This anonymous text, written in the third or fourth century CE in the language of the Egyptian Coptic Christians, is believed to be a copy of an earlier Greek text in the tradition of the Gnostics. The Gnostics were an early Christian sect whose members believed that the path to salvation lay in secret knowledge that Jesus relayed to his inner circle. Their texts were often at odds with the gospels of Matthew, Mark, Luke, and John and were later declared heretical by orthodox Christian leaders. Controversial in its portrait of the relationship between Jesus and Judas, the Gospel of Judas nevertheless shows again that Jesus actively participated in his martyrdom. This is consistent with the active submission typical of martyrdom in antiquity.

Notwithstanding Mel Gibson's movie *The Passion of the Christ*, details of Jesus's crucifixion and death are sparse. According to the gospels of Matthew (27:46) and Mark (15:34), as death approached Jesus cried out, "My God, my God, why have you forsaken me?" His last breath came with a loud cry. In Luke (23:46) Jesus called out, "Father, into your hands I commit my spirit." John (19:30) has Jesus saying, simply, "It is finished." Jesus speaks of Paradise when he tells one of the criminals crucified with him, "I tell you the truth, today you will be with me in paradise" (Luke 23:43).

The term *passion* has come to be used in reference to any Christian martyrdom, but the story of the resurrection sets *the* Passion apart. The shock to Jesus's followers was profound, and for good reason: Reality as they knew it had been reversed. Their leader was first killed, then raised up from the dead. To those willing to believe, the message was that a prophesied event had occurred in the passion of martyrdom. Later, the apostle John spelled it out by referring to Jesus as "the faithful witness, the firstborn from the dead" (Revelations 1:5).

Over the centuries immediately following Jesus's crucifixion, the spread of Christian faith was fueled by stories of suffering and martyrdom. Among disciples, Stephen was the first martyr, as reported by the apostle Luke in Acts 7:5–8. Hauled before the Sanhedrin on charges of blasphemy, Stephen gave them a lecture on God's promise to Abraham and railed at the high priests who betrayed and murdered the Righteous One. Stephen might have survived the priests' shock and anger at his nerve, but he added the blasphemy that "I see heaven open and the Son of Man standing at the right hand of God." Stephen was dragged out of the city and stoned to death while asking the Lord to receive his spirit and to forgive his executioners.

Saul was an approving witness to Stephen's death and an experienced Jewish persecutor of the new Christian sect in his own right. But after his own conversion, Saul (now Paul) spent most of his life as a travelling missionary for the Jesus movement. Letters from the apostle Paul, comprising almost half of the New Testament, continually referred to his own suffering as the servant of Christ and called on Jews and gentiles to follow his path. Many did, some going willingly to their deaths, inspired and comforted by Jesus's promise that "whoever loses his life for my sake will find it" (Matthew 10:39, and again at 16:25).

Thousands of Christian faithful were stoned, crucified, or beheaded during the years immediately following the Passion. Most were illiterate, uneducated men and women, but all were converts whose love of Jesus was the heart of their faith. Among them were Philip, Matthew, Jesus's brother James, Matthias (who filled the place vacated by Judas), Mark, and Peter. It is said that Peter asked to be crucified upside down because he felt unworthy to be crucified in the same manner as the Lord. Much to the surprise of the Romans, the many executions seemed to encourage conversions rather than discourage them. The next two hundred years saw thousands more Christians tortured and dying for Jesus. Some died in extraordinary and brutal ways, taxing the creativity and perseverance of the executioners. Many were eaten alive by wild animals. To those who recorded the events, it seems, the more brutal the passion, the more glorious the martyrdom. The stories of many of these martyrs were compiled in the first great history of the Christian church, written by Eusebius in the fourth century.

As missionaries fanned out, stories of glorious death in the trenches became the inspiration and model for others. During the second and third centuries, when Roman persecution ebbed and flowed, Christian writers more clearly articulated the church's perspective on martyrdom. Some prominent church leaders thought it should be encouraged as much for the sake of the church as for the salvation of the martyr.

The most prolific writer of the second century was the philosopher Justin Martyr. Justin was a native of Samaria, a city and region on the western banks of the River Jordan. He converted to Christianity around 130 CE and moved to Rome, where he became a staunch defender of the faith. He urged fellow Christians to endure the pain and suffering of persecution. "Though threatened with death," he wrote, "we do not deny his name." And he argued that martyrdom could benefit the movement: "It is clear that, although beheaded, and crucified, and thrown to wild beasts ... and fire, and all other kinds of torture, we do not give up our confession. But the more such things happen, the more do other persons and in larger numbers become faithful believers and worshippers of God through the name of Jesus."[2] This instrumental view of martyrdom was echoed in the writings of the North African theologian and convert Tertullian. Sometime around 200 CE,

Tertullian penned this famous line: "The oftener we are mown down, the more in number we grow; the blood of Christians is seed."[3] We will see this idea reprised by many advocates of martyrdom in the centuries that follow.

A growing number of Christians began actively seeking out martyrdom, perhaps influenced by this instrumental view. Pagans were astonished at the willingness of Christians to provoke the wrath of Roman authorities, and it clearly troubled some Christian writers, who began questioning both the motivation and rationality of such acts. Two in this camp were Clement of Alexandria and his famous pupil, Origen. They didn't question martyrdom per se; around 195 CE Clement wrote, "We call martyrdom perfection, not because the man comes to the end of his life ... but because he has exhibited the perfect work of love." But Clement did not approve of people offering themselves up for martyrdom unless God called them. As he put it, "Some furnish occasions for themselves and rush into the heart of dangers.... In contrast, those who are in accordance with right reason protect themselves. Then, upon God *really* calling them, they promptly surrender themselves and confirm the call." In Clement's mind suicide, an otherwise evil and selfish act, was thus sanctified by divine will.

Origen also revered martyrdom, calling it "reasonable in itself and well-pleasing to God." But he did not countenance imprudence: The faithful must be committed but rational. "When a trial comes that is not in our power to avoid," he wrote, "we must endure it with exceeding nobleness and courage. But when it is in our power to avoid it, not to do so is rash." Ironically, this brilliant and celebrated teacher was tortured during the persecutions of Emperor Decius and later died from his wounds. He died a "confessor," a state short of martyrdom. Cyprian, Bishop of Carthage, wrote in 250 CE, "confession is the beginning of glory, not the full desert of the crown." Had Origen died while confessing the faith during torture, he would have achieved the martyr's crown.

St. Perpetua and the Gate of Life

Among Christian martyrs of this period, the story of Vibia Perpetua and her five companions is one of the most interesting.

Perpetua was probably a leader in the Christian community where she lived at the turn of the third century CE. In *Her Share of the Blessings*,[4] Ross Shepard Kraemer observes that women were more prominent in the early days of Christianity than in the Middle Ages, when male opposition to leadership roles for women had crystallized. Arguably, this opposition was conveniently based on a line from Paul's letter to Timothy: "I do not permit a woman to teach or to have authority over a man; she must be silent" (1 Timothy 2:12). Perhaps protected by more gender-neutral pagan traditions, there were Christian women who performed priestly functions as presbyters, or elders. And the story of missionary Priscilla in the book of Acts suggests that women sometimes taught Christian doctrine to men. In any case, the freedom of women to assume leadership roles in the emerging Christian church varied from place to place and may for a time have been greater in the North African community where Perpetua lived.

Newly married and nursing an infant son, Perpetua was caught up in persecutions during the reign of Roman emperor Septimius Severus along with a slave girl, Felicitas, and four young men. Severus, a native of North Africa himself, supported a lawful approach to containing Christianity and did not advocate annihilation of the religion through systematic persecution. Instead, in 202 CE he forbade new conversions to Christianity and imposed stiff penalties on teachers. He believed that Christianity would simply die out through attrition. Nevertheless, Severus's order led some Roman officials to engage in rigorous prosecutions in his name. The story of the newly converted Perpetua is told by an anonymous author in *The Passion of Perpetua and Felicity*, much of it based on a diary purportedly kept by the condemned woman as she awaited execution.[5] If genuine, the account is one of the earliest known pieces of writing by a Christian woman.

Perpetua had all the zeal of a new convert and young leader. During interrogation by the Roman governor Hilarian she repeatedly refused to renounce her faith, proclaiming, "Christiana sum"—I am a Christian. She went "cheerfully" back to the dungeon, even though earlier she had been abused by the guards and probably raped. Her distraught father, a pagan, visited her in prison, and during her trial he begged her to recant for the sake of her child and family if not for herself. She ignored his pleas. Perpetua had several visions during her imprisonment; in the climactic final one she became a man and slew an enormous Egyptian in the arena. She concluded from this that she would fight the Devil and win immortality through the "Gate of Life." The next day, Perpetua and the others were led into the arena to face wild beasts during games held in honor of the emperor's son Geta.

The six would-be martyrs entered the arena "cheerful and bright of countenance; if they trembled at all, it was for joy, not for fear." After two of the men were quickly killed, the wild beasts had a difficult time of it. A bear even refused to come out of its pen. Perpetua and Felicitas survived a ravaging by a "most savage cow." Thrown to her knees, Perpetua sat up and pinned back her hair "for it was not meet that a martyr should suffer with hair disheveled, lest she should seem to grieve in her glory." After stabbing Perpetua as a preliminary to the fatal blow, the gladiator's sword wavered, so Perpetua herself "sat it upon her own neck." The story's admiring author concludes that "so great a woman could not else have been slain had she not herself so willed it."

By the third century, Christian martyrs had become post-humous heroes on earth, and bits and pieces of their corpses were circulated among the faithful as relics and objects of veneration. Like Justin Martyr before him, Tertullian had given the Jesus movement a practical motive for acts of martyrdom: Perpetua and others like her promoted the spread of faith and strengthened commitment to it. And, like Jesus, they pointed the way for others to follow.

Tertullian was certainly an interesting advocate of Christian martyrdom, and some believe he penned the story of Perpetua and Felicitas, including the diary. Before his own conversion, Tertullian had lived a life typical of wealthier Romans: He was well educated, indulged his passions (including adultery), and enjoyed the games where gladiators fought each other to the death and criminals were eaten alive by wild animals. Gladiatorial combat originated in Etruscan sacrificial rites that were part of pagan religious ceremonies during funerals. Introduced to Rome in 264 BCE, the combat was at first a private ceremony honoring the death of an important person. It was not until two centuries later that gladiatorial combat became a sport held in public amphitheaters such as the huge Colosseum, which held fifty thousand people.

The gladiatorial games were festive occasions that Roman emperors soon learned to use for their political value. By attending the games, the emperor could keep in touch with the masses while promoting his popularity. He could also reinforce prevailing law and demonstrate his power over life and death. By allowing the spectators to decide the fate of the loser, emperors cleverly gave the masses a fleeting taste of that power.

The execution of Christians in the amphitheater during gladiatorial games had become a common part of the bloody spectacle by the third century CE. By refusing to renounce their faith and worship pagan gods, Christians not only broke the law but also challenged prevailing beliefs and accepted religious practices. To Romans, the gods brought success in war and prosperity in peace; not to honor them with worship and sacrifices was tantamount to treason.

Yet the struggle between the Roman elite and Christianity ebbed and flowed: Many pagan and Christian communities lived in peace for decades at a time. Although being a Christian was illegal, it was often tolerated or ignored. And the Roman emperors themselves were not consistent in their approach to the new religion. Even the emperor Diocletian, later a ruthless persecutor, was at first friendly toward Christians. Even so, there was no way that Christians could truly be good Roman citizens because they refused to participate fully in Roman life and rituals. In particular, neither the Greco-Roman practice of sacrificing to the gods nor the Roman imperial cult, which had deified the dead Julius Caesar and, later, living emperors, was consistent with Christianity. Conflict between leaders of the Roman state and Christianity was bound to continue unless one side changed its beliefs and behavior.

Persecution of Christians and the Cult of Martyrdom

There were periods of systematic Roman persecution and suppression of Christians, first under Nero, and later under the emperors Severus, Decius, Valerian, and Diocletian. In his *Book of Martyrs*, the sixteenth-century heretic-turned-Protestant

John Fox identified ten periods of systematic persecution by Roman emperors. At other times, persecution was sporadic, perhaps reflecting uncertainty among local officials and fear of doing the wrong thing. Indeed, some provincial governors wrote Rome for advice on how to deal with Christians. In one such exchange, the emperor Trajan ordered Pliny to adopt a "don't ask, don't tell" approach: Only if Christians identified themselves as such and then refused to comply with the law were they to be executed. This policy drew attention to activists in the Jesus movement, many of whom were happy to be arrested and martyred. Their sacrifice awed the rank and file, who were taught that martyrs enter Paradise immediately through the gate of life. Other Christian dead would have to await the general resurrection when Jesus returned.

Despite the insightful reservations of some executioners, the Romans made the martyrdom of Christians a public spectacle. Executions during the games, when the crowd's thirst for blood was heightened and legitimized, demeaned and humiliated the victims in a carnival atmosphere. The executions in Rome itself often took place during a lunchtime interlude in the games. Christians were sometimes forced to fight professional gladiators; more often they were left defenseless in the arena and torn apart by wild beasts. Some emperors delighted in concocting hideous forms of execution; on one occasion, Nero dressed some condemned Christians in shirts stiffened with wax, then had them tied to chariot wheels and set them on fire to illuminate his gardens at night. During Valerian's four-year persecution, three Christian girls were among the hundreds executed: "Maxima, Donatilla, and Secunda had gall and vinegar given them to drink, were then severely scourged, tormented on a gibbet, rubbed with lime, scorched on a gridiron, worried by wild beasts, and at length beheaded."[6]

Executions like these may have thrilled the emperors and many onlookers, but they also had an unintended consequence: The bravery and dignity of many victims impressed some Romans. Tertullian had been so impressed that he vowed to learn more about the religion and ended up converted and an almost fanatical advocate of martyrdom.

Tertullian used the willingness of Christians to be martyred as a gauge of the strength of the growing church. And when he grew angry at signs of accommodation among Christians and pagans, he exhorted Christians to "glory in the palms of martyrdom."[7] Perhaps he reminded fellow Christians of this line in Psalms: "Precious in the sight of the Lord is the death of His saints" (116:15). The greatest victory for a Christian, Tertullian wrote, is to attain the glory of pleasing God, "and the spoil of life eternal." Christians achieve this victory if they are executed while willfully "battling for the truth.... Therefore we conquer in dying; we go forth victorious at the very time we are subdued."[8] Like Jesus, the martyr was cut down only to rise up.

During the time of Tertullian, the torture and execution of Christians was sporadic but occurred throughout the Roman Empire, from North Africa to southern France. The stories increasingly pictured Christianity locked in a deadly battle with satanic forces, each martyrdom a gift of God and a sign of His power. A cult of martyrdom grew within the church, fueled by the proliferation of executions and the stories of heroic self-sacrifice. Lists of martyrs and inspired accounts of their deaths, called martyrologies, were compiled by local churches, and many were eventually combined to form more general lists. The church identified special feast days to mark the events, shrines were constructed, and bodies of the martyred were exhumed and buried under church altars. Pieces from the bodies of some martyrs were used for healing or performing miracles. The body was seen as the earthly connection to the martyr's soul, and thus a link to the heavenly realm.

Many grand legends of Christian martyrs were born during the later periods of Roman persecution. One of the most extraordinary stories comes from the reign of the coemperors Diocletian and Maximian, around 286 CE. The story was heard by the bishop of Lyons, France, who recorded it sometime in the fifth century, and a brief account is contained in Fox's *Book of Martyrs.* A legion of 6,666 soldiers from Thebias in upper Egypt was ordered by Emperor Maximian to help crush a rebellion in Gaul. The soldiers were Christians who believed in rendering to God all that was God's and to Caesar all that was Caesar's. They were willing to follow orders, but not when it came to sacrilege.

Maximian crushed the rebellion in Gaul and then ordered human sacrifices to the gods in thanks. This was not an unusual practice, but the Christians of the Theban legion unanimously refused to participate in the pagan ritual. An enraged Maximian ordered them to comply on pain of death. The soldiers remained steadfast, so Maximian ordered every tenth man slain. The Christians offered no resistance, nor did the survivors change their minds. A second decimation was ordered, still to no avail. The remaining soldiers were given a rousing call to martyrdom by their commanding officer, who sent word to the emperor of their resolve: "We have seen our comrades slain with the sword; we do not weep for them but rather rejoice at their honor. Neither this nor any other provocation has tempted us to revolt. Behold, we have arms in our hands, but we do not resist, because we would rather die innocent than live by any sin."[9] All the remaining soldiers were put to the sword.

It is significant that here again there is no mention of Christians trying to protect themselves or fight back. As the officer noted, the soldiers had the weapons to do so. But martyrdom in antiquity was an act of peaceful submission, which is not the same as saying that it was passive. On the contrary, *the martyrdom was active.* It was active because martyrs exclaimed their faith or refused to deny it; it was active because martyrs welcomed and embraced death; it was active in many cases because the martyr sought out death and sometimes controlled the death experience itself. It was passive only in the sense that martyrs in antiquity did not flee or fight back or otherwise harm the people out to kill them. Writing during the last great Christian persecutions under Diocletian and Maximian, the Christian convert Lactantius put the issue clearly: "In order to defend religion man must be willing to die, but not to kill."[10]

There are other grand martyr legends from the Diocletian and Maximian persecutions, including the martyrdom of ten thousand Christian converts, also soldiers, who were crucified on Mount Ararat and the eleven thousand virgins martyred in Cologne, Germany. The historical authenticity of these and many other martyr legends is doubtful. The *Catholic Encyclopedia* notes that the legend of the eleven thousand virgins rests on a mere ten undated lines carved on a stone located in the Church of St. Ursula in Cologne. The encyclopedia concludes that *some* virgins were doubtless martyred, consistent with the Diocletian persecution, but that all sorts of fantastic embellishments were promulgated during the ninth and tenth centuries.[11] The legend even inspired a widespread cult of St. Ursula. From the twelfth century on, relics purported to be the remains of the martyred virgins were sent as far away as India and China. The value of these tall tales of martyrdom, spread mainly through missionary work, is in the messages they conveyed to generally illiterate followers—and to pagans, and later, Muslims—about the strength of Christian faith and love of God, and the scale by which it was tested.

Even as the Roman persecution of Christians was ending in the fourth century CE under Emperor Constantine, the cult of martyrdom was gaining strength. Relics, including purported ashes of martyrs, were distributed among cities throughout Europe and the Middle East. The bones of the martyr Polycarp, personal disciple of the apostle John and bishop of Smyrna for many years, were considered "more precious than the most exquisite jewels."[12] Priests eulogized martyrs from the pulpit, and churches and shrines were erected in their honor. The anniversaries of local martyrs were commemorated with all-night vigils at their graves. Most important, the martyrs were looked upon as intercessors who could plead before God on behalf of individuals or even whole communities. The martyrs were elevated to sainthood, cherished by the faithful, and used by Christian missionaries as powerful allies in their calling.

Themes from the centuries-old Maccabean legend of Hannah and her seven sons also resurfaced from time to time in Christian stories of dying for God. One story stands out in this regard: the Forty Martyrs of Sevastia (or Sebaste), celebrated in both the Roman Catholic and Greek Orthodox churches on March 9.[13]

Around 320 CE, during the persecutions of Licinius, emperor of the eastern territories of the Roman Empire, a band of forty soldiers from a legion stationed in Sevastia (now Sivas, Turkey) declared their faith in Christ and refused to participate in a pagan sacrifice. The Roman prefect ordered their arrest and torture. Enduring gruesome torments, the soldiers nevertheless refused to renounce their faith and save themselves. They were chained together and forced to lie naked on the icy surface of a pond, where they slowly died from exposure. The prefect placed warm baths nearby in a cruel gesture of temptation. One young soldier succumbed, and renouncing his faith rushed toward the baths. But instead of relief and life, he died just as he stepped into the warm water. At the same time, the legend says, a heavenly light surrounded the remaining thirty-nine soldiers who were on the verge of death. In a move reminiscent of the martyrdom of Carpus and Papylus in Asia Minor, where a pagan onlooker "saw the glory of the lord ... [and] threw herself joyfully onto a stake,"[14] a Roman guard then proclaimed himself a Christian, threw off his clothes, and joined the others on the ice. The number forty thus remained intact.

By the next morning most of the soldiers were dead or close to it. One young soldier who was still alive appeared strong enough to recover from the ordeal. The prefect offered him life if he would forsake his faith in Christ. It is here that the story reaches back five hundred years to the legend of Hannah and her seven martyred sons. Like Hannah, the young soldier's mother stepped forward and begged her son not to bend, but to "suffer a little bit more" and become "a perfect martyr of Christ." She reminded him of the rewards of martyrdom and also of his importance as her own intercessor: "Joy shall receive you after this; pleasure, comfort, elation, other goods, which you shall enjoy reigning with Christ and being an ambassador to Him for me, your mother." The guards meanwhile carted away the soldiers and began to burn their bodies. The mother, desperate for her son's martyrdom, carried him behind the cart and added him to the pile of bodies. Once again, the promise of rewards in the afterlife had outweighed a loving mother's natural instincts. The Christians' burnt remains were later gathered up and distributed far and wide as holy relics.

Early in the fourth century CE, the Roman Empire found itself embroiled in internecine conflict. The causes of this conflict need not concern us, but a couple of events deserve mention. The first occurred when coemperor Constantine the Great had a vision in which he saw a "cross of light" and interpreted this to mean that he should fight his enemies under the banner of Christ. The next day he designed his famous labarum, or military standard, consisting of a gold spear with crossbar, a wreath of gold and precious stones, and the letters X and P (representing the first two letters of the Greek word for Christ, known today as the Christogram) intersecting at the center. His troops carried the standard in their successful battle against the much larger force of coemperor Maxentius, who craved being lone ruler and accused Constantine of being a tyrant. With the Edict of Milan in 313 CE, Constantine ordered that Romans tolerate Christian worship and return confiscated property.

Ten years later Constantine found himself battling his other coemperor, Licinius, who had reverted to his old treacherous ways and was now persecuting Christians to boot. Defeated but still subversive in prison, Licinius was condemned by the Roman Senate and executed in 325 CE. With Licinius gone, Christianity became ever more important in the lives of Rome's subjects and for Constantine himself. He showered favors on the church, including money, and removed his statues from pagan temples, Even so, he allowed many pagan rituals to continue, including sacrifices in private and worship of pagan gods. Jews were also free to practice their religion and were specifically protected from Christian extremists.

Martyrdom did not disappear with these changes, but its occurrence was less common. At least there were no more executions of Christian believers in the Roman arena. Elsewhere, the very nature of missionary work and conversion exposed Christians to varying degrees of hostility from pagan leaders, and some died willingly in this effort, particularly in Persia (modern-day Iran). Upon Constantine's death, conflicts within the church over the Nicene Creed led to the executions of thirty orthodox bishops in Egypt and Libya under orders of his son, the emperor Constantius. But these pale when compared with the later persecutions under his nephew Julian, who renounced Christianity altogether (which is why history refers to this emperor as Julian the Apostate). Fox's *Book of Martyrs* contains this account:

The persecution raged dreadfully about the latter end of the year 363; but, as many of the particulars have not been handed down to us, it is necessary to remark in general, that in Palestine many were burnt alive, others were dragged by their feet through the streets naked until they expired; some were scalded to death, many stoned, and great numbers had their brains beaten out with clubs. In Alexandria, innumerable

were the martyrs who suffered by the sword, burning, crucifixion and stoning. In Arethusa, several were ripped open, and
corn being put into their bellies, swine were brought to feed
therein, which, in devouring the grain, likewise devoured the
entrails of the martyrs, and in Thrace, Emilianus was burnt
at a stake; and Domitius murdered in a cave, whither he had
fled for refuge.[15]

Short on information, as Fox admits, this account nevertheless
ends on an interesting note, for some readers might wonder
whether Domitius really qualifies as a martyr: He did not embrace death willingly, but apparently tried to escape it. Was
this the rational display of prudence recommended by Origen,
or a change of heart prompted by fear? Since Domitius was
elevated to sainthood and added to the growing list of Christian
martyrs, we must presume that church elders saw more of Origen than of fear. Domitius's flight did not disqualify him from
being recognized as a martyr. Yet similar questions continued
to surface in discussions of Christian martyrdom, even as late
as the sixteenth century in France, when some Protestants
escaped from prison to avoid execution for their beliefs.[16]

The story of martyrdom in antiquity, then, is this: Over
roughly eight hundred years, the idea and practice of martyrdom became quite complex. Stimulated by religious persecution and anticipating the glory of resurrection through
suffering for God, the martyr willingly embraced death, even
to the point of provoking it. Rich and poor, men, women, and
children, priests and soldiers refused to renounce their faith
on pain of death; mothers encouraged their sons to die in
glory. Martyrs died not in fear of God but in love with God.
Their self-sacrifice consummated that love. (Some later Christian writers said that the souls of chaste nuns who diligently
sought salvation would be embraced by the "true Bridegroom"
in the "Garden of Delights" and joined to him for eternity. The
thirteenth-century nun and mystic Mechthild of Magdeburg
wrote, "My soul spake to her Spouse: Lord, thy tenderness
is to my body delightful ministration; thy compassion is to
my spiritual nature wondrous comfort; and thy love is to my
whole being rest eternal."[17])

Rituals emerged that bound martyrs together in predictable
legends. The stories became increasingly fantastic. A cult of

martyrdom emerged, growing stronger as missionary work expanded and would-be martyrs heeded the call of religious leaders and, perhaps, the compulsion of divine will. In antiquity, martyrdom was passive only in the sense that the faithful submitted without fight or flight. Martyrdom was an active experience from start to finish, an exercise in self-control and, to a degree, control of others. Martyrdom was never a mere execution but a process in which the person being killed (and often tortured beforehand) had a controlling influence in its unfolding and ending.

The early Christians, unlike their Jewish cousins, never engaged their Roman persecutors in anything resembling organized physical resistance. For the Jesus movement God's battlefield was a spiritual one and, much as they tried, the Romans could not extinguish the fires of devotion. As Justin Martyr and Tertullian had wisely predicted, the willingness of some Christians to die for their faith only made matters worse. Martyrs not only controlled their own destiny but also in their self-sacrifice shaped the destiny of millions. Muslims and Sikhs, the subjects of part II of this book, came to appreciate the power of martyrdom very well indeed.

Part II

The Rise of the Warrior-Martyr

Muslims, Christians, Assassins, and Sikhs

Late in the winter of 1527, the new Mughal king of Delhi and Agra, Zahir-ud-din Muhammad Babur, won a decisive battle at Khanwa in northern India against an alliance of princes known as Rajputs. At first Babur's chances had not looked good: The Rajputs had one hundred thousand soldiers and five hundred war elephants; Babur had a mere twelve thousand men. But Babur had good hole cards, as poker players say. One was the experience gained from his unlikely victory over Sultan Ibrahim Lodi at Panipat under similar lopsided conditions a year earlier. Gunpowder had proved decisive in that battle. Babur's muskets and cannons had felled thousands, and the din caused panic among Lodi's war elephants. That same scene was repeated at Khanwa. Then, when the enemy made a last desperate charge, Babur's precision archers had caught them in a deadly crossfire. The survivors fled in disarray along with their leader, Rana Sanga.

Another, less tangible, hole card had been attitude. Babur had in fact anticipated an even larger enemy force. He had lost a third of his troops in the earlier victory at Panipat, so he worried now that his men might balk in the face of such

overwhelming odds. To counter this prospect, Babur fired
up his men by invoking the concept of jihad. The term *jihad*
comes from the Arabic word for "strife" or "struggle." It has
two traditional meanings among Muslims: Jihad al-Akbar is
the most important, referring to a battle for inner purity, a
cleansing of the soul; Jihad al-Asghar refers to physical battle
in defense of the faith—a righteous fight, or holy war.

To a Muslim, writes M. J. Akbar in *The Shade of Swords*,
"there is no higher form of sacrifice than death in a jihad."[1]
Babur steeled his soldiers by example, renouncing alcohol,
destroying gold and silver wares, and praying to Allah. Then
he addressed the troops, telling them that the glory of martyrdom awaited them. Babur's diary records his words on
that February day:

> Better than life with a bad name is death with a good one! God
> the Most High has allotted to us such happiness and has cre-
> ated for us such good fortune that we die as martyrs, we kill
> as avengers of His cause. Therefore each of you must take an
> oath upon His Holy Word that he will not think of turning his
> face from this foe, or withdraw from this deadly encounter so
> long as his life is not rent from his body.[2]

After the victory, Babur celebrated in verse, claiming the title
ghazi, or warrior of God:

> For Islam's sake, I wandered in the wilds,
> Prepared for war with pagans and Hindus,
> Resolved myself to meet a martyr's death,
> Thanks be to God! A *ghazi* I became.[3]

Here was a very different idea of martyrdom from that
spawned in antiquity. The martyrdom of a holy warrior was
not the result of a peaceful act of submission but an aggressive act of war; a ghazi fought to victory or to death. This was
still death by design, and glorious as well, but now the glory
included killing others along the way. Martyrdom had taken
a new road, a belligerent path that beckoned warriors, not
pacifists. Even though Constantine the Great had promoted
the idea of fighting under the banner of Christ, it was the
destiny of Islam to create holy war and the warrior-martyr.
Ironically, five hundred years later their creation would be

turned against the Muslims in a series of holy wars known as the Crusades.

This is not to say the older ways of martyrdom disappeared; far from it. Dying for God in submissive ecstasy continued along the path laid down in antiquity, and pacifist Christian missionaries volunteered quite regularly. But they were not alone. There were Muslim martyrs of similar stripe, the Sufi mystic Hallaj among them. The Sufis were pious Muslims who wore woolen habits to show their disdain for worldly pursuits and who sought a mystical reunion with the Creator. Sufis would sometimes put themselves into a trance and stay up all night, keeping vigil and chanting passages from the Quran.

Hallaj had traveled as far as India and China calling men to God and leaving the Sufi imprint behind. Yet the Sufis clashed with mainstream Islam. There were stories of miracles, including raising the dead, and their growing fame was responded to with envy and hostility by some Muslim clerics. Although Islam had endured assassinations, wars, and sectarian strife almost from the beginning, it was doctrinal intolerance that came to a head in the tenth century. The passion of Hallaj was but one among many. The thirteenth-century Persian poet Farid al-Din Attar left the following account of the Hallaj legend.[4]

Abu al-Mughith al-Husayn ibn Mansur al-Hallaj was awaiting execution for blasphemy in a Baghdad prison. The year was 913 CE (291 in the Muslim calendar). One day Hallaj helped the other prisoners escape by unlocking their chains with a wave of his hand. When asked why he did not free himself, he replied, "I am God's captive. I am the sentinel of salvation.... I have a secret with Him which cannot be told save on the gallows." Outraged at this new blasphemy and fearing a public riot, the sultan ordered Hallaj beaten until he recanted.

Hallaj did not recant, and the sultan ordered his immediate execution. Wearing a loincloth and burdened with thirteen heavy chains, Hallaj strode out proudly to the gallows. The executioners cut off first his hands, then his feet. Hallaj smiled. He smeared blood over his face with the stumps of his arms so that the onlookers would not mistake pallor for fear. "The cosmetic of heroes is their blood," Hallaj told them. The executioners then plucked out his eyes and cut off his nose and ears. Just before they cut out his tongue, Hallaj cried out, "O God, do not exclude them for the suffering they are bringing on me for Thy sake, neither deprive them of this blessing. Praise be to God, for that they have cut off my feet as I trod Thy way. And if they strike off my head from my body, they have raised me up to the head of the gallows, contemplating Thy majesty." As the executioners cut off his head, Hallaj smiled again. What else would a martyr do upon entering Paradise?

In keeping with other stories of submissive martyrdom over the centuries, the Hallaj account emphasized the ecstasy of dying for God. But if the submissive Sufi martyr smiled in anticipation of heavenly rewards for not resisting or fleeing his oppressors, Babur's warrior-martyrs *would* resist, and they hoped for a distinctly worldly reward in doing so: victory on the battlefield. They were, after all, warriors first.

Chapter 3

The Spirit of Jihad

Islam was revealed to an illiterate Arab trader, Muhammad ibn Abd Allah, over a twenty-two-year period that began with a vision in 610 CE.[1] As was his custom during the month of Ramadan, the forty-year-old Muhammad was spending a few days in contemplation and fasting in a cave on Mount Hira in the Hijaz, a wilderness area bordering the Red Sea and encompassing the oasis cities of Mecca and Medina (known then as Yathrib).

In the frightening first vision, Muhammad felt an overwhelming presence that left him terrified and exhausted. The presence told him to recite the revelations he was to receive. A fearful Muhammad stumbled down the mountainside thinking he was losing his mind. Suddenly, he had a second vision. This time the angel Gabriel told him that Allah, the One God, had commissioned him to be his apostle. Muhammad staggered home and asked his wife, Khadija, to hide him.

For months there were no more visions, yet Muhammad could not shake the persistent memory of that day. Then one day Gabriel reappeared, and soon afterward Muhammad started receiving revelations. Often the revelations came as he searched for solutions to problems confronting his small band of followers. The revelations were committed to memory and later written down by Muslim scribes to form the Quran.

Muhammad lived in Mecca along with other members of the Quraysh tribe, who traced their lineage to Ishmael, Abraham's eldest son. At first Muhammad kept the revelations secret, telling only Khadija and her Christian cousin. In 612, however, Muhammad began to preach, and he soon found converts among the Quraysh and the powerful Umayyad family. These included his ten-year-old cousin and future son-in-law, Ali ibn Abi Talib, and a friend, Abu Bakr. Tribal communities in Arabia at that time often commingled elements of paganism and the monotheistic faiths of Judaism and Christianity. Such was the case in Mecca. Mecca was the site of the Ka'ba, a place of religious ritual long before Muhammad and venerated by many Arabs as the shrine of Allah, the same God worshiped by Christians and Jews. At the eastern corner of the Ka'ba lies the famous Black Stone, possibly a meteorite, that Muslims believe was a gift from Allah. The Ka'ba is the holiest place in the Muslim world and the destination of the hajj, the annual pilgrimage that is one of the Five Pillars of Islam and that every able Muslim is called on to complete at least once during his or her lifetime. (One of Hallaj's heresies was a claim that Muslims could make the hajj in spirit while staying at home.) The other Pillars of Islam are belief in Allah and acceptance of Muhammad as his prophet, prayer, almsgiving, and fasting.

The message Muhammad brought to the people of Mecca emphasized justice, equity, compassion, and modesty. One meaning of the word *Islam* is "surrender." Believers were expected to prostrate themselves before God, to lay aside pride, selfishness, and self-indulgence, and to share their income with the poor, of which there were many. Muhammad also demanded that followers reject traditional pagan deities and worship only Allah, the One God. He called for removal of the many idols placed around the Ka'ba. Yet Muhammad also embraced some elements of traditional ritual. These included the pilgrimage to Mecca during which the Ka'ba was encircled seven times following the direction of the sun around the earth. On the final day of the hajj, pilgrims sacrificed sheep, goats, and other animals, a practice that continues today.

Within ten years, roughly seventy families became Muslims, and they soon faced danger. Tribal leaders resented the new threat to their ancestral beliefs, not to mention their economic practices; they were also fearful that Muhammad's growing influence would undermine their own. A few mistook for political ambition his campaign against polytheism and idolatry and his appeals on behalf of the fragile and the "portionless." At first, the resentment and fear were expressed in ridicule; before long, ridicule turned to anger and persecution. The Quraysh were forbidden to trade with Muslims or to marry them. Slaves, the most vulnerable of converts, were "beaten and dragged through the streets with ropes around their necks ... [and] they were placed in the blazing sun with stones on their chests and left there to die."[2]

The persecution escalated and some Muslim families left Mecca in search of safer climes. Muhammad remained in Mecca and continued preaching and visiting the Ka'ba. Although taunted while he preached and occasionally roughed up, Muhammad was protected from real harm by his uncle Abu Talib. Though not a convert himself, Abu Talib had raised Muhammad from childhood and in the Arab tradition served as his protector. Abu Talib died in 619, a year of sorrow for Muhammad in which Khadija also died, and the family's protection was lost.

Muhammad was now in real danger, and the future of Islam looked bleak. While he continued to preach, facing his tormentors with prayers and the poetry of the emergent Quran, Muhammad also looked for a safer place for his followers and his message. The opportunity to leave Mecca came when leaders from Yathrib converted to Islam during the hajj in 622 and invited Muhammad and his followers to move there. After negotiations with Yathrib tribes, which included Jews and Christians, Muhammad set the emigration, or *hijra*, in motion. His decision to accept the protection of the tribes of Yathrib signaled renunciation of his birthright as a Qurayshi. Insulted by his defection and fearful that he could organize powerful opposition to their leadership and practices if permitted to relocate, the tribal leaders of Mecca set out to assassinate Muhammad. Tipped off, Muhammad and his cousin Ali successfully thwarted the would-be assassins and escaped in the night.

The hijra in 622 marks the beginning of the Muslim era and its official calendar. It also marks the point at which Muhammad's stand toward the enemies of Islam took a significant turn: Patient submission gave way to active resistance. During the early days in Medina, Muhammad received a revelation, as recorded in verses 39–40 of Surah (chapter, or portion) 22 of the Quran: "To those against whom War is made, permission Is given (to fight), because They are wronged.... (They are) those who have Been expelled from their homes In defiance of right—(For no cause) except That they say, 'Our Lord Is Allah....'"[3] In this revelation, God validated defensive use of the sword.

Destiny and Martyrdom at the Battles of Badr and Uhud

Yathrib was soon renamed al-Madinah—Medina, *the* City, a model of the ideal Muslim society. But the going was tough at first. Over the next ten years the Muslim community, or *umma*, of Medina fought well over sixty battles and skirmishes trying to repel its enemies and achieve economic security. Muhammad had a direct role in twenty-seven battles. Arabia was a harsh land where rival tribes targeted each other's caravans and fought to extinction in tribal vendettas. With poverty threatening the survival of the umma, Muhammad followed this tradition by attacking the rich caravans of his former tribe. The outraged Quraysh were quick to respond.

Muslim lore regards the ensuing battle in the oasis of Badr in 624 as the first great Islamic battle of destiny. Almost fourteen hundred years later, in the Occupied Territories of Palestine, the walls of Gaza and the West Bank would recount the battle in the graffiti and slogans of the intifada, or uprising, against the Israeli occupation. The last words of Khubaib al-Ansari, captured by the Meccans at Badr and sold to the sons of a man he had killed in battle, are prominently displayed: "It doesn't matter when or how I am killed as a Muslim as long as my death is for the sake of Allah."[4] These words are also included in the Hamas anthem "O My Homeland."

Badr was an impressive victory for Muhammad and a great humiliation for the seasoned Quraysh: Muhammad led 313 men, only four on horseback, against a well-equipped army three times the size. The Muslims killed seventy and took as many prisoners. It was said that Ali killed twenty of the enemy single-handedly. To Muslims, the unlikely victory at Badr was God's work. It signified His approval of the cause and thus was a validation of jihad.

Permission to fight back was one thing, but purposely committing suicide in the process was another. All warriors faced the possibility of dying in battle, but armor and skill helped many escape death, if only until the next skirmish. Heroic actions on the battlefield such as helping a comrade or covering a retreat made death more likely, but there remained hope of survival, however slim. The notion of martyrdom as an active experience conveys the idea of death by design. Did God's permission to fight back mean that He approved of self-sacrifice on the battlefield?

Muhammad apparently thought so and conveyed this to his men. He feared failure at Badr would mean the end of Islam. So he gave his men a promise that death in battle would be a special kind of death: "No man will be slain this day fighting against them with steadfast courage, advancing not retreating, but God will cause him to enter Paradise." The story continues: "Umayr bin al-Humam was eating some dates when he heard this. He flung them aside and asked 'Is there nothing between me and my entering Paradise save to be killed by these men?' He seized his sword and plunged into the enemy, fighting until he was slain. When the Prophet was asked what made Allah laugh with joy at His servant, he replied: 'When he plunges into the midst of the enemy without mail [armor].'"[5]

The story of the battle of Badr produced two beliefs that became core principles in Islam: God protects those who fight in His name, and He rewards those who die—in Arabic *shuhada* (singular, *shahid*)—with eternal blessings in Paradise. Righteous battle was a win-win situation for believers, and Muslims quickly gained a reputation as fearless soldiers. They did not win every fight, however, and Muhammad had to contend with treachery both inside and outside the umma. In the next important battle, a rejuvenated and determined Quraysh army of three thousand met the Prophet's much smaller army of a thousand at Uhud, just outside Medina, on a Saturday in 624. The Qurayshi leader was Abu Sufyan, and he was so confident that he brought his wife, Hind, along to enjoy the victory.

Things went wrong for Muhammad from the start. The Jews of Medina, bound to the Muslim community through a covenant ensuring equality and mutual assistance, refused to fight on the Sabbath. Then, on the morning of the battle, a third of Muhammad's soldiers deserted. As the battle progressed, Muslim forces appeared at first to be winning. When the Quraysh unexpectedly fell back, ecstatic Muslim archers placed on a hill as a rear guard ran forward to finish off the wounded and strip booty from the dead, common customs in war. The Quraysh rallied and attacked from the rear in a cavalry charge led by Khalid ibn al-Walid. Muhammad would later say that greed had been the Muslims' downfall.

The victorious Quraysh mutilated the bodies of the dead Muslims. This was a common practice in Arabia, but Hind's actions were not. Full of bitterness over the death of her father and two sons at Badr, she had sworn to avenge their deaths by tasting the liver of the Muslim warrior Hamza, an elderly uncle of the Prophet. A North African slave ran Hamza through with his lance on promise of his freedom, and Hind fulfilled her own promise by taking a bite from his bloody liver. Muslims revere Hamza as a Prince of Martyrs.

Abu Sufyan took his forces back to Mecca without finishing the job he had started. The Quran says God spared the Muslims, for "Allah is full of grace To those who believe" (Surah 3:152). The mutilated Muslim warriors were buried where they fell, a graveyard left untouched to this day. Appalled at the mutilations, Muhammad forbade Muslims to disfigure human or animal bodies, and his subsequent rules for warfare prohibited abuse of the women and children of the enemy or their elderly and infirm men.

Muhammad also took the defeat at Uhud as an opportunity to remind Muslims that failure was itself a test of faith (Surah 3:166). Renewal and resistance were the keys to victory. The living must remain steadfast in their faith and resolute in their resistance to unbelievers. As for their brothers who died in battle, the Quran comforted the living with the "glad tidings" of a joyous afterlife in the presence of Allah. Surah 3:169 says, "Think not of those who are slain in Allah's way as dead. Nay, they live, finding their sustenance in the presence of their Lord; They rejoice in the bounty provided by Allah."

The battle of Uhud, more so than Badr, showed Muslims the gateway to Paradise.

The glory of religious battle is thus savored in defeat as well as in victory. But victory is the ultimate goal, and the battles continued. Allah smiled on Islam at the battle of the Trench, so called because Muhammad ordered a ditch dug around Medina to protect against the Quraysh cavalry. It worked. The victory was a substantial one for the Muslim army because the defeated forces represented a formidable alliance of Quraysh, desert Arabs, and rebel Jewish tribes from around Medina that now sided with Mecca against the umma. Among these Jewish tribes were the Qurayzah. After the battle, seven hundred Qurayzah men were slaughtered and their women and children sold into slavery.

The massacre of the Qurayzah Jews would not have appeared unusual or barbaric at the time. In a war of extermination, it was too risky to let enemy fighters escape, and no Arab chief would survive long if he showed mercy to traitors. Such actions were seen as weakness, not kindness. Nor was the killing of these Jews inconsistent with Quranic revelations in which all followers of the One God were revered: "For Allah loveth not transgressors. And slay them Wherever ye catch them . . ." (Surah 2:190–91). The killing of the Jewish rebels after the battle of the Trench was referred to with approval in Surah 33:26: "And those of the People Of the Book who aided Them—Allah did take them Down from their strongholds And cast terror into Their hearts, (so that) Some ye slew, and some Ye made prisoners." There was nothing here that would surprise Jews or Christians familiar with this biblical account of Joshua's actions after the battle of Ai:

> When Israel had finished killing all the men of Ai in the fields and in the desert where they had chased them, and when every one of them had been put to the sword, all the Israelites returned to Ai and killed those who were in it. Twelve thousand men and women fell that day—all the people of Ai. For Joshua did not draw back the hand that held out his javelin until he had destroyed all who lived in Ai. But Israel did carry off for themselves the livestock and plunder of this city, as the Lord had instructed Joshua. So Joshua burned Ai and made it a permanent heap of ruins, a desolate place to this day. (Josh. 8:24–28).

Awed by the success of the Muslim army, many Arabian tribes sued for peace or alliance with Muhammad. There was even a truce between Muhammad and the Quraysh. However, in 630 the truce was broken when the Quraysh attacked one of the Prophet's tribal allies. In response, Muhammad raised an army of ten thousand pilgrims and confederates and marched on Mecca. Looking defeat in the eye, envoys from the city accepted Muhammad's terms and the Quraysh offered no resistance. A solemn Muhammad rode his camel through empty streets to the Ka'ba, where he destroyed the many idols in its courtyard one by one. He rededicated the Ka'ba to Allah and then led his Muslim followers in prayer.

Muhammad undoubtedly surprised those Quraysh who expected retribution, for he left most of them alone, executing only the few former Muslims who had apostatized and turned against the umma. No one was forced to embrace Islam. However, many did convert, and by the time of Muhammad's death in 632, most of Arabia was part of the Muslim umma through alliance or conversion. Although some tribes tried to break away immediately after the Prophet's death, the wretched cycle of tribal warfare that had plagued Arabia for centuries was over. Diverse tribes, including among them Christians and Jews, now lived under the influence and protection of Islam. Peace had come through jihad.

After the Prophet's death, Abu Bakr was elected to rule the Muslim community as the first caliph (*khalifah*), or deputy. He spent most of his short reign (632–634) reasserting the unity of the umma during the so-called *riddah* (apostasy) wars. Then followed a long period of Muslim conquest, beginning with Iraq, Syria, and Egypt. The banner of Islam gave the Arab tribes a common identity, like that enjoyed by Jews, Persians, and Byzantine Christians, and the Quran forbade them to fight each other. This put a stop to plundering each other's caravans, stealing livestock, and enslaving captured women and children. Now the caliphs looked beyond Arabia to secure the future of the Arab people and their faith. Some tribal warriors who flocked to these early wars of expansion doubtless came in the hope of divine remuneration, but most were surely motivated by the adventure and the plunder. By 750, Muslims controlled contiguous territory stretching from Afghanistan in the northeast to North Africa in the west, and across the Straits of Gibraltar into Spain. The Muslim creed (Shahadah) was recited by millions: "There is no God but God, and Muhammad is his messenger."

The Arabs found that "People of the Book" inhabited most of the territories they conquered, and Christians and Jews were allowed to practice their own faith. In the Arab tradition, conquered communities (*dhimmis*) paid a modest poll tax (*jiziya*) in return for protection. They could not be attacked or plundered so long as the tax was paid. Here is how the warrior Khalid ibn al-Walid, who had converted to Islam after the battle of Uhud, put it to the Christian bishop of Damascus during a siege of that city in 636:

> In the name of Allah, the compassionate, the merciful. This is what Khalid would grant to the inhabitants of Damascus, if he enters therein: he promises to give them security for their lives, property, and churches. Their city-wall shall not be demolished; neither shall any Muslim be quartered in their houses. Thereunto we give to them the pact of Allah and the protection of his Prophet, the caliphs, and the believers. So long as they pay the poll-tax, nothing but good shall befall them.[6]

Although the Muslim expansion was driven by practical considerations as much as by jihad, a defeat on the battlefield threatened the umma, and therefore Islam itself. Muhammad, and later Abu Bakr, had promised faithful warriors plunder and Paradise in the afterlife. Victory on the battlefield was a victory for Islam. Whatever else they were doing, the Arab warriors were also God's warriors, protecting Islam whose banner they carried into battle.

Nevertheless, the revelations in the Quran did not generally extol the virtues of warfare or call upon Muslims to fight wars of aggression. The sword should be taken up defensively but not meekly; Muslims should "Fight in the cause of Allah Those who fight you ... And slay them Wherever ye catch them" (Surah 2:190–93). Muslims who turned their backs on their faith or refused to defend it were treated with contempt and a warning: "O ye who believe! When ye meet The Unbelievers In hostile array, Never turn your backs To them. If any do turn his back To them on such a day—Unless it be in a stratagem Of war, or to retreat To a troop (of his own)—He draws on himself The wrath of Allah, And his abode is Hell—An evil refuge (indeed)!" (Surah 8:15).

Participation in a legitimate jihad was thus obligatory for Muslims. Yet this duty came down to a human decision made in the world of war where death was real; so the Quran also spelled out the rewards for the shuhada who died in righteous battle. They were part of a bargain offered by Allah, as explained in Surah 9:111: "Allah hath purchased of the Believers Their persons and their goods; For theirs (in return) is the Garden (of Paradise). They fight in His Cause, And slay and are slain: A promise binding on Him In Truth, through the Law, The Gospel, and the Quran: And who is more faithful To his covenant than Allah? Then rejoice in the bargain Which ye have concluded: That is the achievement supreme." For many Muslims, this verse is the cornerstone of the Islamic justification of martyrdom. "The ideal type of martyrdom," writes Farhad Khosrokhavar in *Suicide Bombers: Allah's New Martyrs,* "involves an active commitment on the part of the Muslim. He will be slain or slay, and will use legitimate violence against heretics or unbelievers who pose a threat to the religion of Allah."[7]

The Quran offers glimpses of the Paradise that awaits "those who are slain In the way of Allah—He will never let Their deeds be lost. Soon will He guide them And improve their condition, And admit them to the Garden which He Has announced for them" (Surah 47:4–6). Paradise is a place of silk and brocade, ornaments and jewels, wine and ginger; of gardens, fountains, cool shade, and flowing rivers. It is a place of purity, beauty, and bliss; of perpetual enjoyment, without fear or grief. It is a place of forgiveness and of honor and dignity. "And besides them will be Chaste women; restraining Their glances, with big eyes (of wonder and beauty). As if they were (Delicate) eggs closely guarded" (Surah 37:48–49). The rewards of Paradise are so great, Muhammad once said, that no one who had experienced them would ever wish to come back to earth, "except the martyr who, on seeing the superiority of martyrdom, would like to come back to the world and get killed again (in Allah's Cause)."[8]

While the Quran promised the martyrs of jihad an afterlife of bliss, their sacrifice was fueled first and foremost by a need to win in this world, the here and now. But there were rules to be followed even in jihad. If the enemy stops fighting or ceases its persecution or oppression of the faithful, "Allah is Oft-Forgiving, Most Merciful" (Surah 2:191). If an enemy sues for peace, Muslims must try to reach an accord. Jihad is primarily an act of self-defense, pursued against an aggressor only until peace and freedom are restored.

It might not have appeared this way to the Persians and Byzantine Christians—and later the Rajputs of India—who were defeated by Muslim armies. Indeed, there were some Muslim religious scholars—*ulama*—who urged offensive war as a means of spreading Islam. They took selected verses from the Quran to justify an aggressive jihad against unbelievers. A favorite one was this part of verse 5 in Surah 9: "But when the forbidden months Are past, then fight and slay The Pagans wherever ye find them, And seize them, beleaguer them, And lie in wait for them In every stratagem (of war)...." And yet, the striking thing about these conquests was not the death and destruction that are inevitable in warfare, but the religious tolerance often shown by the victorious Muslims.

The standard for religious tolerance was established early on, in the conquest of Jerusalem in 638. Arabs had long revered the city as holy, and it was the place where Muhammad, in a vision, met Abraham, Moses, and Jesus at the Noble Sanctuary (known to Jews as the Temple Mount) and ascended to the throne of God. Access to Christian and Jewish holy sites was protected, though Muslims built their own cherished shrines, the Dome of the Rock in 691 to celebrate Muhammad's vision, and the Al-Aqsa Mosque in 701 near the Wailing Wall. Jerusalem became the third holiest city in Islam after Mecca and Medina.

Córdoba, City of Islamic Pride and Christian Passion

The spirit of jihad had largely burned out by the middle of the eighth century, becoming little more than "a slogan used to enliven official speeches."[9] Many Muslims lived side by side with people of other religions and recognized the benefits of normal trade and diplomatic relations with non-Muslim countries. In some areas of Muslim control, the majority population remained non-Muslim, so garrisons of Muslim troops were stationed in newly constructed forts on the outskirts of town and life went on largely as usual for the inhabitants. Where Muslims and conquered Christians lived at close quarters, as in the Andalusia region of southern Spain, the Christians largely kept a low profile. There was no organized persecution and only rare attempts to make them convert. Yet many Christians were attracted to the simplicity and tolerance of Islamic doctrine and to the beauty and promise of Muslim culture, the most advanced in the world. A good deal of assimilation took place.

In 850, the sparkling city of Córdoba in Andalusia was the most populous and prosperous city in Europe. Its Muslim ruler, the emir 'Abd ar-Rahman II, had spared no expense in imitating the style and ceremony of the Abbasid court in Baghdad. He built new palaces, brought in poets and musicians from the East, and imported fine silks and furnishings. Muslims and Christians alike were affected by the cultural awakening. A local priest complained that Christian youths wrote love poems in Arabic but hardly knew a word of Latin. But as the social blending continued, some Christians became alarmed: They saw salvation slipping away and the infidel triumphant.

By and large, religious conversions were from Christianity to Islam, and this is not difficult to understand: There was nothing obvious for the Muslims of Andalusia to gain in conversion, but everything to lose. Apostasy brings forth the wrath of God, says the Quran (Surah 47:25–28). In Islamic law, apostasy, if not recanted, is a capital offense, and the occasional convert to Christianity would inevitably become a fugitive. So it was on the Christian side that faith became an issue in Córdoba. Notwithstanding the lack of persecution, some Christians under Islamic rule felt that a recommitment to Christ was necessary; it came in the form of spontaneous martyrdom. Alan Corré writes, "Occasionally, in Muslim lands, a Christian would feel called upon to publicly insult the Islamic faith and thereby invite Christian martyrdom. The Muslim authorities were happy to assist him in this endeavor with a swift stroke of the sword. Jews did not provoke martyrdom in this way. Moses Maimonides (1135–1204) declared that such misguided enthusiasm was actually sinful, and tantamount to suicide, which was a major crime."[10]

The recommitment fermented in the monasteries and came to a head in 852. In one week alone eight people appeared before the Muslim *qadi*, a judge responsible for administering Muslim religious law, and proudly asserted the conventional Christian objections to Islam: Jesus was God and Muhammad the author of a profane doctrine and harbinger of the Antichrist. The Christians happily collected the death sentence they expected. A monk and a pilgrim then showed up at Córdoba's Great Mosque, one of the largest in the Muslim world, and berated Islam in front of the horrified worshipers. The irate crowd might have killed them there and then had the authorities not intervened. The enemies of Islam were tried and executed for blasphemy and desecration of the mosque. For the crime of desecration, their hands and feet were sliced off prior to decapitation.

The spate of spontaneous self-sacrifices continued as other monks and penitents, including some young women, sought their own salvation as confessors. Fifty-four Christians would be executed as blasphemers or apostates before it was all over. Yet in Córdoba itself many Christians dissociated themselves from the martyrs, perhaps fearing retribution on the Christian community as a whole or because they personally had too much to lose. Furthermore, unlike their predecessors in late antiquity, the martyrs of Córdoba were not tortured beforehand or killed in a prolonged grisly spectacle, and some observers wondered whether these lawbreakers were really martyrs. The Christian scholar and priest Eulogius had this answer for any doubters: "Death may come quickly or slowly; what matters is whether they suffered their passions for the sake of the faith, whether they strove to lose their lives on behalf of Christ, the one who crowns martyrs, so that they might be saved."[11] Eulogius may have written this in hopeful anticipation of his own future; he was beheaded in 859 for protecting a young Muslim apostate named Leocritia, who was also beheaded.

The Muslim rulers of Andalusia reacted to the spontaneous outbreak of blasphemy by imposing some new restrictions on Christians, but otherwise Córdoba continued to enjoy the Golden Age of Islam. By the tenth century, Córdoba had ten times the population of Paris and the first streetlights in Europe. Contemporary accounts list hundreds of mosques, palaces, and public baths, as well as many libraries, one with half a million manuscripts and a staff of illustrators, researchers, and binders. Córdoba also became a center of Jewish scholarship and culture. A wealthy Jewish doctor and diplomat, Hisdai ibn Shaprut, rose to power and influence in the courts of Caliph 'Abd ar-Rahman III and his successor, al-Hakam II. The latter surrounded himself with Jewish poets, philosophers, and scholars, bringing acclaim and wealth to the Jewish community and to Córdoba as a whole. If anyone was thinking about jihad and warrior-martyrs as the eleventh century arrived, it was probably not the Muslims of Córdoba. Yet before the century was over, Europe and much of the Mediterranean region would be mired in holy war.

Chapter 4

The Crusades, the Templars, and the Assassins

Córdoba was one of the few bright spots in a Europe that was still mired in the so-called Dark Ages. Disease, war, famine, and natural disasters had consumed the continent for four hundred years. Life was brutal and harsh, and most people were poor and uneducated. Magic and superstition shared equal footing with religion and faith. The great Frankish king Charlemagne, crowned Holy Roman Emperor in 800 by Pope Leo III, had offered a momentary glimpse of what Europe might become, but his death brought disintegration and invasions by Vikings from the north and Magyars from the east and raids by Muslim pirates who plied the Mediterranean Sea. On the religious front, the major news story was the continuing tension between Eastern Christianity in Byzantium and its Roman counterpart in the West. Tensions boiled over in 1054, when the pope in Rome excommunicated the bishop of Constantinople, spiritual head of the Orthodox Eastern Church, and the favor was duly returned.

The Seljuk Turks then swept into Western consciousness. The Seljuks were nomadic barbarians who had conquered Persia in the tenth century and then converted to Islam. They occupied Baghdad and later expanded their empire north toward Constantinople, capital of Byzantium, and east toward Cairo, headquarters of the Muslim Fatimids. At the battle of Manzikert in 1071, the Seljuk army led by Sultan Alp Arslan routed the mighty army of the Byzantine emperor, Romanus IV.

The emperor was carried away in chains only to be released when a large ransom was paid. His freedom was short-lived, however, for soon afterward he was deposed, blinded, and thrown in prison by his stepson Michael VII. Then, in 1077, the Turks captured Jerusalem from the Fatimids, ending four hundred years of Arab rule. During that period, Christian pilgrims from Byzantium and the West had enjoyed relatively free access to sacred shrines such as the Church of the Holy Sepulchre, revered as the site where Jesus was buried. The new emperor of Byzantium, Alexius Comnenus I, feared that if the Seljuks were not stopped they would eventually destroy Byzantium itself. He appealed for help from the West, banking that the strong historical bond between European Christians and the Holy Land would lure the pope despite their differences.

Christians Embark on Holy War

According to eyewitness accounts reported later, Pope Urban II responded to the Byzantine emperor's appeal for help in a dramatic way: He promoted the idea of a Christian holy war against the Seljuk Turks. "Christianity was in danger. The Church demanded its own martyrs. One jihad had asked for another."[1] Although Jesus had urged his followers to turn the other cheek, the fifth-century Christian convert and bishop Augustine of Hippo had taught that there can be just wars and that war is always righteous if God wills it. St. Augustine came up with his definition of just war because of the escalating violence against Christian interests. So when the pope addressed a church council in Clermont, France, on November 27, 1095, he labeled the Turks infidels and a threat to the True Religion. He called on the Franks to stop fighting each other and to unite in an armed pilgrimage to the Holy Land to save Christianity and to recapture Jerusalem from the infidel.

The idea of a Christian holy war against the Muslims, or "Saracens," appealed to the Germanic Franks because it offered an opportunity to reassert their leadership of Europe, which had dimmed since Charlemagne. Finding new enemies and resurrecting old heroes was an important aspect of this new awakening. To help matters along, the concept of warrior-martyrs dying for God in a battle against evil forces was played up in celebratory songs and poems that emphasized the holy destiny of the Franks. *The Song of Roland,* written anonymously sometime in the eleventh century, is a grand example in the tradition of French heroic poems called "chansons de geste." It glorified the heroic stand of Charlemagne's fictional nephew, Roland, when he was cut off from the main army as it crossed the Pyrenees into France in 778. In the poem, a small band of knights led by Roland, his friend Oliver, and the archbishop Turpin fight their way to heaven in a bloody battle against the Saracens, "those misbegotten men, who are more black than ink is on the pen, with no part white, only their teeth."[2]

It was in reality the Basques that ambushed the rear guard of Charlemagne's army, but this rewriting of history helped stir Frankish hearts and unite them against a common enemy. So did the repeated references to Saracens as pagans. This may have been more ignorance than deceit on the author's part, but it served a useful purpose: Why confuse the Christian audience and possibly dull its ardor? The enemy was cunning and strong, and the battles would be great and long. Before the battle Archbishop Turpin told the knights, "though you die, blest martyrs shall you live; thrones you shall win in the great Paradise."[3] Astride his trusty charger Veillantif, and wielding his great sword Durendal with its hilt filled with holy relics, including "Saint Peter's tooth ... [and] some of the hairs of my Lord," Roland epitomized the warrior-saint locked in mortal combat with evil. He single-handedly dispatched hundreds of Saracens, cleaving skulls and slicing through enemy armor long after Veillantif was felled under him. When the inevitable drew near, a dying Roland made a last-ditch effort to save his sword with its precious relics and then lifted up his glove to God. Angels descended and bore his body up to heaven.

Notwithstanding the glorious battles in *The Song of Roland,* convincing the knights to embark on an expensive venture to faraway lands was no easy task; but the pope had prepared himself well. He appealed to their chivalry, their desire for adventure, their lust for the spoils of war. Despite the lack of any theological basis for his holy war, Urban also appealed to their Christian beliefs. First, he painted an inflammatory picture of the Turks. They were an accursed race, he told the knights, that stole Christian lands, forcibly circumcised Christian men, tortured and raped Christian women, and defiled the altars of Christian churches. He gave gory details, and the knights were appalled and outraged. Then he reminded them of Jesus's promise in Matthew 19:29 that those who lost property or family for His sake would be rewarded a hundredfold. Members of Urban's entourage undoubtedly relayed the message in Emperor Alexius's letter about the great plunder that awaited the victorious Christian knights, including beautiful women.

Finally, Urban offered the Franks immortality: If the knights undertook the armed pilgrimage to the Holy Land, their sins would be forgiven and they would be assured of everlasting glory in the Kingdom of Heaven. The pope said that God approved of such a war "as the only warfare that is righteous. All who die by the way, whether by land or by sea, or in battle against the pagans ... shall receive immediate remission of sins."[4] In the same way that Abu Bakr had motivated recruits for a Muslim holy war four hundred years earlier, the pope linked the hope of divine remuneration with the expectation of plunder. He put it quite bluntly: "The possessions of the enemy, too, will be yours, since you will make spoil of their treasures and return victorious to your own; or empurpled with your own blood, you will have gained everlasting glory." In Proverbs (14:25) it is written, "A faithful witness [recall that in Greek the word is *martur*] shall deliver a soul from evil."

A bishop fell to his knees before the pope in a dramatic gesture of support, begging to join God's war. According to Robert the Monk, the crowd unanimously cried out the macaronic "Deus le volt! Deus le volt!"—God wills it! Since God had obviously put those words into each man's heart, Urban declared it the soldiers' battle cry. The "living sacrifice, holy, acceptable to God," that each man offered by signing up for holy war was symbolized by a piece of cloth bearing the sign of the cross. These were sewn to the right shoulder of a cloak or mantle worn by each crusader.

Once unleashed, "the passion could not be controlled."[5] The ferocity of the conflict that ensued over the next two hundred years was heightened by the symbolic importance of Jerusalem, sacred to three religions. A bloody massacre of Muslims and Jews following Jerusalem's fall to the crusaders in 1099 set the tone of a confrontation between Christianity and Islam, and between Christianity and Judaism, whose effects still linger today. In her book *Holy War,* Karen Anderson goes so far as to say that "from the time of the First Crusade, Western Christians would never again regard Jews and Muslims as normal human beings."[6]

Pope Urban II quickly lost control of his great pilgrimage to wrest the Holy Land from the infidel. To attract recruits from across Europe he had ordered bishops and their priests to preach holy war from the pulpit. The fervor of Clermont was fanned enthusiastically, no more so than by the charismatic monk Peter the Hermit. Muslims were "vile" and "abominable" and, as "enemies of God," deserved extermination. He laced his diatribes against Muslims with orations against the Jews, inspiring a dangerous mix of zeal and hate. He eventually emerged as a leader of the so-called Peasants' Crusade, a group of unofficial armies composed of many ordinary people and a few knights that set off for the Holy Land while the main army was still assembling.

A Portent of Things to Come: The Bloody Massacre of German Jews

Recruits poured in from across Europe. They were on a mission to reclaim the Holy Land for Christendom, but first the opportunity arose to avenge the death of Jesus. In the spring of 1096, Count Emico of Leiningen, a notoriously cruel zealot with apocalyptic aspirations, led a reported twelve thousand German and French crusaders through the Jewish communities in Speyer, Worms, and Mainz. Jewish merchants traveling up the Rhine with the Roman armies under Julius Caesar had settled in the three cities, and for centuries Christians and Jews had lived there in relative peace, the cities thriving economically and culturally. Now many Jews would become martyrs at the hands of bloodthirsty Christians bent on revenge.

In Worms, the crusaders butchered every Jew they could find, plundered their homes, and torched their synagogues.

The Jews of Mainz were forewarned and given sanctuary in the bishop's palace. When the crusaders arrived some Jews fought back, but the resistance was quickly overcome. The palace was overrun, the bishop fled, and the Jewish families were given an ultimatum: baptism or death. Many chose the way of Masada: "The women there girded their loins with strength and slew their sons and their daughters and then themselves. Many men, too, plucked up courage and killed their wives, their sons, their infants. The tender and delicate mother slaughtered the babe she had played with, all of them, men and women arose and slaughtered one another...."[7] Altogether, an estimated four thousand Jews died in the pogrom. Despite the church's official condemnation of the atrocity, the terrifying combination of crusader zeal and virulent anti-Semitism would reappear with each new Crusade, swelling the ranks of Jewish martyrs in Europe.

Christian and Muslim accounts of the Crusades show death and destruction on a huge scale. They also show that the religious motives behind the carnage were often muddled with political motives and personal agendas. Muslims, in particular, had to contend with constant conflicts within their ranks and virtual chaos whenever a caliph or important leader died. There were times when Muslims fought Muslims and Christians fought Christians; there were also times when Muslims and Christians united to fight other Muslims or Christians. Great warriors stood out on both sides: Bohemond, Tancred, Godfrey of Bouillon, and Richard the Lionheart among the Christians; Zengi, Nur ad-Din, Shirkuh, and Saladin among the Muslims.

God's Warrior-Martyrs Defend Their Faith and Kill Each Other in His Name

Throughout the two hundred years of this conflict, the fortunes of war ebbed and flowed. From the Muslim perspective, the Crusades were an attempt by Christians to return Israel to the Promised Land and thus bring about the second coming of the Messiah. Today, al-Qaeda leader Osama bin Laden and the Jordanian militant Abu Musab al-Zarqawi have revived this idea with their warnings of the "crusader" plan to create a "Greater Israel."

The low points for Muslims were the fall of Jerusalem in 1099 and, twenty-five years later, the fall of Tyre. Yet with Muslims caught up in their own squabbles, calls for a jihad to liberate Palestine were initially met with apathy. "Muslims were ready to weep for their brothers but were not prepared to take any practical steps to help them."[8] By 1130, the crusaders controlled territory from Marash and Edessa in the north to Gaza and Aqaba in the south. They built great fortresses across the land, many of which can still be seen in Israel, Lebanon, Jordan, and Syria. In Jerusalem, meanwhile, an order of monk-knights had been established to provide protection to Christian pilgrims. King Baldwin II housed these "Poor Fellow-Soldiers of Christ" in the Al-Aqsa Mosque on the southern edge of the Temple Mount, which crusaders called the Temple of Solomon. The monk-knights formed the Holy Order of Knights Templar, the first military order of the Roman Catholic Church. The Templars would eventually become rich and powerful, with castles strung across the Middle East and Europe and their earlier vows of poverty long forgotten.

To many Christians, the Templars epitomized what the Crusades were all about: They vowed to protect Christ's faithful and were glad to die in His service. The abbot and former knight Bernard of Clairvaux passionately supported this ideal. After Edessa fell to the Muslim forces of Imad ad-Din Zengi in 1144, Bernard called for a new crusade. He made the same argument Muhammad had made after his defeat at the battle of Uhud: God had caused the defeat as a test of faith. Christians must renew their resistance to the infidel. Bernard praised the Templars, in particular, and extolled the virtues of martyrdom: "Rejoice, courageous athlete, if you live and conquer in the Lord, but exult and glory the more if you die and are joined to the Lord. Life indeed is fruitful and victory glorious, but ... death is better than either of these things. For if those are blessed who die in the Lord, how much more blessed are those who die for the Lord?"[9] If the Templars felt any pangs of guilt at killing other human beings, Bernard explicitly cast those worries aside: "The knights of Christ may safely do battle ... inasmuch as death for Christ, inflicted or endured, bears no taint of sin, but deserves abundant glory.... The death which he inflicts is Christ's gain, and that which he suffers, his own. At the death of the pagan the Christian exults

because Christ is exalted...."[10] With the authorization of Pope
Eugenius III, Templars wore a scarlet cross on the front of
their plain white robes signifying the red blood of the martyr.
As the Crusades wore on, few questioned the fearlessness of
the Templars, armed as they were with steel and faith.

In the battles of this holy war, Christian and Muslim alike
fought hard in the name of God and looked for His help in
bringing victory. Combatants on both sides described killing for God with relish. In a letter to his wife, the crusading
Count of Blois wrote about the victory at Antioch, crowing,
"we fought with the fiercest courage ... and with the aid of
the Lord God, we conquered and most assuredly killed an innumerable number of them." The "sacrilegious Turks" tried to
cross a bridge into the city seeking refuge. "We followed them
as closely as possible, killed many before they reached the
bridge, forced many into the river, all of whom were killed,
and we also slew many upon the bridge and very many at
the narrow entrance to the gate.... The number of Turks and
Saracens killed is reckoned at 1,230, but of ours we did not
lose a single man."[11]

On the Muslim side, contemporary Arab chronicler Ibn
al-Qalanisi wrote in a similar vein of Nur ad-Din's victory at
Al-Mallaha:

> God, the mighty, the omnipotent, sent down his aid upon his
> faithful followers and his abandonment upon the stiff-necked
> infidels; we overpowered their horsemen with slaughter and
> captivity, and the swords extirpated their foot-soldiers. They
> were great in number and a vast assembly, but none of them
> escaped ... save ten men.... [Two of the Muslim fighters were
> killed.] ... Each of them passed away a martyr, rewarded and
> recompensated (God's mercy upon them).[12]

Soldiers on both sides imagined God smiling at the carnage.
The dead were infidels or martyrs, depending on your point
of view. But spirits were not always high among the warriors, so when fortunes waned and desperation loomed, hope
was renewed with uplifting stories of martyrs from the past.
Sometimes these heroes were seen in visions. St. George, the
soldier-saint from Palestine who was tortured and beheaded
during the Diocletian persecutions in the fourth century, reportedly appeared to crusaders before the battle of Antioch

and a century later to Richard the Lionheart. Martyred knights who had fallen earlier in the Crusades also appeared in visions, urging soldiers onward.

It is worth remembering that the reality of the Crusades for the warriors, foot soldiers, clerics, and bystanders who experienced them likely did not match the stories created afterward. Stories have a way of getting away from the truth, usually because they are written to get a certain message across to the readers. John Esposito, an American authority on Islam, writes, "The significance of the Crusades is less a case of what actually happened than what the stories taught us to believe. Each community looks back with memories of its commitment to defend its faith and to heroic tales of bravery and chivalry in struggling against the 'infidel.'"[13]

From the battles themselves came stories of suicidal actions in the field. Some Muslims saw suicide as preferable to being caught by the Franks, and mothers were willing to kill their daughters rather than have them fall into enemy hands. In one story an old woman covered herself with a veil, rushed into the fray, and was quickly killed. During the battle for Acre, a crusader held the enemy off even though pierced by more than fifty arrows; he was finally felled when a Muslim flamethrower hurled a bottle of napalm at him, burning him alive. In another story a woman crusader kept firing off arrows from her longbow in suicidal defiance rather than join the retreat.

The thirteenth-century Arab historian Ibn al-Athir reports two stories of martyrdom by Muslim ascetics. One was an elderly theologian who ran out of Damascus to fight the Franks as they approached the city. The emir told him to go back, that his age exempted him from fighting. The old man replied: "I have sold myself and God has bought me." Then "he marched forward and fought the Franj [Franks] until he fell under their blows."[14]

The thirst for blood and the spoils of war, coupled with the passion of doing God's work, led to atrocities on both sides, but the lion's share arguably belonged to the crusaders. The most significant in scope and historical impact occurred when the Christian soldiers finally breached the walls of Jerusalem in July 1099 and poured into the city. It is commonly held that more than forty thousand Muslim men, women, and children were slaughtered in two days. "This killing was not just an ordinary battle of conquest; the crusaders had fallen upon the Muslims ... and slain them like the avenging angels of the Apocalypse."[15] But the killing did not stop there. Jews who had taken refuge in a synagogue were burned alive. A chaplain of the crusading army wrote approvingly of the slaughter.

> Piles of heads, hands, and feet were to be seen in the streets of the city. It was necessary to pick one's way over the bodies of men and horses.... Men rode in blood up to their knees and bridle reins. Indeed, it was a just and splendid judgment of God that this place should be filled with the blood of the unbelievers, since it had suffered so long from their blasphemies. The city was filled with corpses and blood.... This day, I say, marks the justification of all Christianity, the humiliation of paganism, and the renewal of our faith. This is the day which the Lord hath made, let us rejoice and be glad of it, for on this day the Lord revealed himself to his people and blessed them.[16]

Jerusalem was almost emptied of people, and it was Christmas before all the rotting bodies were removed. On October 2, 1187, the very day Muslims celebrate Muhammad's nocturnal journey to heaven, the great Kurdish warrior and statesman Salah ad-Din Yusuf ibn Ayyub, known as Saladin, retook Jerusalem. There was no bloodshed, and Saladin allowed many poor Christians to leave the city without paying the agreed-upon ransom. The contrast in treatment of the vanquished by the two conquering armies has been a source of anger and resentment, but also pride, among Muslims. (Interestingly, some Western academics have lambasted Ridley Scott's recent film on the Crusades, *Kingdom of Heaven,* calling the screenplay an outdated portrayal of the Fourth Crusade. And, they say, the film's portrayal of Muslims as sophisticated and civilized is "utter nonsense." The veneration of Saladin, some argued, panders to Islamic fundamentalism.[17])

There are stories of many other crusading atrocities. One incident occurred during the siege of Acre in June 1191. Richard the Lionheart, out of a combination of pique and practicality, broke an agreement with Saladin and slaughtered twenty-seven hundred Muslim prisoners. He bound the men, women, and children together, marched them outside the city wall, and executed them one by one. The executions took place in full view of Saladin's troops, whose screams of anguish could be heard throughout the night.

Muslim soldiers sometimes slaughtered helpless Christians as well. After Zengi retook Edessa in 1144, his troops immediately massacred approximately six thousand people, and another five thousand were trampled to death trying to escape the slaughter. In the next century there was a Muslim massacre after the reconquest of Tripoli, which was then razed. Some Christians escaped. A young member of the Muslim army, Abu'l-Fida, was present and described what happened next:

> A short distance from Tripoli, in the Mediterranean Sea, there was a small island, with a church. When the city was taken, many Franj took refuge there with their families. But the Muslim troops took to the sea, swam across to the island, massacred all the men who had taken refuge there, and carried off the women and children with the booty. I myself rode out to the island on a boat after the carnage, but was unable to stay, so strong was the stench of the corpses.[18]

In 1291, exactly one hundred years to the day of Richard the Lionheart's slaughter of Muslim prisoners, the Mamluk sultan Khalil retook the Palestinian seaport of Acre. He massacred prisoners and razed the city just as his father had done in Tripoli. This act of brutality and destruction ended Christian control of Middle Eastern lands. The crusading movement had produced plenty of bodies all around, though hardly the end result its proponents had wanted. The thousands of dead Christians, Muslims, and Jews, whether soldiers or noncombatants, were considered martyrs by one side or the other because they died in a holy cause. The true motives of many soldiers, including their leaders, were far from pure, of course. An anonymous German critic of the Second Crusade put it bluntly: "A few could, with difficulty, be found who ... were directed by a holy and wholesome purpose ... to fight earnestly and even to shed their blood for the holy of holies."[19] But the true motives of participants in holy war are always glossed over in service of the idea behind it: death on God's behalf. Those who die on the side of God are considered martyrs even if their embrace of death is incidental or reluctant.

The Shiite Assassins Make
Martyrdom Political Strategy

There was nothing incidental or reluctant about the deaths of Muslim fighters known variously as Batinis, Ismailis, Nizaris, or Hashishin—the Assassins. The term *Hashishin,* from which the English word *assassin* is derived, referred to their alleged ritual use of hashish, or marijuana. The Assassins were a radical Shiite sect founded by the Persian poet and scholar Hasan ibn al-Sabbah. Shiites are "partisans of Ali." They believe that Ali ibn Abi Talib, Muhammad's cousin and son-in-law, should have succeeded the Prophet as first imam, or divinely inspired leader, instead of Abu Bakr. Ali was passed over three times before finally becoming the fourth caliph. Nevertheless, the majority of Muslims, known as Sunni, accepted the line of succession established by the first four "rightly guided" caliphs, which included Ali. Sunnis claim that they adhere to the pattern of life and thought represented by the Prophet.

Some of the beliefs held by the minority Shiites are considered heresies by Sunnis, including that the true imam of the Muslim community should be a descendant of the Prophet through his daughter Fatimah and Ali. The Shiites developed a tradition of protest typified by Fatimah and Ali's son Husayn ibn Ali, who refused to accept the authority of the Ummayads after they seized the caliphate following the death of his father. Responding to calls for help, Husayn and his entourage were massacred by the new caliph as they traveled to Kufa in modern Iraq.

In Shiite tradition, Husayn, like Hamza before him, is referred to as a Prince of Martyrs. Influential Shiite clerics in Iran have recently argued, however, that Husayn's martyrdom differed from Hamza's. Husayn, they say, was a martyr *by his own design*: "He knew perfectly well he was going to lose the battle and perish."[20] Husayn's martyrdom is commemorated by Shiites on Ashoura, the holiest day of their calendar. Processions of believers flagellate themselves during the celebration as a reminder that it is sometimes necessary to die in the fight against tyranny. At the time of the Crusades, Sunni allegiance was to the Baghdad caliphate, Shiite to the Fatimid caliphate in Egypt. "Even men of state like Saladin considered the struggle against the Shiites as at least as important as the war against the Franj."[21]

The lesson on martyrdom given by the Assassins was that a combination of disciplined training and religious fervor— perhaps with the aid of drugs—could turn young men into highly effective suicidal killers on behalf of a political cause. Hasan wanted to create a golden era for the Shiites, but the Seljuk Turks, who had converted to Sunni Islam, stood in the way. With a small band of men who saw themselves as the true followers of Islam, Hasan started his own jihad from Alamut castle, a fortress high in the Elburz Mountains near the Caspian Sea. It is said that Hasan never left the fortress. He devoted his time to prayer and fasting and to extending his sphere of power and influence. He sent missionaries out with armed men to back them up. Neither the religious opposition of the Sunni majority nor the military might of the Seljuks could defeat him. On one occasion Hasan's soldiers defeated a Sunni army of ten thousand men.

Demanding unconditional loyalty and using a combination of ideological indoctrination, physical training, and strict discipline, Hasan honed his closest followers into martyr-assassins for the greater glory of God. "He turned assassination into an art form," writes James Wasserman in *The Templars and the Assassins*.[22] His agents targeted leaders, not average citizens. He maximized the political benefits of assassination while minimizing loss of life. The typical assignment was to kill a specific target in a public place. Assassins often worked alone, and after the assassination they were usually killed on the spot by bodyguards or onlookers. The preferred site for the assassination was a crowded mosque at prayer time, the better to demonstrate the heroic martyrdom of the executioners, who were called fedayeen ("suicide commandos"). Hasan correctly assumed that people would take notice of his jihad.

The Assassins were good at their work, and fear made them powerful. They were feared even by fellow Shiites: "No one dared to criticize them publicly, neither emir, nor vizier, nor sultan."[23] A Spanish rabbi traveling through the region reported that they were "faithful to each other, but a source of terror to their neighbors, killing even kings at the cost of their own lives."[24] The Assassins dressed in red and white robes, just like the Templars, and their notoriety grew with their power, and attempts to rein them in were unsuccessful. Even a carefully orchestrated massacre of two hundred of their members in Damascus was only a temporary setback. Hasan carried out approximately fifty targeted assassinations during his thirty-five-year reign. Fedayeen operations continued after Hasan's death, led by Rashid al-Din Sinan, known as the "Old Man of the Mountain." They included the execution of al-Hawari and al-Khashab, two prominent Syrian *qadi* (judges). Ironically, these were the very men who had first called for jihad against the invading Franks following the fall of Jerusalem and the massacre of its Muslim and Jewish inhabitants.

Like most soldiers, holy warriors were prepared for death but hoped to survive. The Assassins were different, and therein lay their reputation. The fedayeen knew their missions would be suicidal, and they carefully planned their martyrdom. One of the first successful assassinations killed the vizier to the Great Sultan Malik-Shah of Persia in 1092. As he was being killed by the vizier's guards, the Assassin cried out, "The killing of this devil is the beginning of bliss."[25] This is clearly a double entendre: On one hand, the assassination represents the triumph of Good over Evil, and on the other, the assassin's own sacrifice is rewarded with Paradise.

Discipline was extreme and mistakes rare. Even so, not all attacks were successful. In his classic work on the Assassins, Bernard Lewis describes how martyrs were celebrated in the medieval Nizari community—and that unfinished business was a source of anguish. Hearing of her son's death in an Assassin mission, the mother of a Syrian fedayee rejoiced; when her son returned unscathed she fell into a state of mourning and despair.

Two attempts to kill Saladin failed, even though the martyr-assassins penetrated his camp, and in one case his personal tent, before being killed. After this, Saladin started sleeping in a special wooden tower and only people he knew personally were allowed to come near him. Saladin eventually went after the Assassins and laid siege to one of their fortresses at Masyaf in Syria. After some time had passed, Saladin suddenly lifted the siege and left the Assassins alone. No one really knows why, though one story is told that Saladin was scared off by a mysterious nighttime visitation. The more likely explanation is that Saladin wanted to conserve his time and resources for more important enemies.

At one time or another the Assassins were enemy or accomplice of every party in the larger holy war that raged around them. If a holy purpose had first stirred Hasan and his men, it was the politics (and benefits) of power that kept them going. "The intention of assassination," Wasserman writes, "was to create maximum intimidation and a psychological pattern of chronic fear and anticipation among Nizari enemies."[26] In the end their martyrdom was up for sale: The Assassin clan in Syria eventually became hired killers for the Mamluk sultans of Egypt. Those headquartered at the Alamut fortress in Iran ended up victims of the second Mongol invasion of the Near East led by Hulegu, grandson of Genghis Khan. As was their trademark, the Mongols massacred indiscriminately in the process, and in 1257 they dismantled the fortress. Soon after, the Mongols captured and killed the Abbasid caliph in Baghdad, along with hundreds of thousands of Muslim civilians.

The Crusades had given Christian and Muslim warriors plenty of opportunity to die killing for God and thus be recognized as martyrs. But many of the dead were ordinary people condemned by place and time, casualties of religious fears and hate and the political agendas of the day. Among these were some who welcomed death in submissive acts of allegiance to their faith and others for whom death was preferable to life under the infidel. Many were simply overrun and massacred, casualties of holy war and soon forgotten. Given a choice, many would doubtless have chosen life for themselves and their families. But they had no choice and, therefore, no opportunity to take a stand one way or the other. Since they were killed for their beliefs, whether Christian, Muslim, or Jew, they, too, were martyrs. Collectively, the legacy of their bloody witness was a reminder for future generations that they might also someday be called upon to give their lives for their beliefs.

For their part, the Templars and the Assassins had grown powerful during the Crusades, as much through political intrigue and tyranny as through service to the greater glory of God. The strict hierarchical structure and secretiveness common to both groups helped account for their power and longevity, as well as for the fear and loathing they ultimately inspired among many Christians and Muslims. The purveyors of intrigue and tyranny eventually became its victims, however. We saw what happened to the Assassins; the Templars ended up facing charges of heresy, corruption, and sodomy. Early in the fourteenth century many were arrested, tortured, and executed. The order could not withstand the combined assault of Pope Clement V and France's King Philip IV; it was officially dissolved in 1307.

Against a backdrop of holy war and the schism between Shiites and Sunnis, the Assassins had introduced the Middle East to a new type of organized holy warrior, the suicide commando. These warrior-martyrs undertook attacks that made their own deaths virtually inevitable. Unlike other warriors, for whom survival in battle was at least a slim hope and the only way to fight on, the Assassins thought of survival as failure. The Assassins' special contribution to the unfolding story of martyrdom was their founder's clever manipulation of ideological fervor, loyalty, and discipline to ensure that his warriors would happily die killing for the cause. Seven centuries would pass before the world would experience anything quite like it again.

Chapter 5

The Khalsa Sikhs and the "Game of Love"

A distant relative of Genghis Khan, Zahir-ud-din Muhammad Babur, founded the Mughal empire in India. Like other Muslim conquerors stretching back to the first caliphs, Babur brought military and political ambitions together under the umbrella of jihad. He rose from humble beginnings to become ruler of a small kingdom in Turkistan and then set his sights on Afghanistan, gateway to the riches of northern India. In 1504 he captured Kabul.

Over the next few years Babur made a number of forays across the mountains into what is now Pakistan. The lure of Hindustan and the rich plains and valleys of the Indus River simply would not go away, and a determined Babur eventually defeated a large army raised by Sultan Ibrahim Lodi at the battle of Panipat in 1526. The victory gave Babur control of Agra and Delhi; he established himself as sultan and built a mosque in Agra named after his wife, Kabuli. The next year he defeated the Rajputs under Rana Sanga at the battle of Khanwa, stirring his meager troops with the glories of martyrdom in jihad. A group of Afghan chiefs then joined forces with Muslim fighters under Ibrahim Lodi's brother Mahmud and made a stand against Babur on the banks of the Ghaghara River. Once again Babur proved victorious and was now undisputed ruler of northern India.

Even though Babur had fought under the banner of jihad, urging his warriors to look martyrdom in the eye, the primary goal was most certainly political. He fought against other Muslims because they stood in the way of his expansionist dreams. Babur could hardly have imagined that the Mughal dynasty he founded would one day pit the warrior-martyrs of Islam against an opponent for whom self-sacrifice became an attitude, a tradition, and a policy. The seeds of this confrontation were sown early, when an Indian contemporary of Babur's grew appalled and saddened by what he saw around him. This observer was Nanak Dev Ji, founder and first guru, or prophet-teacher, of the Sikh religion. Commenting on Babur's reign, he wrote, "There was so much slaughter that the people screamed. Didn't You feel compassion, Lord . . . ? This priceless country has been laid waste and defiled by dogs, and no one pays any attention to the dead." Guru Nanak noted, furthermore, that "since Babur's rule has been proclaimed, even the princes have no food to eat. The Muslims have lost their five times of daily prayer, and the Hindus have lost their worship as well. Without their sacred squares, how shall the Hindu women bathe and apply the frontal marks to their foreheads?"[1]

Nanak's pain ran deep. His extensive travels and exploration of history, religion, and philosophy had led him to preach the virtues of egalitarianism, tolerance, harmony, and compassion. He believed that in the eyes of the one true God, everyone was equal, hence his famous dictum: "There is no Hindu, there is no Mussalman [Muslim]." Guru Nanak renounced worldly possessions and preached that God is formless, timeless, the Creator of all, and the embodiment of all virtues. He rejected idol worship and preached that salvation comes through action.

Nanak used music and poetry to spread his message among the illiterate masses, and soon he had a small following among Hindus and Muslims. His followers became *Shishya* or disciples, in turn called *Sikhs*, a form of the Sanskrit word used in the Punjab, the northwestern region of India where Sikhism took hold. (*Punjab* means "land of five rivers," referring to tributaries of the Indus River. It is fertile land, often called the "breadbasket" of India.) Nanak Dev Ji formed the institution of guruship to steer the development and spread of the movement. There would eventually be a succession of ten gurus, which became a cumulative guruship whose writings formed the *Guru Granth Sahib,* also called the *Adi Granth.* The tenth and last of the living gurus, Guru Gobind Singh, declared that the *Adi Granth* would henceforth be the embodiment of spiritual leadership in the Sikh movement.

Egalitarianism was not the strong suit of Hindus, with their rigid caste system, nor was religious tolerance a primary trait of the Mughal dynasty. This became increasingly evident as Hindu and Muslim conversions to the Sikh *panth* (literally, "path") grew and successive gurus anguished publicly over the uncharitable condition of Indian society. Guru Nanak had been the first to throw stones, observing that "there was nothing to choose between the Hindus and the Muslims, for both had forgotten the real message of their scriptures and were wholly concerned with mechanical observances of their respective religious rituals and rites. Egotism, backbiting, arrogance, and mutual tension—these had become the traits of their character."[2]

Nanak proposed that the newly born panth be self-sufficient in all matters, a brotherhood of equals who sat together, prayed together, and ate together regardless of caste, race, or wealth. Nanak preached the Sikh gospel wherever he traveled, including places where Islamic law—Sharia—was strictly observed. "What is even more significant, is that the Gurus ... did not hesitate to admit those Muslims to their faith who wanted to join. This was a deliberate defiance of the Shariatic concept of the Muslim state."[3] The punishment for aiding and abetting apostasy in Islamic law is death.

Even so, Mughal opposition to the Sikh panth was at first weak and fitful. Babur and his immediate successors were preoccupied with consolidating their empire, and the small Sikh community was hardly a blip on the radar screen. But things changed radically when Jahangir acceded to the Mughal throne in 1605 during the guruship of Arjun Dev Ji, the fifth guru. Jahangir pursued a hard-line policy toward the Sikh community, whose continuing growth was seen as a political threat to the purified Muslim state he was trying to establish.

Guru Arjun was ordered to change "offensive" hymns in the
Guru Granth Sahib, but he refused. Then when Jahangir ordered him to renounce his faith and embrace Islam or face
death, he again refused. The powerful Sufi mystic Mian Mir
interceded on the guru's behalf and it was agreed that Guru Arjun could avoid execution by paying a fine. But Arjun refused,
saying, "whatever money I have is for the poor, the friendless,
and the stranger." He was tortured for five days with burning
hot steel and sand, and when Mian Mir offered to intercede
yet again, the guru explained his resolve this way:

> I bear all this torture to set an example. . . . The true test of faith
> is the hour of misery. Without examples to guide, ordinary
> persons' minds quail in the midst of suffering. In the second
> place, if he, who possesseth power within him, defends not his
> religion by the open profession thereof, the man who possesseth
> no such powers will, when put to the torture, abjure his faith.
> The sin will light on the head of him who hath the power but
> showeth it not; and God will deem him an enemy of religion.[4]

Guru Arjun's execution was ordered, and the guru was
granted permission to bathe before being beheaded. As he
hobbled into the Ravi River, the current swept him under and
he was never seen again. The fifth guru died a martyr in the
classic way of antiquity. Sikh tradition holds that he was the
first martyr for the faith.

Guru Arjun knew well that if the Mughal policy of oppression and forced conversions continued, the days of the panth
were numbered. His call for the open profession of faith was
a warning to his followers that they should prepare for the
defense of Sikhism by force. His successor, Guru Hargobind,
quickly raised a small army and there were occasional skirmishes with Mughal forces followed by periods of armed truce.
Under Guru Hargobind's stewardship the Sikhs established
a parallel state in open defiance of the Mughal government.
With it emerged a political and military independence that
was welcomed by many, though not all, Sikhs.

But the Mughals were hardly indifferent to Sikh triumphs, and
the new Mughal emperor Aurangzeb was determined to impose
Islamic theocracy on Hindus and Sikhs alike. In the 1670s one
of Aurangzeb's viceroys led a series of forced mass conversions
of Hindus, massacring those who refused to embrace Islam.

Hindu leaders were thrown in jail by the hundreds in the expectation that if they converted, others would quickly follow. The Hindus appealed for help from the Sikhs and their leader Tegh Bahadur, youngest son of Guru Hargobind and now ninth guru. Guru Tegh Bahadur had been raised in the art of warfare as a child but had long since renounced violence, choosing instead a life of peace and meditation. He notified the emperor that he was coming to Delhi and made him a challenge: If Aurangzeb could convince him to convert, the Hindus would follow. The guru told his nine-year-old son Gobind Rai that the sacrifice of a holy man was necessary to convince the Hindus to remain faithful. "Who is more worthy than you?" his son asked with the candor of youth.

Guru Tegh Bahadur was arrested before he got to Delhi and taken before the emperor in chains. His three traveling companions, Bhai Mati Das, Bhai Dyala, and Bhat Sati Das, were also arrested. Aurangzeb invited the guru to embrace Islam, but he refused. He was kept in an iron cage and forced to watch the gruesome executions of his companions. Bhai Mati Das was tied between two pillars and sawn in half, Bhai Dyala was boiled alive, and Bhat Sati Das was wrapped in cloth and set on fire. The guru was asked to perform a miracle to save himself. He refused but then tied a piece of paper around his neck promising that the executioner's sword would not be able to pierce it. On November 11, 1675, Guru Tegh Bahadur was publicly beheaded as he prayed. Words on the piece of paper, legend goes, declared that Tegh Bahadur had given his head but not his resolve. His head was secretly taken back to his young son in Anandpur, where it was cremated. His son would later acknowledge his father's heroic sacrifice in verse: "He gave his head for men of faith without flinching / And chose martyrdom in the cause of righteousness."[5] To modern Sikhs, the martyrdom of Guru Tegh Bahadur "symbolizes the spirit of supreme sacrifice for an ideal, the ideal of the freedom of conscience."[6]

The Khalsa Sikhs and the Instinct of Militant Martyrdom

Hearing of Guru Tegh Bahadur's torture and death in defense of the religious freedom of Hindus, Sikhs from all over northern

India poured into Anandpur to show their solidarity with the martyr's young son Gobind Rai. He would become the tenth and last of the living gurus. Over the next twenty years, Guru Gobind Singh, as he would later call himself, wrote poetry and prepared the panth for armed struggle against oppressors, whoever they might be. He also moved to institutionalize the ideal of unflinching faith in the guru, his mission, and the tenets of the Sikh religion. This he accomplished in 1699 with the creation of a community of baptized Sikhs called the Khalsa, or "pure ones." In his recent book *The Sikhs,* Patwant Singh notes, "The creation of the Khalsa reflected Guru Gobind Singh's conviction that Sikhism was a *tisar* panth, a third religion, distinct from Hinduism and Islam."[7] All men would use the last name *Singh,* from the Sanskrit word for "lion," and all women the last name *Kaur,* from the Sanskrit word for "prince." The use of a common name formally freed the Sikhs from social stratification, and the different female last name emphasized gender equality and independence, unheard of in most of the world, then or now.

The Khalsa was revolutionary also in its commitment to armed struggle and the spirit of martyrdom. This spirit became "anchored in the Sikh psyche as an instinct, indeed as a real passion."[8] To be sure, Guru Nanak had said that faith was worth fighting for, and Guru Hargobind had girded himself with two swords to symbolize his spiritual and temporal power. But it was Guru Gobind Singh who turned the "steel" of Guru Nanak's dictum "truth is pure steel" into a symbol of divine power. The sword offered protection and a way to destroy evil. Armed struggle became policy, and Sikhs displayed a heroic investment in self-sacrifice that much impressed Mughal and Hindu leaders, and later the British.

The ceremony formally creating the Khalsa is etched in the consciousness of all Sikhs. The story goes that on March 30, 1699, the guru raised his *khanda,* or double-edged sword, before a large gathering of Sikhs at Anandpur and asked if there were a true Sikh who would offer his head as a sacrifice to the faith. There was a stunned silence, and some men walked away out of bewilderment or fear. Finally, a man from Lahore named Daya Ram came forward. The guru took him into a tent and minutes later reappeared alone, his sword dripping with blood. He called for another head, and the process was repeated until five Sikhs had volunteered to be sacrificed.

After a while Guru Gobind Singh went back into the tent and the five would-be martyrs emerged alive and dressed in saffron-colored robes and turbans, swords at their sides. Their mettle tested and proved, the five were then initiated into the fellowship of the Khalsa. The guru prepared a nectar of sugar and water, called *amrit*, and the "Beloved Five" knelt before him to receive the amrit while the guru recited passages from the *Adi Granth*. Anthropologist Cynthia Keppley Mahmood writes, "The Sikh who has been admitted into the Khalsa is ... a martyr from the moment of initiation. In the sipping of amrit he or she is committed to play Nanak's game of love, 'with head in hands,' utterly selflessly and therefore without fear for one's personal mortality. It is the moment of initiation, the moment of imbibing amrit, that is actually the significant moment in the creation of the Sikh martyr...."[9]

The five men formed the nucleus of a self-abnegating, martial, and casteless fellowship into which thousands were baptized over the next few days. The guru had composed a line for the occasion, and this became their rallying cry: "The Khalsa belong to God, and God's truth will always prevail." Guru Gobind Singh had "hitched the wagon of the Sikh movement to God," and this became "a never-ending source of inspiration, energy, and optimism."[10]

The baptized Sikhs were required to wear five symbols of the Khalsa, all beginning with the letter K: *Kes*, long hair and beard; *Kanga*, a comb; *Kara*, a steel bracelet; *Kachha*, short breeches; and *Kirpan*, a dagger. These external symbols were taken very seriously, for they signified the wearer's commitment as a witness to the faith. They also made it more difficult for the wearer to blend into a crowd and thus shirk his duty.

Sikhs called their martyrs *shaheed*, borrowing the Arabic word. For Sikhs, as indeed for Muslims, militant martyrdom grew out of political and cultural processes that coalesced around resistance to oppression and became ingrained in the psyche. But what did Sikhs visualize as the reward for self-sacrifice? Martyrs for Islam and Christianity looked to rewards in the afterlife, a blissful eternity in Paradise. Sikhism drew inspiration from Islam, but also from Hinduism and Buddhism. Many Sikhs believe in karma and reincarnation. Deeds in this life influence future reincarnations. The man of

God must constantly struggle to defeat evil, and this struggle inevitably involves suffering and sometimes self-sacrifice. Renouncing the self and devoting one's life to the will of God may result in God revealing himself and ending the cycle of birth and rebirth. But "Sikh shaheeds are never given any assurance of some sort of Heaven," writes Indian historian Surjit Singh Gandhi.[11] Instead, the would-be martyr's reward is the knowledge that self-sacrifice for faith and justice follows God's will or purpose. Guru Nanak had defined God's will as altruistic and loving, and he invited Sikhs to play the game of love: "Shouldst thou seek to engage in the game of Love, step into my street with thy head placed on thy palm; while stepping onto this street, ungrudgingly sacrifice your head."[12]

Social distinctions were abolished in the Khalsa fellowship, and this attracted so many converts from the lower Hindu castes that some Rajputs shared the Mughal alarm at the goings-on in Anandpur. It wasn't long before Mughal warriors and northern Hindu rajas joined forces to crush the troublesome Sikhs once and for all. There were several bloody battles around Anandpur and a long siege of the city. The Sikhs stood their ground until the prospect of thousands dying from starvation led Gobind Singh to accept an offer of safe passage from emperor Aurangzeb. The guru left Anandpur at the end of 1704 with his family and an entourage of Khalsa Sikhs.

The Mughals and their Rajput allies had treachery in their hearts: The Sikhs were attacked soon after leaving Anandpur. Hundreds were killed. In true Khalsa spirit, one group died fighting against suicidal odds in a rearguard action so that the others might escape. Many of the remaining Sikhs died while fording the swollen Sarsa River, and others became separated from the guru on the opposite bank. These included his mother and two young sons, who were later arrested and imprisoned by Nawab Wazir Khan, the governor of Sirhind. The sons were offered inducements to convert to Islam, but they refused. Wazir Khan had them bricked up alive, and when just their heads remained above the masonry, the offers were repeated—and rejected once again. Furious, Wazir Khan ordered the boys beheaded despite pleas for restraint from the Muslim governor of Malerkotla, Sher Muhammad Khan, whose efforts Sikhs honor to this day.

Guru Gobind Singh's Khalsa entourage had been reduced to around forty men, and at the battle of Chamkaur on December 22, 1704, he faced his enemies again. All but three of his men died in hand-to-hand combat, including two of the original "Beloved Five." The three survivors and the guru eventually made their way to the village of Jatpura where they were warmly received by the Muslim chief. For indeed, many Muslims admired the Sikhs for their principled and determined stand against tyranny and oppression. The repressive policies of Emperor Aurangzeb were condemned by many of his fellow Sunnis, including the caliphs of Mecca and Baghdad. Guru Gobind Singh took advantage of shifting allegiances and internal conflicts among Muslim and Hindu leaders to rebuild and strengthen the Sikh community. He even joined forces with Aurangzeb's son Prince Muazzam against another son who was principal claimant to the Mughal throne.

Over the next two centuries, the martial spirit of the Khalsa panth was called on repeatedly to protect the faith and to expand its domain. Many enemy soldiers were killed in these skirmishes and battles, but many Sikhs died as well. Slaughtering the enemy and sacrificing oneself in the process were complementary actions that controlled Sikh destiny. During the brutal mid-eighteenth-century persecution of Sikhs led by Mir Mannu, governor of Lahore, a ditty surfaced that might have been written by Tertullian, the North African advocate of Christian martyrdom: "Mir Mannu is our sickle, we the fodder for him to mow; the more he reaps, the more we grow."[13]

Some Khalsa Sikhs became legendary warrior-martyrs. The fearless feats of Banda Singh, who avenged the atrocities committed by arch enemy Wazir Khan and in just seven years led the Sikhs to new heights of power, establishing the first-ever independent Sikh state, epitomized what it meant to be a Khalsa Sikh. Banda Singh had been converted to Sikhism by Guru Gobind Singh himself just a month before the guru's death. Under Banda the Khalsa became a fearsome fighting machine; after one battle a Muslim chronicler wrote that "not a man of the army of Islam escaped with more than his life and the clothes he stood in. Horsemen and footmen fell under the sword of the infidels who pursued them...."[14]

Banda's death came at the hands of Muhammad Farrukh Siyar, who had assassinated his own nephew to become

Mughal emperor in 1713. The new emperor amassed the largest Mughal army ever seen and ordered that every Sikh captured should be put to the sword if he refused to convert to Islam. The severed heads of hundreds of Sikhs were sent to the emperor "for his pleasure" by commanders in the field. Following an eight-month siege, a starving, diseased, but unbending Khalsa army was overrun by Mughal troops who immediately beheaded three hundred Sikhs and then marched the rest, with Banda shackled to a cage on an elephant's back, in a victory procession through Lahore to Delhi. Along the way other captured Sikhs were added to the procession, and by the time it reached Delhi there were a thousand manacled prisoners preceded by carts carrying two thousand Sikh heads stuffed with straw. Yet the Sikhs "seemed happy and cheerful," wrote one chronicler, and when spectators threatened to kill them, they shouted back, "Kill us, kill us, why should we fear death?"[15]

Executions followed every day for three months, and spectators were amazed to see some Sikhs pushing themselves to the front, crying "kill me first." Finally it was Banda's turn. He could not be bought off, nor would he convert. On June 9, 1716, he was paraded around the city, then his young child was put in his arms and torn apart in front of him. Pieces of the child's warm flesh were stuffed into Banda's mouth and the executioner then hacked Banda to death, limb by limb.

Mughal persecutions continued, and this kept Sikh militancy alive. "None of the revolutionaries, including women and children, abjured their faith in the face of the barbaric tortures current in that age."[16] Estimates suggest that more than two hundred thousand Sikhs died fighting or under torture during the eighteenth century. The tenacity of the Sikhs and their willingness to kill and die for their beliefs impressed the Mughals even as they tried to exterminate Sikhs. It impressed others as well: the British, who had come to India as merchants and by the mid-eighteenth century controlled large blocks of India, including Bengal and Madras; the Marathas, a militant confederacy of Hindu tribes from the Deccan region bent on establishing their own dynasty, and who by 1760 controlled much of central and northern India, including Lahore and Delhi (despite a sitting Mughal emperor); and finally, Muslim invaders from Afghanistan, whose leader Ahmed Shah Abdali made eight separate incursions into India and found himself up against Sikhs at every turn.

One of these Afghan incursions was at the behest of the Indian cleric Shah Waliullah, who had been urging Muslims "to return to the simplicity and spirit of the time of the Prophet and the first two Caliphs." Waliullah sent Abdali a letter urging him to lead a jihad to "smash the unbelievers' army ... so that in the presence of Almighty God ... his name may be recorded in the register of holy warriors...."[17] The ensuing battle at Panipat—the same place where Babur had defeated Ibrahim Lodi 250 years earlier—killed thousands of Hindus and Muslims (who were fighting on both sides) but settled little. The victorious Abdali returned home to Afghanistan, the Mughal emperor remained on the throne, and the Marathas turned to take on the British who were moving on them from the south. On his way home with spoils that included Hindu and Muslim girls, the victorious Abdali was attacked by Khalsa Sikhs and his wagon train plundered. The Khalsas then captured Lahore. Abdali retaliated, and so did the Sikhs; it was one bloodbath after another.

The British, meanwhile, had designs on the whole of India. After defeating the Marathas, they captured Delhi in 1803 and essentially confined the Mughal emperor to his palace. Muslim leaders called for jihad against the British, and the spirit of rebellion took shape under the leadership of Sayyid Ahmad Barelvi, a product of the Shah Waliullah seminary. When Barelvi heard stories that the Sikhs were persecuting Afghans living in the Punjab, he launched a jihad against them as well. He was ambushed and killed in 1831 by a Khalsa force after celebrating a short-lived victory over the Sikhs at Peshawar, where he had proclaimed himself caliph. The Khalsa commander, the youngest son of the great Sikh leader Maharaja Ranjit Singh, buried Barelvi with full honors as befitted a chief. Over the next twenty-five years the spirit of jihad continued to glow in pockets of resistance against the British occupiers, and the Sikhs were eventually drawn into the conflict in a big way.

Intrigue within the ranks of the Khalsa Sikhs led to a string of assassinations, including the murder of Sher Singh, half-brother of Dalip Singh, the respectful executioner of Barelvi. The Sikhs controlled the Punjab, but bitter infighting made them vulnerable to British ambition and the carefully planned buildup of troops to support it. There were two Anglo–Sikh wars, the first starting in December 1845, the second three years later. The Sikhs suffered heavy losses and their cause was undermined by the incompetence and treachery of some of their leaders. Even so, stories of the ferocity and gallantry of the Khalsa Sikhs filled British dispatches from the field. This was little comfort to the Khalsa, who were forced to lay down their arms and turn over the administration of the Punjab to a British-led commission. Christian missionaries quickly appeared from England and America. They enjoyed strong backing from the British commissioners who aimed to pacify the militant Sikhs, to turn them "away from the source of their determination and strength, from their beliefs which gave them the courage to die in their defence."[18]

The plan worked in that some Sikhs converted to Christianity, including a son of Ranjit Singh. But it also backfired in that there were calls for renewal of faith and noncooperation with British rule. Agitation grew on both sides, and in one confrontation the British arrested sixty-six Sikhs, who were then lined up without trial and blown apart by cannon. Their leader, Ram Singh, was forced to watch the massacre, then deported to Rangoon, where he later died "undaunted and unchanging in his convictions and beliefs."[19]

By the end of the nineteenth century, a movement known as the Singh Sabha had taken root and led the counteroffensive against the arrogance of the British colonizers and their missionary partners. Its leaders sought a purification and resurgence of Sikh intellectual and theological life as well as control over its institutions, in particular Sikh temples—*gurdwara*, or "God's places." The first gurdwara was established by Guru Arjun Dev Ji as a repository of the Sikh religion and a reflection of its resoluteness and strength, a symbol of the indestructibility of the faith. It was built at Amritsar and is known to the English-speaking world as the Golden Temple, a reflection of the gold dome and facade of its most important building, the Harmindar Sahib (House of God), also known as the Darbar Sahib (Divine Court).

The Golden Temple had become the hub of the Sikh world by the early eighteenth century, and all Sikhs were encouraged to visit it twice a year. Its importance made it a beacon for pilgrims and oppressors alike. Mughal and Afghan armies tried to demolish it, and Sikhs willingly gave their lives in its defense. No better death was conceivable for a Sikh. The Afghan invader Ahmed Shah Abdali destroyed much of the temple twice, only to see it quickly rebuilt under the direction of the Khalsa. On the second of Abdali's destructive visits he found a mere thirty Khalsa Sikhs standing guard at the entrance. "They had not a grain of fear about them," said one Muslim eyewitness. He continued: "They were resolved to sacrifice their lives for the Guru."[20] Afterward, their bodies were thrown into the sacred pool in front of the temple.

The desecration of the Golden Temple in 1757 had enraged Sikhs, none more so than the Khalsa leader and scholar Baba Deep Singh, who vowed to take revenge. The story goes that Deep Singh drew a line on the ground with his sword and invited would-be martyrs to join him by crossing it. Five hundred Sikhs did so, and en route to Amritsar their number swelled to five thousand. Five miles from the temple an army of twenty thousand Afghan soldiers lay in wait for them, led by the veteran general Jahan Khan. The battle was furious. At one point Deep Singh was almost decapitated, but he fought on until finally collapsing in a pool of blood near the entrance to the Golden Temple. A legend grew that it was his headless body that fought on, his left hand holding his head while his right hand wielded his double-edged sword. The Khalsa unit (*misl*) led by Baba Deep Singh for twenty years was renamed the "Shahid misl" in honor of his martyrdom.

The Massacre at Jallianwala Bagh, Partition, and Operation Blue Star

In an extraordinary display of religious insensitivity, the Christian British had taken control of Sikh—and Muslim—holy places during the nineteenth century. It wasn't until 1925 that Sikhs and Muslims once again became custodians of their own temples. By then, protest marches and daily arrests had become a common sight around the country, especially in the Punjab. The growing militancy of the independence movement was fueled in 1919 by an atrocity that Sikhs will never forget—the massacre at Jallianwala Bagh.

The Bagh was an open area bounded on all sides by high buildings and located a few hundred yards from the Golden Temple. Thousands of Sikhs and Hindus had gathered there to celebrate a Hindu festival and to hear speeches protesting legislation aimed at suppressing the burgeoning movement for Indian independence. The so-called Black Acts had given the English viceroy authority to quell the "seditious conspiracy" through silencing the press, arresting suspects without a warrant, and detaining political activists without trial.

On April 12, 1919, the new military commander at Amritsar, General Reginald E. H. Dyer, had declared all meetings illegal, but many of those gathering at Jallianwala Bagh on April 13 were probably unaware of the order. In any case, they had brought children with them, not arms. At around 5:15 p.m., Dyer entered the Bagh with his troops through a narrow passageway, which was also the only exit. He took up position and ordered his troops to fire into the crowd. Fifteen minutes later the troops had run out of ammunition and more than a thousand lay dead or wounded.

The international outcry following this act of callous brutality led to a parliamentary inquiry in England, but Dyer was later exonerated by the conservative House of Lords. He was given an engraved sword by supporters and more than a million dollars in today's money. The leader of the massacre may have gotten away with murder, but the British governor of Punjab who condoned the action paid later with his life. He was shot in London in 1940 by a militant supporter of Indian independence who had infiltrated a meeting of the East India Association. The assassin, Shaheed Udham Singh, had no chance of escape and was hanged four months later. Udham Singh is revered by many Sikhs as a patriot-martyr, hence the honorific title of *Shaheed.*

Not surprisingly, Indians were outraged by the Jallianwala Bagh incident, Sikhs in particular, as it had occurred in the sacred city of Amritsar. Far from serving British interests, the killings fueled the demands for Indian independence and played into the hands of those who rejected the nonviolent resistance advocated by Mohandas Gandhi. When India finally gained independence in 1947, it was partitioned into a mainly Hindu India and a mainly Muslim Pakistan. The Punjab was divided down the middle, with two million Sikhs left on the predominantly Muslim side. "What the Sikhs had acquired through shedding their blood on countless battlefields [had been] bartered away."[21] Worse still, they found themselves in the middle of ferocious and bloody battles that erupted on both sides of the partition line. Sikhs on the side that would become West Pakistan became victims of a brutal campaign of ethnic cleansing by the dominant Muslims. Many fled, others were stranded, and hundreds of thousands were killed in the course of a few months.

Queen Victoria's great-grandson Lord Mountbatten was India's last viceroy, and he oversaw the partition. He did little to prevent the killings or the migration of millions of Hindus, Sikhs, and Muslims who rushed to join their own kind before and after partition. And there was more horror: "The estimate of 600,000 who paid for their lives in Punjab because of British indifference to their fate does not take into account the countless bodies burnt, buried or dumped in rivers, nor thousands of women abducted during the frenzy that self-serving men had helped unleash on innocent men, women and children."[22] Many Sikhs never forgave Mountbatten, and there were doubtless celebrations when he was assassinated by Thomas McMahon of the Provisional Irish Republican Army on August 27, 1979. McMahon, who probably knew little of Sikh history, had planted a bomb on Mountbatten's pleasure boat off the coast of Donegal, Ireland.

Sikh fortunes in India in the decades after independence continued the saga of suffering, sacrifice, and killing. The largely Hindu leadership in Delhi held most of the 545 seats in parliament, the Sikhs only thirteen. Efforts to establish a Punjabi-speaking state were delayed and only succeeded after a bitter six-year struggle that left many Sikhs dead and thousands imprisoned. The end result, however, was a truncated state that left out many Punjabi-speaking Hindus and further reduced its political clout in Delhi. In any case, there was plenty of fodder for militancy in the new India, and Sikhs, Hindus, and Muslims were soon offering up martyrs to their respective causes.

The main Sikh party, the moderate Akali Dal, found itself in constant conflict with powerful Hindu elements in the capital, as well as with more extreme Sikh groups in the Punjab. When Prime Minister Indira Gandhi suspended the Indian constitution and rule of law in 1975 and declared a state of emergency, it was Akali Sikhs that rose up in great numbers to protest. Forty thousand were jailed, and the Sikhs had made a dangerous enemy who would never forget. Repeated defeats inside and outside government slowly but surely pushed many Punjabi Sikhs into a dream of secession and a Sikh homeland. People began to say that the Sikh panth itself was in danger. A preacher then appeared on the scene with fiery speeches about threats to the faith and the need to return to Sikh orthodoxy. This was Jarnail Singh Bhindranwale, head of a seminary founded by the revered eighteenth-century warrior-martyr Baba Deep Singh, to whom Bhindranwale reportedly compared himself. Over the next few years he took on "wayward" Sikhs and aggravated the simmering conflict between Hindus and Sikhs over secession. He became a hero to many Sikhs, especially the separatists.

Bhindranwale's attacks against fellow Sikhs came to a head in 1978. A modern Sikh sect, the Nirankaris, were holding their annual convention in a sports stadium in Amritsar on the day commemorating the founding of the Khalsa by Guru Gobind Singh. Bhindranwale was angry that a "heretical" sect would choose such an important date for its meeting and he organized—but did not participate in—a protest march aimed at disrupting the convention. When the marchers entered the stadium, Nirankari guards shot at them, killing a number of orthodox Sikhs. Bhindranwale retaliated with violent attacks against Nirankari missions throughout the Punjab, with the tacit support of the Punjabi state government. The national government seemed unperturbed by the sectarian conflict, even when Punjabi Hindus began to complain that the state government was bowing to Sikh fanatics and terrorists. In truth, it was all playing into the hands of Indira Gandhi, who would be reelected prime minister in 1980 and had a score to settle with the Sikhs.

With a mixture of violence and religious oratory Bhindran-wale continued his campaign for a sovereign Sikh state of Khalistan ("Land of the Pure"). While the government played down the secessionist movement, claiming it was nothing but a few hoodlums acting on their own, many Sikhs began to believe that it was a real possibility. Even some members of the Akali Dal party jumped on the bandwagon. Hindu alarm soared. The Hindu press warned of the collapse of secular democracy and the rise of rule by terror. As if to prove the point, Bhindranwale's followers murdered the Hindu owner of a newspaper chain. When Bhindranwale was arrested for complicity in the murder, a wave of bombings and murders followed, including the hijacking of an Indian Airlines passenger jet. Violence continued throughout the Punjab after Bhindranwale's release a month later, peaking in 1983 with bombings of Hindu temples and gatherings, revenge attacks by enraged Hindus, and sabotage of rail lines that caused deadly train accidents. There were also bombings in Delhi, the capital of India.

A nationwide backlash against Sikhs was inevitable. Bhindranwale and some of his followers moved into the Golden Temple compound at Amritsar. Gandhi sent the army into the Punjab, and security forces conducted combing operations to flush out Sikh militants. "Four thousand two hundred and fifty detainees distributed over one thousand villages in the five central districts gave each village a share of four to five."[23] Many detainees returned to their villages with stories of police excesses, including torture. The tension between the Sikhs and Gandhi's government was at the breaking point. A high-ranking police official was shot dead at the Golden Temple, the Akali Dal launched a campaign of noncooperation with the government, and the Indian army moved toward the Golden Temple. Things came to a head during five days in June 1984. The event is referred to by Sikhs as *ghallughara,* meaning "holocaust."

June 3 commemorates the martyrdom of Guru Arjun. Thousands of Sikh pilgrims were visiting the Golden Temple compound on that day in 1984. The compound contains a number of buildings, including the Akal Takht (Eternal Throne), a semicircular building fronted by pillars in which important gatherings are addressed, and the Sikh Reference Library, holding priceless religious works. These buildings look upon the sacred Pool of Amrit, in the midst of which sits the shimmering Golden Temple, where the *Guru Granth Sahib* is read continuously. The compound also contains a number of offices, along with hostels for visitors. Bhindranwale was first housed in one of the hostels but had moved into the Akal Takht, which he fortified with machine guns.

In preparation for its assault, the Indian army cut off all communication between the Punjab and the outside world on June 3, and a total curfew was imposed on the streets. On June 4, with Muslims, Hindus, and Sikhs in its ranks, the army moved into the compound and exchanged gunfire with the militants inside the Akal Takht. Pilgrims were encouraged to leave, but few did, some doubtless fearing arrest or worse on the outside, others in a show of support for Bhindranwale. No one, not even the army, expected the carnage that followed.

Ferocious fighting continued through June 5 and 6, as the Sikh militants held the army at bay with withering fire from machine guns and explosions from hand grenades thrown from doors and windows. The army brought in tanks, and the militants responded with rocket-propelled, armor-piercing shells fired from Chinese launchers. By the end of June 6, the Akal Takht was virtually destroyed. On June 7, 1984, the army finally entered the building and found bodies strewn everywhere, including those of Bhindranwale and his top lieutenants. Faced with death, Bhindranwale is reputed to have compared himself to Baba Deep Singh, saying, "I am privileged to be able to give my head right here."[24] Toward the end of the fighting, fire had erupted in the Sikh Reference Library and it was gutted, the priceless contents destroyed. One witness recalled, "I stood there watching the smoke. . . . When I found out later that it was the library that had burnt I kept seeing that smoke, smelling that smoke in my mind. It seemed to me that I could feel the pages burning, the precious pages of my Guru Granth Sahib. . . . Many people had died, but I was crying most about my Guru."[25]

Operation Blue Star, as the Indian army called it, enraged and galvanized Sikhs. In all, around five thousand had died, and there were reports of army atrocities against pilgrims and other civilians. Bhindranwale and his dead followers were hailed as martyrs, and two thousand Sikh soldiers in the Indian army rebelled. The violent aftermath would claim more lives in two years than the entire seven years of Bhindranwale's militant secessionist campaign—including that of Prime Minister Indira Gandhi. Less than five months after the assault, she was assassinated by two of the Sikh soldiers assigned to the prime minister's protection detail as bodyguards.

Anti-Sikh pogroms followed; with the connivance of police and other government officials, Hindu mobs attacked Sikh men, women, and children across northern India and in Delhi itself. In one attack, men poured kerosene through ventilation openings in a Sikh home and then brutally attacked and burned alive all the adult males in the family. The bloodbath continued for four days while the army remained confined to its barracks.

Between 1984 and 1992 violence escalated in the Punjab as more Sikhs joined the ranks of their militant brothers in the fight for independence. During those years, more than eleven thousand people died in violence officially attributed to Sikh "terrorists." More than half of the dead were themselves Sikhs. To many Indians, writes Sharda Jain in *Politics of Terror in India*, "a microscopic minority of brainwashed fundamentalists, parading under the garb of religion," were responsible for the terror. The government line was that these "communal zealots ... spread hatred against Hindus, Nirankaris and non-communal Sikhs in the name of liberating the *panth* and to get an independent state for the Sikhs."[26]

In response, India launched a worldwide campaign against terrorism. To the Indian government and world leaders generally, "all distinctions between militant protest, the struggle for freedom, religious nationalism and self-determination" were erased with the catchword *terrorist*.[27] This gave the government a justification for state repression, but it became a vicious circle in which the militants saw violence as their only option and the government responded with greater violence. Meanwhile, Sikhs the world over struggled to understand the unfolding violence in terms of Sikh teachings and the vitality of the global panth.

But the Indian government underestimated the Sikh militants' commitment to their cause and their willingness to sacrifice themselves for it. Sikh militants see themselves as following in the footsteps of Baba Deep Singh. Their attitude is maintained through the combination of "prayer and action, action and prayer," the *miri* and *piri* represented by the sixth guru's two swords. They hold to Guru Nanak's revelation that martyrdom is an expression of love as well as witness: In their farewell letter before being hanged for the assassination of the general who led Operation Blue Star, two Sikh militants "imagined the hangman's rope as the embrace of a lover, longed for death as for the marital bed, and hoped that their dripping blood ... would fertilize the fields of Khalistan."[28] Despite a history stretching back to antiquity, the love expressed in a martyr's act is often underestimated, if it is recognized at all. On occasion it is even more powerful than a mother's love for her child. In her stunning ethnography *Fighting for Faith and Nation: Dialogues with Sikh Militants,* anthropologist Cynthia Keppley Mahmood relates this story:

> One man I interviewed had just gotten out of India a month before I met him, and in the intervening time his wife and infant son had been arrested. Police apparently tied the child to a block of ice in order to make this militant's wife tell them where he was. Rather than succumbing to the temptation to try to spare her child, she asked for a glass of water and when it arrived, she smashed it on the desktop and slit her throat with the ragged edge. She died on the spot.... "She was so full of love, she martyred," [said the husband].... Life as a game of love means life unafraid of death, for oneself or for others.[29]

Notwithstanding the influence of Guru Nanak and the Sikh tradition of martyrdom embodied in this account, the Sikh martyrs who in earlier times had killed and died for justice and faith might have had misgivings about the direction Sikh militancy was moving during the 1980s and 1990s. More and more civilians were being killed. The most infamous incident was the bombing of Air India Flight 182 off the coast of Ireland in 1985. All 329 people on board were killed, most of them Canadians. (On March 16, 2005, a Canadian trial lasting two years ended in the acquittal of two Indian-born Sikh militants charged in the bombing. The judge questioned the credibility of prosecution witnesses.)

This bombing was not a suicide attack, but it showed that militants were ready to kill civilians in large numbers. A decade later the militant Sikhs of Babbar Khalsa International, or BKI, began to use human bombs. In the first known attack, Dilawar Singh blew himself up in the assassination of the Punjab's chief minister. Fifteen others also died in the explosion. Over the next six years a number of attacks involving suicide bombers were thwarted by vigilante Indian security services, but some BKI militants managed to carry out their assignments nonetheless. This was no longer self-sacrifice in a battle of armed warriors (albeit a lopsided one); the martyrdom was becoming predatory, the killing indiscriminate.

In their statements about martyrdom operations, Sikh militants draw on the Khalsa spirit and tradition of self-sacrifice: "We celebrate martyrdom and honor those who have martyred for the cause.... Even our enemies praise the way we sacrifice our lives if necessary. Someone who offers his life for the people becomes part of them, strengthens them. A sincere martyrdom is a very good thing, we think. That is why in the end we will succeed."[30]

Warrior-Martyrs: Killing and Dying for God and Community

We have traveled across many years and many miles to meet the warrior-martyrs, those who willingly give up their lives in militant campaigns on behalf of God or community, most often both. The stories we have encountered were written by participants and by onlookers, and sometimes by historians many years later. I believe this all-too-brief account has identified all the important developments in the concept and practice of martyrdom from the seventh through the twentieth centuries.

With the approval of the Prophet Muhammad and the Quran, Muslims honed the practice of martyrdom into an act of self-sacrifice in the service of jihad, or holy war. Enemies of Islam must be resisted, and those who die fighting in God's cause are rewarded with an afterlife in Paradise. Christians took up this idea with a vengeance when Pope Urban called upon the Franks to save Christianity from the Seljuk Turks and to reclaim Jerusalem from the Fatimids. The will of God played heavily in both camps, as indeed it had done in the mind of Socrates centuries before. But now it was holy war, and willing warrior-martyrs on both sides embraced death while trying to kill God's enemies.

As all this was going on, the submissive martyrdom perfected in antiquity remained the path of believers who refused to abjure their religion under threat of torture and death or the promise of earthly rewards. When it came to torments and tortures, the inventive Persians and Romans of antiquity were arguably bested by the Mughals of India. And for sheer numbers, the crusaders stand out, having made martyrs of thousands of Muslims and Jews, many of whom were massacred or took their own and their children's lives to avoid falling into the hands of the infidel.

Once invented, the idea of holy war traveled far and wide. It motivated warrior-martyrs with the promise of plunder and Paradise, and it served the political and territorial ambitions of its leaders. The Assassins honed the idea into an offensive strategy centered on the discipline, indoctrination, and rigorous training of suicide commandos. The Sikhs tuned the idea yet further with the birth of the Khalsa, who bowed unselfishly to the will of God and committed their martial spirit to the protection of faith, community, and justice. Guru Gobind Singh had made the martyrdom of Sikh warriors both an instinct and a social expectation.

These developments in the concept and practice of martyrdom showed the changing character of suicidal defiance in deadly conflicts where religious belief was a driving force, though often not the immediate cause. Ironically, the warrior-martyrs among Muslims, Christians, and Sikhs were followers of the same God the Creator. They saw themselves in a battle against Evil, killing on God's behalf and dying on God's behalf. For Khalsa warriors this was reward enough; for the warriors of Christianity and Islam, an afterlife in Paradise beckoned, as it had for the religious martyrs of antiquity.

Stories and legends of great warrior-martyrs became part of the history and culture of all three religions. They also gave inspiration and heart to the soldiers that battled against impossible odds or slogged through the marshes and mountains of inhospitable foreign lands. When commanders sensed a dimming of hope or faced unlikely victory, the spirits of legendary martyrs were called upon to stiffen the backs of ordinary men looking death in the face. From the endless battles and skirmishes new warrior-martyrs emerged gloriously and became legends in their own right. But most of the dead were called martyrs anyway, because they died on the "good" side in holy war.

Needless to say, conflicts between unequal powers invite the weaker side to find strategies that challenge the inevitability of

defeat. The more lopsided the disadvantage, the more desperate the situation, and desperation is the breeding ground of
militant martyrdom. It should be no surprise that the drive to
win—for some, simply to survive—encouraged innovations in
the technology and delivery of death and led to the blurring of
distinctions between soldiers and civilians. A no-holds-barred
endgame looks very appealing to the serious underdog, and
only strict religious or moral values may preclude it. It should
also be no surprise, then, that these rules were challenged
by Sikh militants fighting to establish Khalistan. In drifting
toward their endgame they found a way to justify using bombs
that killed civilians. A Sikh bomb maker whose devices killed
countless civilians in an Indian marketplace was proud of
his actions and unapologetic. "If the entire Sikh tradition
is at stake, a few lives here or there seem to weigh rather
less—whether these are of martyrs or of victims."[31]

Part III

Martyr-Warriors

Japan's Kamikazes

On January 6, 1945, just before noon, Commander George F. Davis was standing on the bridge of his ship, the American destroyer *Walke*. The USS *Walke* was part of a large naval force heading for a showdown with the Japanese on Luzon Island in the Philippines. The destroyer had been assigned to support minesweeping operations in the Lingayen Gulf. Japanese fighter-bombers had attacked the Allied ships the night before and again that morning. The pride of the Australian fleet, the cruiser HMAS *Australia*, affectionately called "Aussie," had been severely damaged and would be forced out of action two days later from the accumulated effects of five direct hits. The destroyer USS *Stafford* had also been hit and was taking on water. Other ships damaged by the Japanese planes included the powerful American battleships *New Mexico* and *California*.

Davis and his crew searched the skies for signs of enemy aircraft. Suddenly, four Japanese Zeros were spotted flying toward the destroyer a mere hundred feet above the waves. Commander Davis rushed out to the exposed wing of the ship's bridge so he could better direct defensive operations.

He ordered his gunners to open fire. The leading plane was quickly hit and crashed into the sea below; the second was hit as it passed near the destroyer's bridge. It, too, plunged into the sea.

The third Japanese plane continued toward the ship, aiming directly at the bridge. It hit with a furious crash. Wounded by the explosion, Davis was immediately drenched with gasoline and enveloped in flames. Officers and men rushed to beat out the flames. The wounded and horribly burned Davis, still on his feet, beseeched his crew to save the ship. Only when the fourth Japanese plane was shot down did Davis allow himself to be taken belowdecks. He died a few hours later.

The four Japanese pilots were kamikazes. Their mission was to crash bomb-laden planes directly into enemy ships. The kamikazes were trained to be martyrs. There was no expectation that they would survive; if they did, their mission was counted a failure. The medieval Assassins had shown a similar single-mindedness, but their accomplishments on the field of battle were limited by design as well as technology. Their suicide missions typically targeted specific individuals who were killed with knives or swords in face-to-face attacks. In contrast, a damaging attack on a ship by one kamikaze pilot could kill hundreds of enemy soldiers as well as put the ship out of commission. This, at least, had been the plan, and it was a strategy of war that ended up turning hundreds of Japanese recruits into martyr-warriors—that is, martyrs first, warriors second. The kamikaze campaign was unprecedented in planning, organization, scope, and impact. That the memory of the Japanese airmen who sacrificed themselves in these missions was later sullied by persistent criticism in the homeland they died for was also unprecedented.

Chapter 6

The Divine Wind

In Japanese, *kamikaze* means "Divine Wind." That was the name given to ferocious storms that came up off the coast of thirteenth-century Japan and twice forced back a Chinese invasion fleet under the great Mongol emperor Kublai Khan. A miracle such as the Divine Wind that had saved Japan from foreign invasion seven hundred years ago was needed again in the fall of 1944. Allied forces under the command of Admiral Chester Nimitz and General Douglas MacArthur were fast approaching the Philippines, and if these islands fell, the blow to Japanese defenses would be catastrophic. The Americans had assigned almost two million troops, nearly eight thousand aircraft, and more than seven hundred ships to the Pacific theater, a clear signal of their resolve.[1] As far as the Japanese high command was concerned, this was going to be a fight to the death, a view shared by the emperor and evidently the Japanese people as a whole.

The early Japanese victories, including Pearl Harbor, were long forgotten. By mid-1944 the army was encouraging desperate acts to stem the advance of American soldiers throughout the Pacific islands. The deputy chief of the Imperial General Staff, General Jun Ushiroku, ordered the use of "human bullets" to stop the American tanks. In New Guinea, and later on the island of Saipan in the Marianas, some Japanese troops strapped land mines or satchel charges to their bodies and flung themselves under moving tanks. The tactic failed, and the Japanese army soon after renounced the practice as an ineffective waste of courageous soldiers.

These heroic acts of self-sacrifice by Japanese soldiers were born of desperation yet also fueled by a Japanese military tradition based on honor and unflinching loyalty—the Bushido code of the samurai, or warrior class. The code of the samurai was drawn from the three great religions in Japan: Shintoism, Buddhism, and Confucianism. "Shintoism taught the warriors that they were descendants of divine beings and that upon death they, too, would become 'gods.' From Buddhism they learned to accept the transitory, fragile nature of life and to view death as crossing into another plane of existence. From Confucianism came the concept of absolute loyalty to their lord."[2]

From the first day of training, military recruits had to memorize the "Five Principles of the Soldier," part of the Imperial Rescript to Soldiers and Sailors that laid out their obligations and which they had to study daily. The principles emphasized loyalty, propriety, valor, righteousness, and simplicity. They were taken very seriously. A French professor living in Japan wrote, "A lieutenant once killed himself, in a passion of responsibility, because he had made a mistake in the public recitation of the Imperial Rescript."[3]

Early in 1941, the year of Japan's attack on Pearl Harbor, General Hideki Tojo, minister of the army and soon after prime minister, had ordered the distribution of a code of ethics in battle to every member of the armed forces. The code, called Senjin Kun, included the following directives: "A sublime sense of self-sacrifice must guide you throughout life and death.... Do not fear to die for the cause of everlasting justice. Do not stay alive in dishonor. Do not die in such a way as to leave a bad name behind you!"[4]

To die an honorable death was a soldier's highest duty. The newly appointed commander of the Japanese First Air Fleet, Vice-Admiral Takijiro Onishi, was a firm believer in the code. Onishi was responsible for the air defense of the Philippines. He saw a naval air force decimated by the battle for the Marianas and facing an enemy feasting on victories.

The Marianas "turkey shoot," as it was called by U.S. sailors, had cost Japan four hundred planes, nine aircraft carriers, and most of its newly commissioned airmen; the cabinet and Prime Minister Tojo had resigned in shame. Though highly motivated and filled with youthful enthusiasm, Onishi's airmen were ill-trained and out-gunned for the battles that lay ahead, and time was of the essence. As the admiral searched for new strategies to help save the Philippines and their important Japanese bases, he recalled earlier conversations with fellow officers about the possibility of suicide attacks from the air.

Suicide attack was not a new idea to the Japanese navy. In 1943, a midget submarine, the *Kairyu* ("sea dragon"), had been built. Filled with TNT or carrying live torpedoes, the submarine was supposed to ram enemy ships, its crew sacrificed in the process. However, with a top speed of only 7.5 knots, the *Kairyu* was considered too slow to be effective and was never used in battle. Later, a human torpedo was developed by two young navy lieutenants, Hiroshi Kuroki and Sekio Nishina. Crammed into a small cockpit in the midsection of the specially elongated torpedo, the pilot used a simple periscope to guide his 1½-ton warhead to its target. It was called the Kaiten, which meant "turning of the heavens," to suggest the reversal of fortune resting on its shoulders.

The Kaiten was used in battle a number of times. One attack occurred on November 20, 1944, when five Kaiten were launched from submarines in the Ulithi lagoon, halfway between New Guinea and Guam. Lieutenant Nishina was one of the pilots. He carried with him the ashes of his coinventor Kuroki, who had died earlier during a failed test dive. Running at 20 to 30 knots, the doomed pilots adjusted their direction at the last minute, hoping to hit the enemy targets amidships for maximum damage. Four of the Kaiten were sunk by American fire or missed their targets, exploding harmlessly along with their martyr-pilots. The fifth hit an American oil tanker, the *Mississinewa*, which exploded in a fireball as 400,000 gallons of aviation gasoline ignited. Three officers and forty-seven other personnel were killed—and the sunken *Mississinewa* continues to leak oil to this day.

Gleeful military officials in Tokyo trumpeted news of the Kaiten attack, claiming that the human torpedoes had sunk two battleships and damaged a number of cruisers and destroyers. This exaggerated claim was typical of Japanese domestic propaganda throughout the war. In fact, there was no documented Kaiten sinking of an Allied fighting ship until July 24, 1945. On that day, the destroyer USS *Underhill* was escorting a convoy of troop ships taking soldiers for much-needed rest and relaxation after fighting in the battle for Okinawa. As the destroyer steamed south, it was attacked by four Kaiten launched from the Japanese submarine *I-53.* Two Kaiten were sunk by the *Underhill,* but a third exploded into the destroyer's starboard bow, just forward of Engine Room Number One. The damage was severe enough that the navy scuttled the ship rather than let it fall into enemy hands.

Apart from these suicide attacks from the sea, there were also the last-minute heroics of Japanese fighter pilots who died by ramming enemy planes in flight. Ramming attacks were usually made when a pilot ran out of ammunition or was seriously wounded, or when his aircraft was badly damaged. Survival was moot in any case. The typical attack was to ram the enemy plane head on. One of the most famous ramming attacks was by Japanese flying ace Lieutenant Naoshi Kanno. It was famous not because it succeeded in downing the enemy plane but because both Kanno and his plane survived.

In the summer of 1944, Kanno and other Zero fighter pilots from the 201st Air Group were assigned to intercept Allied heavy bombers over the seas near Yap Island, directly east of the Philippines. A routine day of aerial battles changed when Kanno found himself unable to shoot down a B-24 bomber after repeated attempts. Ability and honor at stake, a desperate Kanno settled on ramming it and turned his fighter into the path of the American bomber. Fearing that the head-on crash would destroy his own plane but not the enemy's, Kanno decided to sheer off the B-24's rudder by veering away at the last moment and flying sideways along the body of the much larger bomber. After two failed attempts his plan finally succeeded. The sudden impact caused Kanno to black out; he came to just in time to pull his damaged Zero out of a tight spin and to see the B-24 crash into the ocean. He returned to base with a fantastic tale to tell.

Another kind of suicidal air attack was actually under development when Admiral Onishi was assigned to the Philippines. This involved the Ohka (exploding cherry blossom), a cigar-shaped, manned flying bomb carried under the belly of a Japanese "Betty" bomber. The Ohkas were to be piloted by members of the 721st Naval Flying Corps, known as the "Thunder Gods." Once released from the Betty, the 2,140-kilogram Ohka was designed to glide toward its target at 250 knots with the pilot controlling its dive and direction. With its 1,200-kilogram bomb, the Ohka could deliver a devastating blow to an enemy warship. Yet, when it was finally used in March 1945, and later during the battle for Okinawa, the Ohka proved largely ineffective. The slow Betty bombers were an easy target for Allied fighters, and there were never enough Japanese fighters available to protect them.

The use of suicide attacks was controversial among officers of the Japanese high command. To be sure, most subscribed to the belief that an honorable soldier seeks the opportunity to sacrifice himself for emperor and country. The prewar rise in militarism and the godlike reverence the emperor commanded added credence and passion to the warrior code. In schools, children were taught to die for the emperor, and the slogan "Jusshi Reisho" (sacrifice life) had become a common cry by 1944. Death in service to the emperor was an honor Japanese soldiers understood, even prayed for. Faced now with defeat rather than the victory they had been taught to expect, many officers and enlisted men were desperate for a way to die honorably. In the final months of the war, one general showed his troops the way with these orders: "healthy soldiers will kill three enemies; sick soldiers will kill one, incapacitated soldiers will fight and die in place; under no circumstances will one allow himself to be taken prisoner."[5]

But the idea that suicide attacks could be an acceptable part of military strategy and an official government policy did not sit well with many naval officers. A consistent opponent was the new prime minister, Kantaro Suzuki, a retired admiral. "Using men in a situation where there is no chance of survival is not a proper military operation," he insisted.[6] Even if one had no moral qualms, who could support a strategy that would purposely eliminate scores of Japanese pilots and their planes?

It was this problem that Admiral Onishi struggled with as he began to formulate his plan for the air defense of the

Philippines. It was clear that Japan's military situation was desperate. American naval strength was far superior, and although Japan was churning out hundreds of aircraft every month, there were not enough trained pilots to fly them. Even getting planes from the factories to the Pacific airfields was a problem. In Onishi's eyes, it was a handful of Japanese planes against the enemy's thousands. Besides, conventional air attacks on Allied warships were obviously not succeeding. Japan's beleaguered forces needed a new and potent weapon, and the weapon must be effective against the backbone of the Allied advance: aircraft carriers.

Banishing doubts and grasping at hope, Onishi ultimately brought three additional arguments to his superiors in support of organized suicide attacks. The first combined the failure of conventional fighting methods with the observation that the likelihood of Japanese pilots returning alive from sorties against the enemy was getting smaller and smaller. In other words, most pilots were going to die. The Imperial General Staff might not call them suicidal, but every sortie cost more and more Japanese planes and crews, and the pilots certainly knew the score.

A second argument, perhaps even more compelling, was that Onishi had a specific plan in mind. He explained it on October 19, 1944, to six officers of the 201st Air Group, part of the First Air Fleet, stationed in Mabalacat, on Luzon Island in the Philippines. After the war, Captain Rikihei Inoguchi, senior staff officer to Admiral Onishi, recalled the admiral's words: "In my opinion," Onishi began, "there is only one way of assuring that our meager strength will be effective to a maximum degree. That is to organize suicide attack units composed of Zero fighters armed with a 250-kilogramme bomb, with each plane to crash-dive into an enemy carrier.... What do you think?"[7]

Onishi knew his audience: There was no debate about the purpose or the means, only its likely success. Though young, these were seasoned officers who knew that Onishi's assessment of the military situation was correct. The 201st Air Group itself had fewer than thirty Zeros left, a third of its original strength. The officers agreed that the plan should be pursued. Perhaps they knew that Onishi would hardly have expected, or tolerated, any other response. "Traditional values of Japanese 'spirit' in warfare reinforced the natural tendency of subordi-nates not to voice suggestions to higher-ranking officers that they did not want to hear."[8] Hierarchy is taken very seriously by the Japanese and rigorously enforced in the military. The late Maurice Pinguet of Tokyo University explains:

> From the dawn of their history, the Japanese have maintained a vertical solidarity which remains operative today.... Chinese observers were noting this fondness for hierarchy as far back as the third century. The Japanese find equality disquieting: it can so easily lead to contests of prestige, which their polite formulae are constantly seeking to exorcise by negation. Equal-ity must be overwritten by differences of rank or age.... The strength of the clan depended on these vertical links whose intensity of feeling mounted every step of the hierarchy. The power of a noble house was directly proportionate to the devo-tion it inspired.[9]

After putting forward his plan, Onishi retired for the night, leaving subordinates to work out the practical details of what came to be called the Special Attack Corps, popularly known as Tokkotai. Picking the pilots and, more importantly, their leaders, was taken up first. Lieutenant Naoshi Kanno was immediately suggested as a leader, but he was unavailable. Lieutenant Yukio Seki was chosen. Seki had proven himself as a carrier-based bomber pilot and had been reassigned to the Philippines a month before. He was well-liked by his commanders and showed leadership qualities. Seki could have been ordered to lead the first Special Attack unit, but that approach did not seem right under the circumstances. Instead, he was asked what he thought about the plan in a private meeting with the executive officer, Commander Asaichi Tamai. After pausing a few seconds, perhaps because he had recently married, Seki begged to be the leader.

Tamai had already found the unit's pilots. Most of the 201st pilots were enlisted men and, after consulting with their squadron leaders, Tamai had called them all together. Admiral Onishi's plan was explained, and every pilot's hand went up to volunteer. Here was a chance to live the samurai code, to sacrifice one's life for the emperor. Or perhaps, as Commander Tamai suggested to Inoguchi later that night, each pilot was thinking of it as a chance to avenge a fallen comrade. Either way, the honor was gladly embraced by these young men. The Special Attack Corps was born. The next day, Inoguchi suggested their name: *shimpu,* meaning "divine wind," also known as kamikaze.

Onishi wanted his kamikaze units to be operational as soon as possible. His plan was to use his suicide squads as a key offensive element in the larger Sho, or "Victory," Operation already under way. The Sho had been planned earlier that summer, following the Allied breach of Japan's main defenses in New Guinea and the Marianas. The idea was to concentrate all available forces from both army and navy against the next major enemy offensive. Intelligence said it would come in the Philippines, and in mid-October the Imperial General Staff had activated the Sho when it was clear that U.S. forces were moving into Leyte Gulf. Carriers were crucial to the Allies' advance. They helped the United States control the skies, and their bombers wreaked havoc on Japanese ships and bases. So far they had withstood all that Japan could throw at them. Onishi's plan was to neutralize them for at least a week, giving the Sho forces breathing room.

A third argument in favor of the Special Attack units was not really an argument but a demonstration. In late September, the 26th Air Flotilla based in Manila had come under heavy bombardment from carrier-borne American planes. Its commander, Rear-Admiral Masafumi Arima, did his best to repel the attacks, but worse was to come. When the high command in Tokyo declared the Sho activated, it did so with a message Admiral Arima took to heart: The destiny of the homeland depended on the next great battle, and everyone was expected to do his best.

On October 15, an American task force was sighted 240 miles east of Luzon. All available planes were ordered to attack the task force. As the second wave of planes was about to take off from Manila, Admiral Arima boarded the lead plane, declaring that he would lead the attack. He had stripped off all insignia of rank; admirals were not supposed to fly missions, certainly not ones that would cost the navy their services. Nor would he want to give the enemy the pleasure of knowing that a senior Japanese officer had been killed.

When the American warships were sighted, Arima picked out an aircraft carrier, the USS *Franklin,* and crashed his plane into the ship, hitting the deck-edge elevator. Three sailors were killed and twenty-two wounded. Known as "Big Ben" to its crew, the *Franklin* was not seriously damaged, but a large plume of smoke was reported by horrified Japanese staff officers who had observed the action from a reconnaissance plane.[10] Word of Arima's heroic suicide spread quickly. An admiral had shown that he was willing to kill himself for his country in true samurai spirit. Enlisted pilots throughout the Japanese army and navy were buoyed by the story. More importantly, here was evidence that carriers were vulnerable to suicide attack, just as Admiral Onishi had been saying.

Organization, Tactics, and Results of Kamikaze Martyrdom

On October 20, 1944, when the Shimpu Tokkotai became a reality, it was no longer a far-fetched idea to the Japanese high command. The initial Special Attack Corps was composed of twenty-four pilots, half assigned to crash-diving, half to escort. There were four units: Shikishima (a poetic name for Japan), Yamato (the ancient name for Japan), Asahi (morning sun), and Yamazakura (mountain cherry blossoms). The rest of the base and many of its officers knew nothing of its mission, for the kamikaze pilots had been sworn to secrecy. Onishi hoped eventually to promote the shimpu concept throughout the army and navy as a grassroots movement, originating with the pilots themselves. This would come soon enough, he thought, with success in battle.

The Yamato unit was quickly sent to the island of Cebu, escorted by Commander Tadashi Nakajima, who had orders to establish another Special Attack unit upon arrival. The importance of the Sho Operation was once again emphasized, with the American carriers singled out as specific targets. Volunteers were requested from among the noncommissioned officers and their men. Nakajima told the Cebu pilots, "We know that you are willing to die in defense of our country. We also realize that some of you, because of your family situation, cannot be expected to offer your life in this way.... Whether a man volunteers or not will be known only to me."[11] There were plenty of volunteers, and officers wanted to be included as well.

Because many of their comrades had already died in conventional missions, the kamikaze pilots had no illusions about any airman's chances of survival as the war wound on. The young pilots had plenty to avenge. In addition, the mounting casualties and continuing Allied advance further pointed up the limits of conventional attack. This bolstered the promise of the new strategy and underscored the dedication and special training required of airmen in the Special Attack Corps.

Successful hits on enemy warships depended on how the kamikaze fighters approached their target. So pilots were given additional flight training and taught the benefits of high- and low-altitude approaches. They also learned the best angle of attack and the specific parts of the enemy carrier they should aim for. Pilots then had to learn how to disengage the bomb safety device and the best time to do it. Early on in the kamikaze campaign some pilots released the safety but never found an enemy target; they had to jettison the bomb before returning to base or risk being blown up on landing. Word went out that no bomb, plane, or pilot was to be wasted in this way.

Many kamikaze airmen showed off their piloting skills by reaching enemy targets despite heavy resistance from Allied warships and planes. During the attacks on HMAS *Australia*, for instance, a handful of kamikaze pilots successfully evaded an Allied Combat Air Patrol consisting of fifty-eight fighter planes. Seven ships were hit. Yet the very best aviators rarely made it into the ranks of the suicide pilots. Instead, they were assigned as kamikaze escorts. Escorts had to shield the suicide planes from enemy fighters until they entered their final dive toward the target. Escort pilots could not initiate air attacks on enemy fighters, nor could they retaliate if attacked from the rear. These actions would likely slow the escorts down, leaving the kamikaze planes exposed. At the point of the final dive, the suicide pilots would speed up while the escorts concentrated on intercepting enemy fighters. If the escort pilots had to sacrifice themselves in protecting the suicide fighters, so be it. However, those escorts that made it back to base survived to fly another mission.

Some escort pilots struggled with their emotions. They had volunteered for the Special Attack units only to find themselves helping others to their deaths. Furthermore, they could not seek out the enemy but had to use their flying skills defensively. In the end, many escort pilots were killed, but not in the way they had first imagined when they volunteered for the Shimpu Tokkotai.

The first kamikaze to officially die in glory was Lieutenant Yukio Seki, leader of the Shikishima unit at Mabalacat. On October 21, 1944, scout planes reported an enemy task force with carriers east of Leyte Gulf. In what became a ritual for many kamikaze pilots, Seki cut off a lock of his hair to be sent home and lined up with the other pilots for a farewell drink of water. It is unclear whether Seki wore the white *hachimaki* headband on this suicide mission, but the headband also became part of the ritual and a symbol of the kamikaze. Centuries earlier, the hachimaki had been worn by samurai warriors to signify a fight to the death. Many kamikaze pilots decorated theirs with poetic verse. In addition to the headband, the pilots often wore white *senninbari,* long strips of cloth on which a thousand women had sewn a stitch to signify their solidarity with the Shimpu pilot and his sacrifice.

But this was not to be the day of Seki's martyrdom, nor the next, nor even the next two. For four successive days kamikaze missions were scrubbed because the enemy carriers could not be found. Finally, on October 25, Seki's unit took off again, five bomb-laden planes accompanied by four Zero escort planes. Before long the group sighted more than a dozen enemy carriers. Lieutenant Seki led the way, and crash-dived into a carrier, followed immediately by another plane that hit almost the same spot. Seki's escort pilots reported smoke and flames rising a thousand feet into the air. They also said that the suicide pilots had damaged another carrier and had sunk a cruiser.

Reconstruction of that day's kamikaze attacks from Japanese and American naval records suggests that only the U.S. escort carrier *St. Lo* was actually hit and sunk by Seki's group, though not necessarily by Seki himself. The sinking of *St. Lo* might have been foretold: U.S. naval historian Admiral Samuel Morison notes that S*t. Lo* "had been commissioned as *Midway,* but when that name was wanted for the new class of big carriers it was taken from her—which as all old sailors know brings bad luck." When hit by the kamikaze, "great sections of the flight deck and elevator and entire planes were hurled hundreds of feet into the air. The ship blazed from stem to stern, and at 1125 [hours], the unluckily named *St. Lo* foundered under a cloud of dense smoke."[12] According to one account it took only one Zero with one bomb to sink the *St. Lo;* the pilot flew in at about one hundred feet and held his plane on course despite intense fire from three of the ship's guns.[13]

Other U.S. warships were hit by kamikazes on that day, including four other escort carriers. But these were damaged by kamikazes from the First Air Group of the Japanese Fourth Air Army, which actually arrived on the scene first. Neither kamikaze unit knew of the other's role in the battle. In any case, the American warships were spread out over many miles, and there were hundreds of conventional aircraft from both sides zooming about in the air. The darting red lines of thousands of tracer bullets and the smoke from hundreds of multicolored explosions and fires made for a surreal scene.

The battle for Leyte Gulf, which Morison calls "the greatest naval battle of all time," was an overwhelming American victory and it cost the Japanese dearly: an estimated 10,500 sailors and airmen, 500 hundred aircraft, 4 carriers, 3 battleships, 6 heavy and 4 light cruisers, 11 destroyers, and 1 submarine. It destroyed the Japanese Combined Fleet as an effective fighting force. In contrast, U.S. losses were modest: 3 escort carriers, 2 destroyers, 1 destroyer escort, slightly more than 200 hundred aircraft, and 2,800 servicemen.[14]

Despite the Allied victory, one lesson that the Japanese took away from Leyte Gulf was that the Special Attack units accomplished much more than the conventional forces relative to their numbers. On October 25, for instance, Japan had used only nine kamikaze aircraft but three hundred conventional planes. The lesson the Americans took away was the realization that they now faced a frightening new strategy in naval warfare. For military reasons, the American public was told nothing about the kamikazes until April 13, 1945, nearly six months after they first appeared. It is not difficult to imagine what those reasons were. This was a terrifying development for which there was no precedent and therefore no tested plan of defense; why unnecessarily alarm the public until its effectiveness had been assessed and successful defensive measures developed? Perhaps more important, keeping things quiet would make it harder for Japanese military intelligence to evaluate the effectiveness of the kamikazes in attacking the warships and the morale of the Allies.

An American sailor who was in the battle of Leyte Gulf recalls his feelings about the new situation: "The only way to stop a suicide piloted plane was to shoot it down before it hit you. Now there could be no margin for error. Prior to the kamikaze attack style we would shoot at the Japs and they would bomb us, sometimes everybody missed! It was horrifying to try and comprehend someone intentionally diving through a hail of deadly anti-aircraft fire with the sole purpose of killing themselves in a blinding explosion."[15] Or, as a steward's mate on the USS *Wichita* put it, "We don't mind them planes which drops things but we don't like them what *lights* on you!"[16]

The success of the first major kamikaze action, much trumpeted by Onishi and his supporters among the Imperial General Staff, could not save the Sho Operation. Japanese forces had taken huge losses, while the Allies were continuing to advance. In spring 1945, the long battle for Okinawa was joined. With fear of an impending Allied invasion growing, and grasping at its reported successes in the Philippines, Emperor Hirohito ordered expansion of the Shimpu Tokkotai. The plan, code-named Operation Kikusui ("floating chrysanthemums"), was to bombard the U.S. fleet with more than two thousand suicide aircraft. This massive kamikaze operation required organization and training far beyond anything contemplated by Onishi. The largest battleship in the world, the 72,000-ton *Yamato*, was eventually thrown into the mix with a suicidal mission of its own: Try to make it from the Kure navy yard on the Japanese mainland to Okinawa, 350 miles away, with minimal escort, no air cover, and only enough fuel for a one-way trip.

The *Yamato* never got there.[17] Spotted by reconnaissance planes still over two hundred miles from Okinawa, the battleship and its handful of escort vessels soon came under attack from U.S. dive-bombers and torpedo planes. Over a two-hour period on April 7, 1945, the *Yamato* was hit by eight medium bombs, twelve torpedoes, and seven armor-piercing bombs. The pride of the Japanese navy sank at 2:23 p.m., preceded by three of its escort destroyers. Almost twenty-five hundred sailors were lost on the *Yamato* alone. The next day Tokyo announced its counteramphibious doctrine for homeland defense. At the center of it was the Special Attack Corps.

Indeed, the kamikaze pilots were enjoying growing support from the Japanese high command for one reason: Their commanding officers reported success after success in those otherwise dark days of the war. Most of these reports were exaggerated, but even so, there were notable successes: Between January and the end of March 1945, suicide pilots damaged dozens of Allied warships and sank two U.S. aircraft carriers—the *Bismarck Sea* and the *Ommaney Bay*. During the early battle for Okinawa, kamikazes sank thirteen destroyers and disabled another eight over a six-week period; they also sank nine landing ships. They damaged scores of Allied warships, including the U.S. carriers *Intrepid, Wake Island, Hancock, Enterprise, Sangamon,* and *Bunker Hill* and the British carriers *Formidable* and *Victorious.* The British carriers *Indomitable* and *Indefatigable* were also hit by suicide planes, but their thick deck armor enabled them to continue normal operations as soon as the wreckage had been cleared away.

The massive onslaught by the kamikaze pilots of the Special Attack Corps, which continued unabated until the end of June, was very costly for Japan: More than seventeen hundred pilots and their planes were lost. When combined with the Philippines campaign, well over twenty-five hundred airmen had died in kamikaze operations. Radio Tokyo, the voice of Japanese propaganda, heralded the bravery and dedication of those who volunteered for suicide missions. They were portrayed as gods, and the whole country bathed in their glory. Yet in truth not all the kamikaze pilots had been volunteers. As the missions continued and all the original pilots were gone, doubts and fears replaced some of the contagious enthusiasm among the early volunteers. Under Operation Kikusui, suicide attack was compulsory for many of the pilots assigned to it. One kamikaze pilot whose plane crashed harmlessly into the sea told American rescuers that his unit of conventional dive-bombers had been summarily changed into a suicide unit by its commanding officer. Meanwhile, back in training camps and at recruitment stations on the mainland, would-be bomber pilots were increasingly pressured to volunteer for the Special Attack Corps.

Admiral Onishi, his fleet commander Vice-Admiral Matome Ugaki, and most of the army generals expected that Japan would fight to the very end. The training schools were turning out new pilots by the hundreds, and some still hoped to volunteer for a heroic death with the Special Attack Corps. Despite the earlier emphasis on the special skills required for successful kamikaze operations, during the Okinawa campaign commanders began assigning novices to their Special Attack units. Often this decision was driven by the lack of any alternative—there simply were no trained pilots available. At other times, it was a darker choice driven by expediency. Recalling his assignment as chief of staff to Ugaki, Rear Admiral Toshiyuki Yokoi commented shortly after the war, "I knew that two of the eight units were practically untrained and so were *not fit for anything but suicide duty.*"[18] Many of these pilots were university students.

From the beginning, kamikaze pilots sometimes had to abort their missions and return to base. It might have been the weather, or mechanical problems, or because the enemy could not be found. In the past, their return was greeted with a mixture of sympathy and relief—sympathy because their moment of glory had been delayed, relief because pilot and plane had survived for another mission. One might have expected the returning pilots to be angry over the missed opportunity, but as this line from a letter home shows, some clearly had mixed feelings: "Beyond the clouds, death lay in wait for me, but I have just regained the hope of living here on earth for a little while longer. Should I thank the clouds, or curse them for preventing us from carrying out our mission?"[19] By June 1945, returning pilots were increasingly scorned and accused of cowardice by senior commanders. Ryuji Nagatsuka, a kamikaze pilot who survived the war, recalls this reaction from his commanding officer after a failed mission: "You have dishonored our squadron and I am ashamed of you.... Why didn't you die like heroes?"[20]

The taste of defeat was everywhere. On July 26, 1945, the U.S., British, and Chinese governments issued the Potsdam Declaration. It gave the emperor of Japan a single choice: unconditional surrender or total annihilation. It was ignored. Two days later the U.S. destroyer *Callaghan* was sunk by a kamikaze attack. The suicide plane in that incident was an old training biplane specially fitted with a bomb. The *Callaghan* was the last Allied vessel sunk by the Shimpu Tokkotai. On August 6, 1945, the U.S. B-29 bomber *Enola Gay*, piloted by

Lieutenant Colonel Paul Tibbets, dropped the atomic bomb "Little Boy" over Hiroshima. More than seventy thousand were killed immediately (another 130,000 would die over the next five years), and the city was virtually destroyed. Still no surrender. Kamikaze attacks on Allied warships continued. Only after a second atomic bomb, "Fat Man," was dropped on Nagasaki and the Soviet Union declared war on Japan did Emperor Hirohito accept the Potsdam Declaration and surrender unconditionally. The date was August 15, 1945.

On that same day, suicide pilots were preparing as usual for raids on Allied warships near Okinawa. Admiral Ugaki, disconsolate over the pending surrender, decided to order a last kamikaze mission. He would lead it. Eleven two-seater bombers were made ready, and Ugaki rejected all entreaties not to go. Ugaki also disobeyed Emperor Hirohito's direct order to lay down arms and surrender. Stripping himself of all insignia of rank, just as Admiral Arima had done nearly a year earlier, Ugaki jumped into the lead plane, taking along a short samurai sword and a pair of binoculars.

Four hours later a final radio message was received from the admiral. It said, in part, "I alone am to blame for our failure to defend the homeland and destroy the arrogant enemy.... I am going to make an attack at Okinawa where my men have fallen like cherry blossoms. There I will crash into and destroy the conceited enemy in the true spirit of *Bushido*, with firm conviction and faith in the eternity of Imperial Japan.... Long live his Imperial Majesty the Emperor!"[21] Despite radio messages from the planes indicating they were making their final crash-dives, there is no official record of a kamikaze attack on a U.S. warship on this date. Four of the planes were forced down because of mechanical problems. The other seven planes, including Admiral Ugaki's, were never seen again.

The father of the kamikaze plan, Admiral Onishi, died in agony. For two days before the surrender, Onishi had tried to convince the Imperial General Staff, and even the emperor, that the war could still be won. His pilots were still willing to die: There were more than three hundred Special Attack aircraft and crew ready to go. It was the duty of every Japanese citizen to fight on for emperor and country, even if it cost twenty million lives! Few people listened, and Onishi wept openly in dismay. A few hours after Emperor Hirohito broadcast the terms of the surrender and called on his subjects to lay down their arms, Onishi committed hara-kiri. Using a sword in the ceremonial manner of seppuku, he drew it quickly across his stomach and then upward to his ribcage. He then tried to cut his throat but was already too weak. The next morning an aide found him still conscious in a pool of blood. Onishi refused medical help and offers of a final coup de grâce. It took him eighteen hours to die. His suicide note read, in part, "I wish to express my deep appreciation to the souls of the brave Special Attackers. They fought and died valiantly with faith in our ultimate victory. In death I wish to atone for my part in the failure to achieve that victory and I apologize to the souls of these dead fliers and their bereaved families."[22]

For Onishi, the storm was over. His creation, the Shimpu Tokkotai, cost the lives of nearly three thousand young Japanese pilots and made no difference to the final outcome of the war. But the Allies paid dearly as well. Kamikaze attacks sank thirty-nine allied warships, including three carriers. They damaged at least two hundred and seventy-five allied warships, including thirty carriers. And they claimed the lives of well over a thousand Allied sailors and injured thousands more. But the greatest accomplishment of the kamikaze martyrs was their impact on the morale of both sides: Allied seamen waited in dread for the next attack, and Japanese fighters bathed in the memory of the Divine Wind, in denial of defeat and ever hopeful of eventual victory.

The Meaning, Value, and Purpose of Kamikaze Martyrdom

Like those of the Christian, Muslim, and Sikh martyrs before them, the self-sacrifices of the kamikaze pilots were understood, admired, and often envied among the people that mattered to them and understood their purpose. Most of these pilots had willingly embraced the opportunity to die for their emperor and country. Of course, history is replete with individual acts of suicidal heroism during the heat of battle. In modern times these acts are often recognized with posthumous awards for gallantry. A case in point: During the battle for Midway Island in June 1942, U.S. Marine pilot Captain Richard

E. Fleming purposely dove his damaged bomber into the rear turret of the Japanese cruiser *Mikuma*. He was posthumously awarded the Medal of Honor. But this was new and different; the Special Attack Corps had been organized for self-sacrifice on a large scale, planned in advance with special procedures for recruitment and training. Maurice Pinguet observes:

> Never in the long history of human warfare had soldiers been asked to do such a thing. Every battle has its perilous volunteer missions with small chance of coming back alive: the volunteer knows that, but the little voice which whispers "you might make it," illusory as it may be, is a large part of physical courage.... Now, for the first time, it meant deliberately choosing absolutely certain death, a few days or even weeks in advance. It was an appeal to pure, free good will, devoid of any illusion, any emotion.[23]

But the pilots cared very much what people thought of them. This is obvious from their letters home. They wanted to be understood, to put doubts to rest, to assure family and friends of their love and respect and of their joy in dying for emperor and country. These young, often well-educated Japanese men wanted their martyrdom to matter in the here and now.

It was not a matter of justifying one's suicide. Unlike Christianity and Western culture in general, Japanese culture had never objected to voluntary death in principle. Indeed, the Japanese believed that suicide was an acceptable choice under a variety of circumstances: suicides of responsibility, suicides of sympathy, suicides of companionship, suicides of devotion, and suicides of self-effacement. The kamikaze pilots wanted it understood that their deaths were consistent with the spirit of sacrifice: a willing gift to the nation, a reward in itself but also a benefit to others. Theirs was the shared martyrdom of heroes, and they asked for nothing more than to be remembered for their honorable self-sacrifice.

Japanese propaganda helped make their case just as it gave encouragement to would-be martyrs waiting in recruitment lines. Roosevelt and Churchill had been utterly demonized in the Japanese media. Many Japanese believed that if the Allies won the war, their beloved emperor and their own families would face unimaginable atrocities. Protecting the homeland at all costs was the first duty of every Japanese man—and, if need be, of every woman and child as well. If the enemy should prevail, suicide was a preferable alternative to becoming an American slave. Here were the Jews of Masada all over again, with one difference: The ancient Jews could point to many real atrocities committed by the Romans, but the Japanese had provoked war with the United States by bombing Pearl Harbor. Yet the power of this argument would be demonstrated time and again in the course of the war, perhaps most notably on July 9, 1944, when hundreds of Japanese civilians living on Saipan killed their families and themselves rather than surrender. The Japanese press praised them as heroic martyrs and the same bloody ending was repeated throughout the Allied advance.

It was, above all, Japanese history that girded the heroic sacrifice made by the kamikazes. Youth were indoctrinated with tales of the samurai and the Bushido code of honor. What soldier could not recount stories from Japan's past, when heroic warriors selflessly laid down their lives for the emperor, their country, or their master? They had learned these stories in elementary school and again in the pilot training schools; the stories taught them the circumstances under which honorable self-sacrifice differs from mere suicide. The stories were often topics of discussion as pilots waited for the next kamikaze sortie, as were more recent tales of heroism such as those of the great generals who defeated superior Russian forces at Port Arthur during the Russo-Japanese War of 1904–1905, the pilots of the midget submarines who were killed during the Pearl Harbor attack, and the gallant crash-dive of Admiral Arima. These stories were told and retold throughout the life of the kamikaze campaign.

Did some pilots have questions or doubts? Of course they did. Though hardly a thought was given to death when they volunteered, during the hours or weeks before their missions it seemed natural to explore the meaning of their sacrifice, which for these mostly eighteen- to twenty-four-year-olds was an untimely death. Some pilots understood their martyrdom by demeaning their life: Death was a way to escape, to be free. Most saw martyrdom as a way to *maintain* life, the life of the emperor and of Japan, especially its traditions and spiritual values. Both views gave death purpose, and this was comforting. As one surviving kamikaze pilot explained, "my own death had a significance, a purpose, and a value. To my great astonishment, these reflections began to relieve my mind after a while, and helped me to regain my tranquility."[24] Thus, when it was time to take off and fly to their deaths, the pilots showed the "composure and tranquility which comes only to those who are aware of their own significance and power."[25]

Expectation of salvation, resurrection, or an afterlife in Paradise was not part of the equation for kamikaze pilots. They would not acquire life through martyrdom as Christians and Muslims believed. Yet many pilots spoke of living on in spirit, a traditional belief of the dominant Shinto religion. Admiral Onishi had told the first group of kamikaze volunteers that they were already gods, and that their spirits would fly to the Yasukuni Shrine near Tokyo and live on forever. The Yasukuni Shrine had been established in 1869 by the emperor Meiji as a tranquil resting place for the spirits of soldiers killed in battle. In their last letters home, kamikaze pilots often spoke of this. Thus Ensign Susumu Kaijitsu wrote, "Please watch for the results of my meagre effort. If they prove good, think kindly of me and consider it my good fortune to have done something that may be praiseworthy. Most important of all, do not weep for me. Though my body departs, I will return home in spirit and remain with you forever."[26] Moments before leaving for his kamikaze attack, Flying Petty Officer First Class Isao Matsuo wrote his parents saying, simply, "I shall return in spirit and look forward to your visit at the Yasukuni Shrine. Please take good care of yourselves."[27]

Some Western writers apparently believe that the posthumous honor of a place at Yasukuni was the most important incentive for volunteering to join the Special Attack Corps. This is unlikely because *all* Japanese soldiers killed in service to the emperor are honored at the shrine: Nearly two and a half million names are inscribed there. Voluntary death is not a prerequisite. Yet Admiral Onishi had mentioned the shrine to his first volunteers, and many pilots talked about it among themselves and in their letters. Such talk certainly underscores the reverence accorded the shrine and the importance—some would say, privilege—attached to the kamikaze mission. It also pays homage to the Buddhist belief in karma: Actions in this life can determine one's destiny in future incarnations.

The kamikazes were the latest manifestation of a Japanese tradition of voluntary suicide in the service of a noble purpose. Onishi had called their deaths beautiful. In the last months of the war, the airwaves were full of their virtues and accomplishments. Parents wept tears of pride when they learned that a son had volunteered for the Special Attack Corps and died in glory. It was simple: Their son had willingly embraced death to help save the beloved emperor and country. As Lieutenant Shigejuki Suzuki put it in a letter home, "The great day that we can directly be in contact with the battle is our day of happiness and at the same, the memorial of our death."[28] What could be a better show of devotion and duty? If there were doubts about the success of the missions, the public had no sense of them; the emperor himself made Special Attack operations the key to homeland defense. The propaganda value of the kamikazes had been understood from the beginning: Their sacrifice was expected to inspire others, to create strength out of vulnerability. This was consistent with the tradition of martyrdom from at least the time of Tertullian.

After the war things changed. Not only did the Japanese question their leaders' conduct of the war but also the kamikaze strategy in particular came under attack. Comments about sending young men fruitlessly to their deaths were heard, and outrage grew over complaints that many pilots, particularly toward the end, were simply drafted into suicide missions. Rear Admiral Yokoi, in the thick of kamikaze attacks at Okinawa, paints a picture that must have startled and disturbed many Japanese:

> Early in the Okinawa campaign pilots could go to their deaths with some hope that their country might realize some benefit from their sacrifice. But toward the last, the doomed pilots had good reason for doubting the validity of the cause in which they were told to die. The difficulties became especially apparent when men in aviation training were peremptorily ordered to the front and to death. When it came time for their take off, the pilots' attitudes ranged from the despair of sheep headed for slaughter to open expressions of contempt for their superior officers. There were frequent and obvious cases of pilots returning from sorties claiming that they could not locate any enemy ships, and one pilot even strafed his commanding officer's quarters as he took off. When planes did not return there was

seldom any way of knowing the results of their sacrifice. There was no conclusive means of determining if they had crashed into a target.[29]

There is really no way of knowing the extent of coercion or, more to the point, the degree to which pilots felt coerced, among units of the Special Attack Corps. For most of the kamikaze campaign "there was no shortage of volunteers, in fact there was a waiting list."[30] In light of the almost universal criticism of the kamikaze operations outside Japan, and particularly among the Allies, it is possible that some postwar Japanese commentators exaggerated the degree of coercion because they thought it would help dispel a racist argument, loudly proclaimed by anti-Japanese propaganda during the war, that the "yellow bastards" were a subhuman species who thought nothing of life, including their own.[31] Blaming the kamikaze operations on misguided leaders who coerced soldiers to undertake suicide missions shifted the focus from Japanese culture and Japanese history to a few deviant militarists.

One thing is certainly clear: For most of the war the Japanese public was not told the truth about the war's progress. Perhaps exaggerating so as to emphasize this point, Japanese naval expert and war correspondent Masanori Ito has claimed that during the entire war all but three news releases by the Imperial General Staff were falsehoods.[32] In the case of the Special Attack Corps, Radio Tokyo routinely gave exaggerated reports of Allied losses from kamikaze missions. Such reports not only bolstered public confidence in the progress of the war but also helped justify the suicide missions for the pilots and the families left behind. Without a concrete benefit from martyrdom it was certainly harder to sell the idea. When Tertullian called for early Christians to join the ranks of martyrs, he did so in the expectation that the church would become stronger as a result. This was the practical benefit of martyrdom, and it could be measured in conversions. So long as the Japanese public believed the propaganda there was no reason to doubt the practical value of kamikaze operations or the underlying code of Bushido.

The emphasis on the practical benefits of martyrdom and martyrdom stories was not new: As we saw in earlier chapters, it first emerged in antiquity and was refined within Islam and alongside the rise of Sikh militancy. New, however, were the organization, training, and policy aspects of martyrdom associated with the Shimpu Tokkotai, particularly as the prospects of a final Japanese victory faded away. It is now clear that World War II witnessed yet another transition in the idea and practice of martyrdom: from occasional aggressive acts of willful self-sacrifice in a fight for group survival to systematic, policy-driven, and repetitive acts of self-sacrificial aggression on a mass scale. Under these conditions, external mechanisms to create compliance and maximize results become more salient.

The willingness to die young is nudged along by a certain amount of moral blackmail, as Maurice Pinguet astutely observes. It must have been hard for young pilots to resist when squadron leaders invited them to volunteer and to then reply one by one in a private meeting. Or consider the importance of group pressure: "Suicide seems less difficult when a whole group can do it together."[33] The mass suicides by Japanese civilians on Saipan and Okinawa and the suicidal banzai charges by Japanese soldiers on Iwo Jima and elsewhere are latter-day examples of the kind of contagion experienced nearly a thousand years before when 432 samurai warriors disemboweled themselves following their master's lead.

Part IV

The New Predatory Martyrs

Around 5:30 a.m. on September 11, 2001, a thirty-three-year-old Egyptian and his twenty-two-year-old Saudi companion left the Comfort Inn in Portland, Maine, for the short flight to Logan International Airport in Boston. In the Egyptian's travel bag were a copy of his last will and testament and instructions on how to behave during their upcoming mission for Allah. If the men had followed the instructions, their bodies were washed, shaved, and perfumed, and they were smartly dressed, shoelaces firmly tied. At Logan the young men hurried to Gate 26 where the rest of their group waited to board American Airlines Flight 11 to Los Angeles. They passed through a gate security check with no trouble at all.

The Egyptian known as Mohamed Atta settled into his business-class seat, unaware that his travel bag had missed the connection. The plane taxied slowly toward the runway for its 7:59 a.m. takeoff. "In the plane," the instructions read, "you should pray to God, because you do this for God, and everyone who prays to God shall prevail.... When the airplane moves, as soon as it starts to move slowly, start praying the prayers of the traveling Muslims, because you travel in order to meet God and to enjoy the journey."[1] Within twenty minutes of takeoff, Atta and his companions had hijacked the plane and were flying into the annals of modern martyrdom. The awful result is well-known to everyone.

The attacks on the World Trade Center and the Pentagon on 9/11 exemplify what I call *predatory martyrdom.* Predatory martyrdom adds an important development to the martyr-warrior theme embodied in the kamikaze campaign during World War II—the indiscriminate killing of civilians with little or no warning. In their suicide attacks, predatory martyrs hide behind masks of innocence and then kill themselves along with women, children, the elderly, the infirm, and anyone else who happens to be in the target zone. Indeed, the assailants and their sponsors are happy to take as many people with them as they can. The weapon of choice is an explosive device transported to the scene and triggered by the martyr. To put the predatory death toll from 9/11 in perspective, the al-Qaeda martyrs "caused more civilian deaths in one hour than the Northern Ireland conflict caused in the past half century or collectively all those that perished in Pearl Harbour."[2]

As we have seen time and again, martyrdom is both expressive and pragmatic. The act of dying for the cause is valued in itself and as a means to something else. Numbers count in reckoning the value, and this is especially true with predatory martyrs; the greater the number of enemy killed, the closer seems the victory and the more glorious is the martyr's sacrifice. Al-Qaeda leader Osama bin Laden said of Atta and his companions, "When people see a strong horse and a weak horse, by nature they will like the strong horse. . . . Those young men . . . said in deeds, in New York and Washington, speeches that overshadowed all other speeches made everywhere else in the world. The speeches are understood by both Arabs and non-Arabs—even by Chinese."[3] The death and destruction on 9/11 had actually surpassed bin Laden's expectations, and in a videotaped conversation soon afterward he agreed that the martyrs had done a great job for Islam. As proof he recounted media reports of a great surge of interest in Islam, including many conversions.

Osama bin Laden and al-Qaeda were not the first to commit mass killings through suicide attacks. That honor belongs to Hezbollah, a little-known organization back in 1983, when it claimed responsibility for suicide bombings of the U.S. embassy in Beirut, and later, of American Marine barracks and

French paratrooper barracks that left approximately three hundred dead and many more wounded. The martyrs were Shiite Muslims intent on driving Israel's Western allies out of Lebanon. Their actions had a global impact, putting Hezbollah on the front pages of newspapers everywhere. U.S. president Ronald Reagan vowed to avenge the killings and in so doing highlighted the significance of the martyrs' actions and inflated their prestige in the world of militant groups waging war against superior forces. To the supporters of Hezbollah, the bombing of the U.S. Marine barracks was seen as a great victory against Israel's most powerful ally.

In the jungles of Sri Lanka, a charismatic leader battling for the independence of his people looked upon Hezbollah's achievement with admiration. He would soon embark on the systematic use of suicide attacks as a means to advance his own cause. The admirer was Velupillai Prabhakaran, founder of the Liberation Tigers of Tamil Eelam, or LTTE. From 1987 to 2000 he orchestrated more suicide attacks than any of the other nine militant groups around the world known to employ the strategy—in fact, more than all the others combined. The story of the freedom fighters of LTTE, nicknamed the Tamil Tigers, will serve to introduce the unfolding world of predatory martyrdom.

Chapter 7

The Black Tigers of Sri Lanka

Near-Predatory Martyrs

The jungle country of Sri Lanka, "resplendent island," lies off the southeastern tip of India. The ethnic Tamils are united by language, and legends claim ancestry going back ten thousand years. Today, more than three million Tamils form the majority population in the north and east of Sri Lanka and, like their Tamil cousins in southern India, most follow the Hindu religion. The largely Buddhist Sinhalese (about 13 million) are in the majority in the remaining two-thirds of Sri Lanka. The Sinhalese control the government in accordance with a plan dreamed up with the exiting British colonial rulers in 1948 and capitalized upon by successive Sinhalese leaders. A series of discriminatory laws were passed during the 1950s and 1960s restricting Tamil access to government employment, arms, and education and declaring Buddhism the state religion. Peaceful protests were organized by Tamil leaders, but there were also signs of growing militancy, especially among students.

The government responded harshly, inciting anti-Tamil riots that killed or wounded thousands and destroyed homes and businesses, even entire villages. The violence against Tamils radicalized the protest movement, and in 1977 Velupillai Prabhakaran carved his corps of freedom fighters out of the increasingly militant conflict. His repeated calls for Tamil independence fell on deaf ears, and six years later civil war erupted. Observers soon linked his growing reputation for brutality to the traumatic experience of seeing one of his uncles burned alive during riots in 1958. There was much to goad him on, in any case: In 1979 the government passed the Prevention of Terrorism Act, which allowed the army to hold prisoners for up to eighteen months with no outside contact. Tamil civilians were rounded up and kept without access to lawyers or family.

In 1983, anti-Tamil violence flared into riots after thirteen government soldiers were ambushed and their bodies mutilated near Jaffna. Sinhalese rioters burned homes and Tamil-owned businesses. The civilian unrest increased support for the Liberation Tigers of Tamil Eelam (LTTE) among Tamils. In reaction, government forces killed thousands of Tamils and many more fled to the jungles of Sri Lanka or to the southern Indian state of Tamil Nadu, whose refugee camps housed one hundred thousand by 1990. It wasn't hard for Prabhakaran to find recruits for the cause of Tamil independence. Although numerous Tamil resistance groups were vying for support early on, by the late 1980s he had become the only real game in town.

The Tamil Tigers turned to guerrilla warfare against the government and its allies. A fan of war films and Clint Eastwood westerns, Prabhakaran used his charisma and growing reputation for ruthlessness to create a force of dedicated fighters. He described his approach in a 1986 interview with *Newsweek* reporter Sudip Mazumdar: "Discipline and order are most important. We emphasize personal morality and a sense of patriotism. Our cadres carry cyanide pills with them to avoid falling into enemy hands. . . . We have imposed a strict moral code on ourselves, not to use even liquor."[1] Prabhakaran did not tell *Newsweek* that he was toying with the idea of forming a special squad of fighters who would attack the enemy by blowing themselves up. A year later the Black Tiger suicide fighters became an elite and secretive corps of the LTTE. Their identities were revealed only upon their deaths.

Among Tamils, two special days commemorate LTTE fighters. One is November 27, known as Martyr's (or Heroes) Day; the other is July 5, known as Black Tiger Day. The latter is the anniversary of the first suicide attack in 1987. On that day a Captain Miller (his nom de guerre; his real name was Vallipuram Vasanthan) followed Hezbollah's example in Lebanon and drove a truck full of explosives into a government army camp on the Jaffna Peninsula and detonated it. The explosion killed the driver and more than forty government soldiers. A life-size statue of Miller was erected in Jaffna in 2002 to celebrate his martyrdom.

Over the next fourteen years, at least 240 Black Tigers would blow themselves up for Tamil independence, leaving hundreds of civilian casualties in their wake. The Tamil Tigers have been called "unequivocally the most effective and brutal terrorist organization ever to use" suicide attacks.[2] The label *terrorist* may be a misnomer inasmuch as the Sri Lankan and Indian governments have called LTTE fighters "enemy combatants." In a November 27 Martyr's Day speech in 1997, Prabhakaran scorned those who call his martyrs "terrorists": "Our tradition of venerating martyrs as war heroes has always irritated the Sinhala chauvinist state. The Sinhala chauvinists find intolerable the very fact that those whom they categorize as terrorists are venerated and glorified by the Tamils as war heroes."[3]

Prabhakaran adopted suicide attacks as a legitimate strategy of warfare, much like the Japanese in World War II. Unlike the kamikazes, however, the targets were diverse, from soldiers to politicians and occasionally to anyone else deemed a threat. Collateral damage often included women and children, and sometimes other Tamils. Even so, the Black Tigers received strong support among Tamils. In *Dying to Win: The Strategic Logic of Suicide Terrorism,* Robert Pape suggests why: "The most prominent factor driving Tamil community support for individual self-sacrifice is fear of Buddhist extremism."[4] For thirty years, Tamil leaders fanned fears of a Sinhalese master plan to turn Hindu Tamils into Buddhists.

Although the Tamil resistance was a secular nationalist movement, religious themes were cleverly used by Prabhakaran to generate support for the cause and to justify martyrdom operations. For example, the Bhagavad Gita, purportedly written more than four thousand years ago and an essential text in Hinduism, emphasizes the soul's immortality and that death on the battlefield is just the shedding of the body. Death is the beginning of new life. Hindu temples and shrines are commonly bedecked with flowers and oil, and the friends and relatives of Black Tigers were encouraged to erect shrines in honor of the martyrs. All of this helped give Hindu legitimacy to the militancy of the independence movement. Since some LTTE members were Christian, however, the organization did not associate itself officially with the Hindu religion.

Prabhakaran's speeches dealing with the martyrdom of the Black Tigers show a familiarity with Tertullian and underline the instrumentality of the martyr's action. "We have sowed the seed of an ideal," he once said, "[and] we grow it by irrigating with the blood of our martyrs. This seed will grow into a luxurious tree and make our martyrs' dreams a reality."[5] He told his supporters that "a liberation fighter does not die. That fire of ideal which was his life never burns out; [it] becomes a historical force and captures the heart of others. It wakes up the national spirit of a race." In a 1992 speech announcing an escalation in guerrilla attacks, Prabhakaran said, "Freedom is a sacred right that can be won by shedding blood." His martyrs die killing for the Good, and should be revered, he said, adding, "None can equal our martyrs in their dedication and deep commitment to the goal, and [in the] tremendous courage that transcends the fear of death." On Martyr's Day later that year, he said, "Our heroes have sacrificed their lives for a just cause. Their demise does not constitute an ordinary event of death. Rather, their death signifies a profound spiritual aspiration for national freedom." On Black Tiger Day in 1999, posters proudly displayed this familiar slogan: "We are not dead; we have been sown."[6]

Women and Children Become Suicide Bombers

In the mid-1980s the LTTE began a concentrated effort to recruit women and children as fighters, and some found their way into the Black Tigers. The women suicide squads were called Black Tigresses, sometimes Birds of Paradise. It was a woman who undertook the Tigers' most notorious assignment, the assassination of former Indian prime minister

Rajiv Gandhi. Gandhi had sent Indian troops into Sri Lanka in July 1987, ostensibly to mediate the struggle. The Indian Peace Keeping Force (IPKF) was soon fighting both sides and became perpetrator and victim of countless atrocities along the way. Among Tamils, the IPKF became known as the Innocent People Killing Force.

The Jain Commission Report on Rajiv Gandhi's assassination later concluded that "the role of the IPKF had changed from being the guarantor of peace, as originally envisaged, to being a de facto military force fighting against the LTTE."[7] Within two years, anger at the IPKF presence on the island brought Sinhalese and Tamil forces together in a rare period of cooperation to rid the island of what many saw as an occupying force. The effort succeeded, but by then Gandhi was no longer prime minister.

Suicide missions against political leaders were nothing new to the LTTE, but there had been no attacks outside the island. The occasion for the first was a preelection address on May 21, 1991, at Sriperumbudur in Tamil Nadu. Gandhi was running for a second term as prime minister and was there to support a candidate in his party. It is believed that Prabhakaran ordered the assassination because he feared Gandhi would reintroduce the hated IPKF into the Sri Lankan conflict. Revenge may have had something to do with it as well.

The martyr-assassin was a young woman known by various names, including Dhanu. She was from the northeastern city of Jaffna, in the heart of Tamil territory. That day she was wearing a white dress typical of those worn by pregnant women in India. No one could tell that across her stomach she was also wearing a denim belt holding six improvised explosive devices (IEDs). In her left hand she held a flower garland; in her right hand, the triggering device for the bomb.

As Gandhi approached the dais along a red carpet strewn with flowers, the bespectacled Dhanu quietly stepped up beside three other women holding garlands. When Gandhi approached she put the garland around his neck and knelt to kiss his feet. As he bent over to raise her up she detonated the grenades, killing them both instantly. The IEDs contained the plastic explosive C4-RDX and 3,300 steel pellets to increase the deadly effect. Dhanu's head landed twelve yards from the blast site, while her hands were later found nearly seventy-five yards apart. In all eighteen people were killed, including nine police-men and a Tamil coconspirator who was taking pictures of the event. The assassination had been a carefully planned attack involving not only Dhanu but also a stand-in named Subha and at least eleven others. The mastermind was believed to be an LTTE intelligence officer known as One-Eyed Jack on account of his glass eye; he was observed at the scene of the assassination posing as a journalist.

The martyrdom of Dhanu became legendary among the Black Tigers and especially among Tamil women with griev-ances against the government and the Indian Peace Keeping Force. The story circulated that Dhanu had been gang-raped two years earlier and her brothers killed by the IPKF. For a Hindu woman, rape is worse than death because it means she cannot marry or have children. "In this strongly patriarchal society, ... acting as a human bomb is an understood and ac-cepted offering for a woman who will never be a mother. Family members often encourage rape victims to join the LTTE."[8]

In her recent book *Dying to Kill: The Allure of Suicide Terror,* Mia Bloom suggests four motives for women to join the Tamil Tigers: to avenge ruined honor, achieve status, express per-sonal rage, and reverse an enduring sense of helplessness. A Tamil contact told Bloom, "One woman joined after her boy-friend was arrested, killed, and the corpse left in the village market for the public to see...."[9] Needless to say, many Tamil women suffer from at least one of these conditions.

Estimates put the percentage of LTTE suicide attacks using women at 30 to 40 percent, a figure surpassed only by the Kurdistan Workers Party (PKK), which carried out or attempted twenty-one suicide attacks in southeast Turkey between 1996 and 1999, fourteen of them by women. According to an Israeli expert, "all of them deceptively used the innocent appearance of a 'pregnant' woman in order to by-pass the heavy security arrangements while approaching their targets."[10] If the above estimates are correct, as many as a hundred women have participated in Black Tiger suicide attacks.

The picture is murkier where child martyrs are concerned, but there is no question that the Tamil Tigers recruited Baby Tigers extensively during the late 1980s and throughout the 1990s. Some children were eager to join up and others compelled; some were too young to know the difference. The international Human

Rights Watch (HRW) reported in 2004 that "the LTTE has had a history of forcibly recruiting children and placing them on the front lines during combat operations."[11] A *Frontline* report by PBS in May 2002 described the main recruitment effort as follows. Children as young as six were taken from refugee camps and put in a special school known as the Red Garden. After two or three years of indoctrination and training at the school, dubbed by Prabhakaran the University of the Tamils, the children were taken into a hidden camp in the jungle where they were all trained as fighters, some for suicide missions as human bombs. The young trainees were routinely shown videotapes of past suicide attacks.

A Tamil newspaper editor told *Frontline*, "Once chosen as a Black Tiger, or suicide killer, there is no way of getting out of the whole thing.... He cannot go back, because saying 'I can't do this' will bring shame for him. Everybody will say, 'What are you? You are nothing. No, you have to die for the leader.'"[12] In addition, there is evidence that some Tamil parents have encouraged children to join—or not stopped them from being recruited—because they have too many mouths to feed.

While generally quiet on their recruitment of children—they didn't admit the practice until recently[13]—LTTE leaders typically describe their child fighters as willing volunteers in search of refuge or revenge after government aircraft and tanks destroyed their villages or killed their parents. In 2002 the LTTE and the Sri Lankan government agreed to a cease-fire, and in 2003 the LTTE promised to end the recruitment of children and to send its remaining child fighters to rehabilitation centers set up by the United Nations Children's Fund (UNICEF). Yet the 2004 HRW report also says that the LTTE is still actively recruiting—and sometimes kidnapping—children into its ranks. UNICEF agrees, claiming that seventy-four boys and fifty girls were recruited during April and May 2004. Still, the LTTE has no monopoly on the atrocities in this conflict. In its "Asia Watch" reports over the years, the HRW documented vicious attacks by all sides and observed back in 1990 that "the utter brutality ... was unprecedented, creating an atmosphere of terror."[14]

A 2002 cease-fire between the LTTE and the government gave hope that political negotiations would find a permanent solution to the conflict in Sri Lanka. Once on Interpol's list of most-wanted fugitives for ordering the assassination of Rajiv Gandhi, Prabhakaran began appearing in public and entertaining journalists and foreign diplomats in the role of peacemaker. Though convicted of murder in absentia by an Indian court in 1994—"Nothing happens in the LTTE without my permission,"[15] he once declared—Prabhakaran is no longer a wanted man, though the LTTE remains on the U.S. State Department's list of foreign terrorist organizations. In his speeches Prabhakaran embraces the search for peaceful solutions ("we are deeply committed to the peace process," he said in 2003[16]) but he also reminds people of the self-sacrifices made by LTTE martyrs on behalf of independence.

A 2004 speech by the political head of the LTTE warned that death and sacrifice could once more be in the offing: "Our fighters are strengthening their security," he said. "All divisions of the Liberation Tigers have restarted their duties. We hope you, the people, will understand your obligations and act accordingly. The people should remain firm in their commitment to national struggle and their loyalty to the national leadership."[17] This left little doubt that suicide attacks would reappear in Sri Lanka.

And they have. First came a July 2004 attack by a woman suicide bomber that killed six police officers but failed to assassinate the target, the Tamil minister for Hindu cultural affairs. This attack was vigorously condemned by LTTE leadership; however, the impetus for continued political negotiations was shored up by a catastrophe—the December 2004 tsunami that killed more than thirty thousand people in Sri Lanka alone. Yet peace remains elusive. In his Heroes Day message of November 27, 2005, Prabhakaran accused the Sri Lankan government of racist policies and subversion of the peace process. He warned that 2006 would see a renewal of the struggle for national liberation if Tamil political aspirations remained thwarted.[18] Then on April 25, 2006, a woman pretending to be pregnant blew herself up in an attempt to assassinate Lieutenant General Sarath Fonseka, commander of the Sri Lankan army. Ten people were killed, and the officer and twenty-six others were wounded. The government blamed the Tamil Tigers.[19]

If Prabhakaran has in fact revived Black Tiger operations after a four-year hiatus, his decision underscores once again the pragmatic element in martyrdom. After decades of deadly struggle, his suspension of martyrdom operations—and then his willingness to revive them—not only draws international attention to the conflict but also shows that the LTTE cannot be crushed by the government's military superiority.

Notwithstanding Prabhakaran's clever use of religious themes and practices, the martyrdom of his fighters has not been driven by religious ideology or the promise of rewards in the afterlife but by the pragmatics of military inferiority. A ruthless charismatic leader demanded absolute loyalty and gave his Tigers reason to hope for victory and a better world for their families—if they were prepared to kill themselves for it.

Recruitment into the Black Tigers has been aided by decades of wanton destruction. The prevalent belief among Tamils that independence is the only sure way to stem the violence has been reinforced by the Sinhalese government's suppression and periodic massacre of Tamils, which in turn produced a burning desire for revenge in some victims. The patriarchal values that denigrate women had also played into Prabhakaran's hands, sending him female volunteers for martyrdom after their gender roles were undermined by sexual assault or widowhood.

The version of martyrdom adopted in the jungles of Sri Lanka—I call it *near*-predatory—produced civilian casualties largely in the form of collateral damage. Mia Bloom interviewed hundreds of Tamils during three months in 2002 and found few that supported the indiscriminate killing of civilians, the hallmark of true predatory martyrdom. The targets of Black Tiger missions were primarily members of the military or politicians. The 9/11 attacks and the suicide bombings associated with the current conflicts in Chechnya and the Middle East are more purely predatory in that the target is often civilian by design. Innocent people going about their daily routines have become the prey of the predatory martyr.

Nowhere is this truer than in the Israeli–Palestinian conflict. Here, nationalism, militant Islam, a history of cruel encounters between Arabs and Zionists amid callous manipulation by the United States and Britain, growing humiliation and despair due to the Israeli occupation of the West Bank and Gaza, and most recently spiraling violence in the Occupied Territories have conspired to turn young Arab men and women into human bombs whose targets are Jews on buses, in coffee shops, at malls, at the beach, or in nightclubs.

As the last two chapters have clearly shown, religious ideology is not a necessary element in campaigns of militant martyrdom, though it may facilitate or encourage them. The Japanese kamikazes and the Sri Lanka Black Tigers pursued a military strategy of suicide attacks for a nationalist cause, not a religious one. Yet religious ideology often plays a key role in facilitating militant resistance in nationalist struggles. This is especially true when the dominant religion of the superior power differs from that of the weaker side. When the underdog in a conflict is driven by both nationalist fervor *and* religious ideology, militant martyrdom is often the result. The spate of recent Chechen suicide bombings illustrates the point. (A notable exception was the decades-long conflict in Northern Ireland. The IRA never used martyrdom operations in its fight against Britain and nationalist Protestant groups. However, for about a month in late 1990, the IRA did kidnap members of civilian families and then force one into the role of suicide bomber by threatening to kill the others. It was a public relations disaster, writes Ed Maloney in *A Secret History of the IRA,* and strengthened the hand of those seeking an alternative to violence.[20])

Militant Martyrdom and the Coupling of Nationalism and Religious Ideology

Leaders of the decades-long Chechen struggle for independence from Moscow turned to suicide bombings in the latest phase of the conflict. According to the Chicago Project on Suicide Terrorism, there were nineteen successful suicide attacks on Russians from June 7, 2000, to December 9, 2003.[21] Truck bombs, belt bombs, and bombs carried in bags were the three methods of attack, and most were carried out by women, known as Black Widows. Like the women suicide bombers in Sri Lanka, many had lost husbands to the conflict, and their martyrdom was fueled to a degree by revenge, that emotion no doubt heightened by a patriarchal culture. In the summer of 2004, three more suicide attacks by women gained world headlines. In one operation, Amanat Nagayeva and Satsita

Dzhbirkhanova blew themselves up aboard Russian passenger planes, killing ninety people; in the other, a woman believed to be Nagayeva's younger sister blew herself up outside a subway station in Moscow, killing at least ten people.

Chechnya is located in the North Caucasus, a mountainous region between the Black Sea and the Caspian Sea long coveted by Russia, Iran, and Turkey as the geographic crossroads between Europe and Asia. The so-called First Chechen War erupted in 1994 after Chechnya declared independence from Russia following the collapse of the Soviet Union. Russian Federation president Boris Yeltsin sent troops in to bring the rebel state into line, and by 1996 as many as eighty thousand people had died in the fighting. After the war, which changed little, the region fell into chaos, wracked by poverty, disorder, and a spate of kidnappings. Radical Islamic groups surfaced, bringing money "and at least the illusion of discipline."[22] The late warlord Shamil Basayev joined them, not primarily for religious reasons, argues Sebastian Smith in *Allah's Mountains: The Battle for Chechnya*, but to increase his military strength—and therefore his regional power. In a humiliating affront to Moscow, Basayev's guerrillas occupied parts of neighboring Dagestan and declared them independent from Russia.

Most Chechens followed a Sufi version of Islam, which they practiced unobtrusively while retaining their secular identity. The new Islamic influence came from the Wahhabis, followers of the strict, orthodox Sunni Islam of Saudi Arabia and the main financial backers of the Chechen guerrillas during the war. The Wahhabis had stayed on afterward, living ostentatiously amid the postwar poverty and throwing their money and influence around.

Not that the Sufis were committed pacifists. For more than one hundred years, a Sufi militant group in neighboring Ingushetia known as Batal Hadji had led resistance to the "Russian infidel." In an interview with Sebastian Smith, Batal Hadji's aging leader, Akhmed Belkhoroyev, explained the role of Islam in the group's separatist struggle:

When they [the Russians] started to crush us, our religion made us strong, it bound us into one people. We broke bread between each other. In Kazakhstan, if we knew one village was starving we would sneak out at night past the guards and bring food. Allah strengthened us. In the Koran, it says that if the infidel come[s] to your land and destroy[s] your people, you must declare ghazawat, holy war. That's what happened in Chechnya and here. During our deportation, the Russians came with bulldozers and destroyed all our graveyards and ancient monuments. They wanted to take away all our culture. But we came back and we rebuilt everything. Now they're destroying Chechnya again. But the Chechens and Ingush cannot be put down. They always recover and take their revenge.... In 1974 I did the hajj to Mecca. I was the first of the Chechens or Ingush to do it.... In 1975 I persuaded them to open mosques, one in each region.... But I didn't bring back Islam—it was already here. It was here, in secret, all the time.[23]

In 1999, Moscow responded to the chaos in Chechnya and the growing influence of Wahhabism by sending in thousands of Russian troops, tanks, and planes to quash the "Islamic terrorists." Western leaders applauded the action of the Russian Federation's new president, Vladimir Putin, or they said little at all. The Chechen capital city of Grozny was virtually destroyed in the ensuing fighting. Despite holding off one hundred thousand Russian troops for more than two months, the Chechen resistance desperately needed a way to undermine Russian confidence while shoring up their own.

Shamil Basayev may have embraced Wahhabism as a power grab, but he had also immersed himself in jihadist literature and is known to have been an admirer of the late Sheikh Abdullah Azzam. Azzam was Osama bin Laden's spiritual mentor and a leader of the resistance to the Russian occupation of Afghanistan. Mia Bloom writes that Basayev "even talked of taking the fight beyond the borders of Chechnya to establish a pan-Islamic state across the northern Caucasus."[24] Basayev used his links with Saudi Arabia and Arab mujahideen training camps in Afghanistan to reenergize his guerrillas and to find new ways to respond to the overwhelming power of the Russian military. The Chechen resistance turned to a campaign of suicide attacks.

Suicide bombings offered a way to target Russians on their own turf and also provided a spectacular way to draw world attention to the dual nationalist and religious causes. The first attack took place on June 7, 2000, at a Chechen police station used by Russian Special Forces. Two women blew themselves up in a truck laden with TNT. An article of unknown origin and authorship circulating on the Internet soon afterward crowed:

> The Russian army ... watched helplessly as a female warrior of Allah drove a knife through the heart of the leadership of Russian's elite forces.... [The] sacrifice [of Sister Hawaa Barayev] for the sake of Allah and the Muslims is a warning to the unbelievers not only in Chechnya, but across the world, that the people of Allah will no longer accept the tyranny of infidels. It is a warning to all those who think they can commit crimes against Muslim women and children without being accountable for such crimes.... [T]hey will be hunted down by the soldiers of Allah....

According to *BBC World News* on June 8, 2000, "rebel spokesman" Movladi Udugov said that twenty-two-year-old Barayeva's last message was, "I am going willingly to my death in the name of Allah and the freedom of the Chechen people." The blending of religious ideology and nationalism is pretty clear in these statements.

There is a current tendency to lump all militant groups together, but this obscures differences among them, including ideas about the kind of suicide mission that is acceptable and the kind that is not. Appearances to the contrary, even groups that adopt predatory martyrdom as a military strategy say they have standards. The Tamil Tigers aside, the standards adopted by most militant groups are legitimized by religious doctrine and honed by experience. So militant Islamic groups ranging from Hamas to al-Qaeda appeal to the Quran and the commentaries of the hadith, as well as to historical events to justify their predatory suicide attacks. Commonly, militant resistance arises when people feel themselves unjustly oppressed. Oppression can take many forms, of course, but the emotional results tend to be the same: fear, humiliation, anger, resentment, and a sense of hopelessness that in the end only resistance or death can assuage.

Violence is the hard end of resistance, and it is potentially very costly to all concerned. Violence is usually adopted when nonviolent resistance is thwarted or otherwise ineffective.

Militant groups claim that the life and ideals of their people are on the line, so they try to turn the tables on their oppressors using whatever weapons they have at hand or can invent. Suicide bombing is generally regarded as a weapon of last resort. A Palestinian who trained suicide bombers put it this way: "Jihad and the resistance began with the word, then with the sword, then with the stone, then with the gun, then with planting bombs, and then transforming bodies into human bombs."[25] The Middle East has been the breeding ground of predatory martyrdom, so a visit there is vital to our journey.

Chapter 8

Dispersal and Occupation

A Festering Anger
Haunts Palestinians

The heartache that is obscured in the impersonal phrase "Israeli–Palestinian conflict" was born soon after World War I, when it became apparent that Jews had more political acumen and clout than Arabs and that Western nations were determined to protect their own interests no matter what. Both Arabs and Jews aspired to homelands in Palestine, and each staked historical claims. Jewish nationalism, represented by the Zionist movement, was grounded in biblical rights to a promised land for God's Chosen People, Eretz Israel—the Land of Israel. Palestinian Arab claims were those of a majority population in the land, some of whom could claim to be indigenous. They were bolstered by the dream of an Islamic empire stretching from the Tigris and Euphrates Rivers in modern Iraq to Egypt, and from the Mediterranean to the Arabian Sea. By the beginning of World War I, the Arab population of Palestine numbered roughly 650,000, and the Jewish population around 60,000, two-thirds of whom were recent immigrants from Europe, mostly Russia.

At the beginning of the twentieth century, the Turks controlled Palestine as part of the Ottoman Empire. When Turkey
joined Germany in World War I, the British government seized
the opportunity to increase its influence in a postwar Middle
East by promising support to the nationalist interests of Arabs
and Jews in exchange for their assistance in the Allied war
effort. At war's end, however, it was the Jewish biblical connection with Palestine that was recognized by the League of
Nations, and it was a Jewish homeland the League of Nations
promised to establish. The misgivings and warnings of some
Arab nationalists seemed to have come true: "Do you not hear
the commotion all around you? Do you not know that you live
in a period when he who sleeps dies, and he who dies is gone
forever? When will you open your eyes and see the glitter of
the bayonets that are directed at you, and the lightning of
the swords which are drawn over your heads? When will you
realize the truth? When will you know that your country has
been sold to the foreigner?"[1]

It is doubtful the Allies could have defeated the Ottoman
Empire without Arab help. In 1916 Faisal ibn Hussein, son
of the emir of Mecca, led the Arab revolt against the Turks
that made British colonel T. E. Lawrence famous and paved
the way for General Sir Edmund Allenby's eventual capture
of Jerusalem in December 1917.

When it came to settling up, neither the British nor their
allies came through for the Arabs of Palestine, despite a 1919
agreement between Faisal and the Russian-born British Zionist Chaim Weizmann that pledged support of both Arab and
Jewish states in Palestine. (The British eventually installed
Faisal as king of Iraq, and his brother Abdullah was made emir
of a new territory, Transjordan, known as the Hashemite Kingdom of Jordan after its independence from Britain in 1946.)
Instead, under the terms of the Palestinian Mandate ratified
by the League of Nations in 1922, the international powers
guaranteed efforts to establish a national home for the Jewish people while merely "safeguarding" the civil and religious
rights of Palestinian Arabs and other non-Jews. There was no
mention of an Arab state, and no Arab agency was established
to develop or oversee the interests of Palestinian Arabs. In
fact, the word *Arab* was not mentioned at all, and the word
Arabic appeared only in Article 22 of the mandate: "English,

Arabic and Hebrew shall be the official languages of Palestine. Any statement or inscription in Arabic on stamps or money in Palestine shall be repeated in Hebrew and any statement or inscription in Hebrew shall be repeated in Arabic."[2]

A festering anger among Palestinian Arabs had already found expression in periodic acts of violence. Attacks on Jewish areas of Jerusalem and Jaffa in 1920 were merely a portent of what was to come. The Arabs refused to cooperate with the British and by doing so unwittingly undermined their own interests. When the British proposed that an Arab agency be set up to facilitate Arab interests, it was turned down, Arab leaders fearing it would signal their acceptance of the mandate. Arab factionalism, an endemic problem for centuries, hardly helped their cause. In the meantime, Jewish immigration was encouraged, and the results were seen in economic development and a rising standard of living that benefited Palestinian Jews as well as Arabs living in urban areas. Even so, the Jews tended to come out ahead in the economic and political competition of the day, despite periodic British efforts to address Arab concerns.

Events in Europe, however, would raise the Palestinian conflict between Arabs and Jews to new heights. Anti-Semitic policies in Poland, Hungary, and Romania had already encouraged thousands of Jews to emigrate, but the rise of Adolf Hitler would add hundreds of thousands to the list. Many went to England and the United States, and others went to Palestine. By 1936 the Yishuv, or Jewish community, numbered over 400,000, around 30 percent of the total population of Palestine.

When a militant nationalist Arab preacher was killed by the British in 1935, his followers took to the streets and widespread chaos soon followed. A general strike was called, and violence against British troops escalated. A royal commission headed by Lord Robert Peel issued a report in 1937 that recommended for the first time partitioning Palestine into separate Jewish and Arab states. While Jews looked favorably on the plan, Arab nationalists rejected it, arguing that no partition of Arab lands was acceptable. The violence continued, and British installations came under attack from Arab fighters brought in from Syria and Iraq. Arab leaders were arrested and deported, and the British turned for help from the underground Jewish defense force known as the Haganah.

A British captain and fundamentalist Christian named Orde Charles Wingate trained the Jewish forces, creating "Special Night Squads" of Haganah fighters whose job was to counter the hit-and-run attacks favored by the Arabs. Around fifteen thousand Jews were armed and trained, including Moshe Dayan and other later leaders of Israel's armed forces. Wingate's belief in biblical prophecy made him an ardent supporter of the Zionist cause, and while the Jews called him *ha-yedid,* meaning "friend," he was hated by Palestinian Arabs, who eventually pressured the British into transferring him out of Israel with the stipulation that he never return.

With the outbreak of a second world war looming on the horizon, the British needed the cooperation of Arab states and the Muslims of India. In May 1939, the British suddenly reversed policy and declared that Palestine would become an independent state and part of the British Empire by 1949. Arabs and Jews would "share in government in such a way as to ensure that the essential interests of each community are safeguarded." Furthermore, Jewish immigration would continue for five years at a rate that would bring the Jewish population to one-third of the whole, but after that "no further Jewish immigration will be permitted unless the Arabs of Palestine are prepared to acquiesce in it."[3] The Arabs took small solace in the new plan, their independence deferred yet again, but the Jews were furious and refused to cooperate with British authorities. World War II put a temporary halt to any significant Jewish uprising, as the Zionists cast their lot with the Allies. The defeat of Erwin Rommel's Afrika Korps by British general Bernard Montgomery at El Alamein in November 1942 was a turning point in the war. Suddenly the pressure was off and the drive for a Jewish homeland renewed.

The British restrictions on the admission of new Jewish immigrants to Palestine remained in place even after Hitler embarked on his "Final Solution" and the horrors of the Holocaust became apparent. Jews felt that if they wanted a state, they would have to take on the British. The Zionists enlisted the help of American Jews, some 4.5 million people. However, neither the British nor the U.S. government wished to antagonize the Arab world, whose support they needed, so the response to Jewish appeals was muted to say the least.

Once the war had ended, two things put the Palestinian problem on the front burner. The first was the fate of thousands of displaced Jews in Europe; the second was the increasing violence directed at the occupying force by militant Zionists the British had themselves armed and trained. Among these was Polish-born David Ben-Gurion, later the first prime minister of Israel. In the background lurked another key issue: control of Middle Eastern oil and strategic ports such as Haifa. The British and U.S. governments wanted oil in safe hands and away from the Soviet Union.

Even as they poured more troops into Palestine, the British faced an intransigent Ben-Gurion who promised that hundreds of thousands of Jews would be willing martyrs for the cause of independence. For their part, the Arabs felt no responsibility for the Holocaust and saw no reason that they should pay a heavy price for it by admitting thousands of displaced Jews into Arab lands. Meanwhile, the old claims remained the same: Arabs wanted Palestine to be an independent Arab state; the Jews wanted a national homeland. Seeing no end to the conflict and fearing an all-out war in Palestine, Britain took the issue to the new United Nations on February 14, 1947. A special committee of eleven "neutral" nations was set up and the input of Palestinian Jews and the recently formed Arab League requested. The Arab Higher Committee for Palestine refused to participate, arguing that the recommendations of eighteen previous commissions of inquiry had been either unfavorable to the Arab cause or ignored.

The committee split on its recommendations, and Australia abstained altogether. The majority proposal legitimized the Palestinian Mandate and called for an Arab state, a Jewish state, an international enclave in Jerusalem, and economic union between the two states within two years. The division of land favored the proposed Jewish state, both in relative size and fertility. On the other hand, it would not include Jerusalem or the biblically significant town of Hebron—and 407,000 Arabs lived within the proposed state's borders.

While the Jewish reaction was mostly positive, the Arab League rejected the proposal on principle and threatened war if the United Nations implemented it. Britain took a neutral position, while the United States supported the plan. After making slight modifications to the partition plan, on November

29, 1947, the UN General Assembly voted 33 to 13 to adopt it, and in doing so gave legal authority to the Yishuv to establish a Jewish state in Palestine. Six months later the British were gone, and at 4 p.m. on May 14, 1948, Ben-Gurion declared the State of Israel a reality.

Fierce fighting between the Haganah and a volunteer Arab Liberation Army sent in via Syria in January 1948 was already in full swing. After May 14, Egypt, Iraq, and Lebanon officially joined the fray, and this became known as the first Arab–Israeli War or, in Israel, the War of Independence. Some Palestinian Arabs had already joined the fight, though many were distrustful of outsiders, and for good reason: Both Jordan and Syria had their eyes on Arab territory. And the elders of some Arab villages had promised not to get involved in exchange for Haganah protection.

As the fighting raged throughout Palestine, bombings, assassinations, and riots killed women, children, and elderly on both sides. Rapes and mutilations were also reported. Yet to many Arabs one incident stands out: the Jewish attack on Deir Yassin. This was a small village just outside the boundary of the proposed Jewish state; it was a quiet village that had earlier signed a nonaggression pact with the Jerusalem branch of the Haganah. The attack on April 9, 1948, involved a force of 132, many still in their teens. It was a combined action of Haganah, including its crack Palmach unit, and Menachem Begin's underground paramilitaries known as Irgun Zvai Leumi. Irgun had conducted the 1946 bombing of the King David Hotel, the British military headquarters in Jerusalem. That attack had killed nearly one hundred, including Arab and Jewish civilians. Begin did not accompany his fighters to Deir Yassin.

The incident at Deir Yassin is widely described as a massacre, and there is survivor testimony that women and children were raped and the dead mutilated. One survivor interviewed by British police four days after the attack said, "A man [shot] a bullet into the neck of my sister Salhiyeh who was nine months pregnant. Then he cut her stomach open with a butcher's knife."[4] On the other hand, there are Jewish claims that Deir Yassin was not a massacre with atrocities but simply a fierce and deadly firefight; but this is not the opinion held by most scholars, including some from Israel. A Haganah commander at the scene who later became a member of the Israeli parliament did not personally see any rapes or mutilations, but in a 1998 interview he said that "almost all the dead were old people, children or women, with a few men here and there. They stood them up in the corners and shot them. . . . They also shot people running from houses, and prisoners. Mostly women and children."[5]

In 1948 hatred and paranoia filled the air, and the word *extermination* was bandied about on both sides. Massacres and the accompanying destruction of Arab homes were not simply an expression of rage or the unrestrained excesses of youthful fighters; they were part of a Haganah strategy to paralyze the enemy and frighten Arabs into leaving their villages. This is arguably why an inflated figure of 254 deaths was given to the press by the Irgun commander at Deir Yassin.

Deir Yassin had an immediate impact, not simply because it provoked Arab retaliation—a Jewish convoy of mostly medical personnel was attacked four days later, leaving scores dead—but because it convinced many Arab villagers to flee for safety. Between April and December 1948, more than six hundred thousand Arabs fled Jewish-controlled areas, most of them into the West Bank and the Gaza Strip but many also into Lebanon, Syria, and Jordan. There is little question that the Israeli army engaged in a systematic practice of ethnic cleansing, later described by Israeli prime minister Yitzhak Rabin as "one of the most difficult actions we undertook," requiring "prolonged propaganda activities" to soften the psychological impact on the Israeli soldiers themselves.[6] In a few days in July 1948, the twin cities of Lydda (now Lod) and Ramla were cleansed of some sixty thousand Arab inhabitants.

The new state of Israel was not inclined to let the refugees return anytime soon. Palestinian Arabs remained largely a stateless people; only those living inside Israel or in Jordan were eventually offered full citizenship. Most of the refugees in the West Bank and Gaza were fellahin, unskilled workers and rural peasants. They filled poorly constructed and unsanitary refugee camps and in the first years did little or nothing to improve them, expecting someday to return home. Someday has not yet come, and may never come. The Palestinians who left their homes were called *naziheen,* the "displaced ones." "Displacement is like death," Palestinian poet Mourid Barghouti writes. "One thinks it only happens to other people."[7]

The refugee issue is one of the flash points in the current Israeli–Palestinian conflict and illustrates the long-term impact of Deir Yassin and other attacks on Arab villages. The physical destruction at Deir Yassin was repeated many times in 1948; according to Israeli government records disseminated first by the late civil rights activist and author Israel Shahak, the Haganah demolished 385 of 475 Arab villages in 1948. In Arab eyes it is proof of the Zionists' commitment to the extermination of Palestinian Arabs and their property. The memory is conjured up today whenever an Israeli tank demolishes a Palestinian home in the West Bank or Gaza Strip.

Other horrors were to come in the years following the War of Independence, some at Arab hands, some committed by Jews. Needless to say, this account focuses on the Palestinian view of the conflict and their aspirations for an independent state. Palestinians found plenty of grist for the mill. From inside the new state of Israel there were complaints that Arab residents were not being treated fairly. Although by 1951, Israeli Arabs were allowed to vote and run for office, they could not serve in the Israeli army, their movements were restricted, and their land could be expropriated for security reasons. Arabs also claimed that the Israeli government denied them civil rights by not investing equally in the educational, social, and economic well-being of Palestinian communities. UN-sponsored armistice agreements drawn up in 1949 between Israel and neighboring Arab states further aggravated tensions because the resulting demilitarized zones cut through some Palestinian farms and villages.

Over the next twenty years a pattern of resistance and retaliation emerged along the borders of Israel. Incursions into Israel from Jordan and Syria were carried out by individual refugees or ad hoc groups whose motives varied from revenge to a desire to see their families or reclaim possessions. From the Egyptian side things were better organized and more deadly, with refugees trained for fedayeen missions at special camps. The fedayeen fighters crossed into Israel as spies, saboteurs, and killers. The Israeli response to Palestinian incursions was to mount counterattacks using regular army units. Ariel Sharon led one of the first large-scale retaliatory attacks in 1953. His soldiers destroyed fifty houses and killed more than sixty men, women, and children in the Jordanian village of Qibya. While the United Nations condemned the attack in a lopsided vote, Ben-Gurion insisted that Arabs only understood and respected the use of force, so the best defense was offense. Ariel Sharon would adopt essentially the same approach when he became prime minister of Israel fifty years later.

With an eye on their own interests, Syria and Egypt, and later Iran, actively funneled money and arms to Palestinian guerrillas while British-educated King Hussein of Jordan took a backseat, fully aware of his vulnerability to the superior forces on the other side of his long border with Israel. In Cairo, Yasser Arafat was among a group of Palestinian students who had founded the guerrilla group al-Fatah. In Arabic *Fatah* means "conquest," and read in reverse it is also an acronym for Harakat al-Tahrir al-Falastini, or Movement for the Liberation of Palestine. By the mid-1960s, Fatah was the preeminent Palestinian resistance organization, conducting many raids from Egypt, and later from Syria. (An interesting aside: Like Osama bin Laden, Arafat came from a prominent Arab family, was well educated, and had built a successful career in the construction industry.)

A second organization dedicated to armed struggle was founded in 1964. The Palestine Liberation Organization (PLO) recruited Palestinians from around the Arab world for its army, and in 1966 its chairman, Ahmad Shuqayri, agreed to coordinate operations with Fatah. The PLO established headquarters in Old Jerusalem and training camps in the West Bank and Syria. Raids were launched into Israel from Jordan, and in November 1966 Israel retaliated with tanks and aircraft, killing eighteen and destroying the homes and infrastructures of three villages in the southern Hebron area. Once again the United Nations condemned the Israeli attack, bolstering Palestinian claims of Zionist aggression.

The war of 1967, known as the Six-Day War, was a humiliation for the Arab states, particularly Egypt, whose air force was virtually destroyed while on the ground. With Arab armies massing along its borders, the Israeli air force made a preemptive first strike on Egyptian airfields on June 5. Its army of citizen soldiers quickly defeated the Egyptian army and seized the Gaza Strip and the Sinai Peninsula. By June 10, Israel had seized the West Bank and the Old City of Jerusalem from Jordan and had captured the Syrian-controlled

Golan Heights. The war was over, and Israel quickly annexed East Jerusalem.

The Arab states were defeated but not the zeal of militant anti-Zionists, whose numbers grew as a million more Arabs now found themselves under direct Israeli control. In November 1967, the UN Security Council passed Resolution 242, calling for the return of occupied territories and a "just settlement of the refugee problem." Israel insisted that any plan to return territories should be linked to peace treaties and the normalization of relations with Arab states as well as a guarantee of navigation through the Straits of Tiran. The refugee problem would be solved by resettlement outside the borders of the State of Israel. The Arab heads of state had already made their position clear at a postwar conference in Khartoum: "no peace with Israel, no recognition of Israel, no negotiations with it."[8]

Despite sympathy from abroad and the seemingly supportive stance of most Arab states, at least one prominent activist felt that the Palestinians should go it alone and called for a popular uprising. George Habash was a Greek Orthodox pediatrician who founded the Arab Nationalist Movement in 1952 and in 1967 created the Popular Front for the Liberation of Palestine (PFLP). A refugee of the ethnic cleansing in Lydda, Habash wanted to establish a secular democratic socialist state through armed struggle. The PFLP gained the world's attention when fedayeen commando Leila Khaled hijacked a TWA plane to Damascus in 1969. She followed this with an unsuccessful attempt to hijack an Israeli plane on September 6, 1970. Khaled was overpowered by security guards and the plane was flown to Heathrow Airport in London. This incident was part of a larger operation in which the PFLP also hijacked three other passenger planes, one of which was blown up in Cairo and the other two flown to a British RAF base in Jordan, where they were subsequently blown up as well. Leila Khaled was arrested by British police. In a matter of hours the PFLP hijacked a British plane en route from Bombay to Beirut and threatened to kill all the passengers unless Khaled and other fedayeen fighters held in Germany, Switzerland, and Israel were released. Khaled was released twenty-eight days later in exchange for a British hostage, and she returned home to become a member of the PFLP's Central Committee.

The hijackings had an immediate impact. They showed that PFLP militants were prepared to attack Western interests, and they embarrassed King Hussein of Jordan, who had long feared that the Palestinian refugees in Jordan would become uncontrollable, a state within a state. Hussein declared martial law and ordered an immediate crackdown on the Palestinian Liberation Army, now under Arafat's control. Despite the help of two hundred tanks from Syria, as many as three thousand fedayeen were killed in battles with the Jordanian army commanded by the Bedouin general Habis Al-Majali. September 1970 became known as "Black September" because Arabs were now fighting each other instead of Israelis. Indeed, British government documents released in 2001 show that King Hussein had asked Britain to pressure Israel into attacking the Syrian army on his behalf.

The name *Black September* was adopted by a fedayeen unit tied to Fatah and the PLO and secretly under the control of Yasser Arafat. One of its first actions was the assassination of the newly appointed Jordanian prime minister, a staunch foe of the Palestinian guerrillas. Black September took on missions that were likely to be suicidal, but they escaped if they could. On September 5, 1972, its commandos killed eleven Israeli athletes following a daring raid at the Summer Olympics in Munich. Their leader was Mohammed Oudeh, known also as Abu Daoud. Just before 5 a.m., Israeli wrestling coach Moshe Weinberg awoke to find armed men in stocking masks at his door in the Olympic village. He shouted a warning, but it was too late. He and weightlifter Joseph Romano were killed as they attempted to block the door. The fedayeen then took nine Israelis hostage and demanded the release of Arabs held in Israel and Germany and their own safe passage out of Germany.

After an apparent deal was struck, the hostages boarded a bus to a NATO airstrip where two helicopters awaited. German snipers also waited, with orders to kill the kidnappers and rescue the hostages. A bloody firefight erupted at the air base during which the Black September militants killed all nine hostages, blowing up six with one of the helicopters. Three Arabs were captured but later released in a deal for the return of a hijacked Lufthansa plane and its passengers. In the now-famous "Wrath of God" operation (on which the recent Steven Spielberg film *Munich* is based), Israeli prime minister Golda Meir secretly sent agents from Mossad, the Israeli secret service, to hunt down and kill those responsible for the deaths of the Israeli Olympians. Eight were eventually found and killed, three in Beirut by a combined operation involving Mossad and Israeli Defense Forces (IDF) agents led by Ehud Barak. In hiding for years, Abu Daoud survived the Israeli operation and emerged as a key player on the Palestinian National Council.

The Black September operation in Munich was one of the most notorious actions of the Palestinian fedayeen, but more were to come. Throughout the 1970s and 1980s, hopes for a Palestinian state were repeatedly dashed and attacks against Israel and its allies continued. When Egypt's president Anwar Sadat addressed the Israeli Knesset in 1977 and then signed the 1978 Camp David Accords with Israel's Menachem Begin, Palestinians found little to embrace. The accords promised "negotiations" among Jordan, Israel, Egypt, and "representatives of the Palestinian people" on the future of the West Bank and Gaza, but made no mention of Jerusalem or the future of the Golan Heights.

The negative reaction of almost all Arab states was spelled out within months as diplomatic relations with Egypt were severed and Egypt was first suspended from the Arab League and then expelled from a number of important Arab and Muslim organizations. While Palestinians doubtless took some comfort in this, they surely seethed at the comments of Israel's right-wing Likud Party, Begin's own: "The autonomy agreed upon at Camp David does not signify a state, or sovereignty, or self-determination [for Palestinian Arabs]. The Arab nation enjoys self-determination thanks to the existence of twenty-one Arab states."[9]

Far from easing the Palestinian–Israeli conflict, the Camp David Accords gave militants new fodder and new recruits. Headquartered in Lebanon since its expulsion from Jordan, the PLO had been recruiting and training fighters from among the large refugee population there. The new developments played into Arafat's hands. He stepped up rocket attacks across the border and fedayeen forays into Israel from PLO-controlled camps and villages. In June 1982, the Israeli army invaded Lebanon with the intention of crushing the PLO once and for all. Following a plan developed by defense minister Ariel Sharon, the army reached the outskirts of Beirut in four days, destroying Syrian artillery, tanks, and planes along the way. The PLO fedayeen withstood a two-month siege before finally abandoning the city and dispersing across the Middle East and North Africa.

Thousands of Palestinians remained in crowded Lebanese refugee camps. On September 15, 1982, Sharon allowed Christian soldiers of the Maronite Phalange Party to enter the camps of Sabra and Shatila to avenge the assassination of their leader, Bashir Gemayal, who had been elected as Lebanese president only a month earlier. The Phalangists blamed Arab Muslims for the assassination. For four days the Phalangists massacred hundreds of Palestinians in the two camps while Israeli solders watched from rooftops overlooking the camps and did nothing. Sharon was forced to resign, but the outrage fueled new anger against Israel and its Christian allies among Palestinians and Arab Muslims generally. Even today Lebanese Muslims remember the atrocity as if it happened yesterday. Israel eventually withdrew from Lebanon at the urging of the United States and the Christian government of Lebanon, but Israeli troops remained in a security zone overlooking the Bekaa Valley. Those troops became the target of systematic attacks by Palestinian fedayeen, including suicide attacks with car bombs and portable improvised explosive devices (IEDs).

However, the first suicide bombings using vehicles targeted Western peacekeeping forces, not Israelis. On April 18, 1983, a van carrying two thousand pounds of explosives blew up the seven-story building housing the U.S. embassy in Beirut. Sixty-three people died, including seventeen Americans. Six months later, U.S. and French military barracks were attacked. The attack on the Battalion Landing Team Headquarters in the U.S. Marine compound occurred when most of the building's occupants were asleep. A yellow Mercedes-Benz truck flew between two marine guard posts, evaded concertina wire and a variety of roadway obstacles, and then crashed into the building's lobby, where its driver—smiling, witnesses said—detonated twelve thousand pounds of explosives. The blast lifted the building off its foundation and caused it to implode on itself. The attack was hailed as a great victory against Israel's most powerful ally.

These suicide attacks were carried out by Hezbollah, "Party of God," a loose conglomerate of militant Muslim groups inspired by the Islamic revolution in Iran that had toppled the Westernized Shah Mohammad Reza Pahlevi in 1979. The Shiite government in Iran now supplied Hezbollah with men, money, and arms in its continuing effort to rid the Middle East of Western influence.

Hezbollah took its name from Surah 58 of the Quran, which promises that those who resist the Evil One and believe in the goodness and justice of Allah will be admitted to Paradise and achieve eternal happiness as the Party of Allah. "Resistance, Resistance, Resistance" is the fighting song of Hezbollah. The group operated from the Bekaa Valley and periodically joined forces with other militant groups, the Sunni Islamic Jihad among them. Hassan Nasrallah directed the war against Israel; interviewed in a documentary film by Robert Fisk of the British newspaper *Independent,* Nasrallah speaks approvingly of the Hezbollah fighters who seek martyrdom "with hopeful heart, smiling and happy."[10]

The Shiite rebellion against the Western presence in Lebanon brought predatory martyrdom to the Middle East. Although the attacks were nominally against foreign governments and their soldiers, civilians were also killed by the suicide bombers, including Lebanese Muslims. This was the beginning of a new trend that soon spilled over to the Israeli–Palestinian conflict.

Chapter 9

Intifada

Predatory martyrs appeared in the militant Palestinian campaign against Israel during the first of two popular uprisings called intifada (literally, "shaking off"). In December 1987, an Israeli shopper was stabbed to death in Gaza. The next day four residents of the Jabalya refugee camp were killed in a traffic accident involving an Israeli vehicle. Rumors spread that the accident was revenge for the earlier stabbing. Riots broke out in Jabalya and soon grew into an intifada that engulfed the Israeli-occupied territories, including Jerusalem.

King Hussein of Jordan called the intifada a "courageous uprising" and vowed to support it during a speech in which he renounced his own claims to the West Bank. Now headquartered in Tunisia, Yasser Arafat and the Palestine Liberation Organization (PLO) slowly took control of the intifada as a way to unify the splintered Palestinian resistance and reassert its leadership. In the first few weeks of the uprising, Palestinians threw stones, Molotov cocktails, and the occasional hand grenade at Israeli Defense Forces (IDF) troops; set up barricades; and burned tires. The beleaguered but better-equipped Israeli troops responded with automatic rifles, machine guns, and tanks. Thirty-eight Palestinians were killed, and many more were injured. The UN General Assembly condemned the Israeli action in yet another lopsided vote.

Over the next year the violence escalated on both sides, but most of the dead and wounded were Palestinians. To put this in perspective: "The death rate of rock-throwing Palestinians in the first year of the intifada was six times the annual per capita death rate of American solders in Vietnam."[1] Many of the dead were teenage boys emboldened by the flood of anger, resentment, pride, and testosterone. Known as *shabab,* and often wearing the traditional Arab headdress (kaffiyeh) to mask their faces, the teenagers alternated between being graffiti artists and guerrillas in the worsening tragedy unfolding in the Occupied Territories.

In Gaza, hundreds of ordinary Palestinians would eagerly await the face-off with Israeli soldiers. When it happened, "screams in Hebrew were answered by screams in Arabic."[2] Television crews from overseas were sometimes on hand to film the clashes. During the first intifada, the Israeli army imposed many curfews and sometimes cut off the electricity. "There would be long periods of silence," wrote two American observers, "and then you might hear the gut-wrenching boom of tear-gas grenades, the roar of tanks and gravel throwers, amid the shouts and screams of 'Allahu Akbar' [God is great] of guys rushing into battle with rocks in one hand and onions (the local antidote for tear gas) in the other."[3]

Some Palestinian leaders saw the intifada as an opportunity to enhance their power and influence. A mainly secular struggle for nationhood and redress of wrongs soon became entangled with the zeal of militant religious fundamentalism. Important in this shift was the emergence in Gaza of the Islamic Resistance Movement, otherwise known as Hamas (for Harakat al-Muqawama al-Islamiya), which in Arabic means "zeal." Hamas was an underground arm of the Muslim Brotherhood, a Sunni movement founded in Egypt by Sheikh Hassan al-Banna in the 1920s. Al-Banna had dreamt of a pan-Islamic state based on Sharia (Islamic law based on the Quran). In Gaza, one of his disciples was Sheikh Ahmed Yassin, a quadriplegic cleric. Yassin saw in the intifada an opportunity for Islam, and Hamas could be its vehicle. Under Yassin's spiritual guidance, Hamas challenged the secular PLO for the hearts and minds of Palestinians while providing Islamic militants with an alternative to the Iranian-funded and Syrian-backed Palestinian Islamic Jihad, another offshoot of the Muslim Brotherhood.

For Yassin the establishment of an Islamic state in Palestine was the first step toward uniting Arab and non-Arab Muslims. He called for jihad against Israel. In 1990 a military wing was established, called the Izz al-Din al-Qassam Brigades in memory of Sheikh Izz al-Din al-Qassam, a militant Syrian Muslim killed by the British in 1935. Qassam organized bands of guerrillas in the hills around Haifa in a revolt against the British and their Zionist partners; it is said that he sold all his belongings to buy a rifle so he could wage jihad against the infidel. Qassam is revered by Palestinians as a warrior-martyr; his smiling face is a common sight on buildings in the West Bank and Gaza. Qassam posters usually include this verse from the Quran: "And say not of those who are slain in the way of Allah: 'They are dead.' Nay, they are living, though ye perceive it not" (Surah 2:154).

While praising the PLO's efforts on behalf of Palestinian liberation, Hamas immediately distanced itself from the PLO, saying its secular stance "completely contradicts" the ideology of Islam. "Hamas is one of the links in the Chain of Jihad in the confrontation with the Zionist invasion," reads the Hamas charter. Nationalism is "part and parcel of religious faith.... The Islamic nature of Palestine is part of our religion, and anyone who neglects his religion is bound to lose."[4] For Hamas, the Arab–Israeli conflict boils down to a religious confrontation between Islam and Judaism from which Islam must emerge victorious. Mahmoud Zahar, a founder of Hamas who secretly became leader in 2004 following Israeli targeted assassinations of Yassin and Hamas cofounder Abdel Aziz al-Rantissi, explained the jihad this way: "They [the Jews] made their religion their nation and state.... They have declared war on Islam, closed mosques and massacred defenseless worshippers at al-Aqsa and in Hebron. They are the Muslim-killers and under these circumstances we are obliged by our religion to defend ourselves."[5]

Hamas waged its war against the Jews with growing intensity, all the time preparing the next generation of predatory martyrs through religious and social services throughout the West Bank and Gaza, but especially in the teeming refugee camps. Children were easily drawn into the revolutionary fervor of the intifada: Its sights and sounds were all around them, in school, plastered on every wall, and blaring from loudspeakers. Cards depicting the latest martyr to die at the hands of Israeli soldiers (if not at his own) were traded like American baseball cards. Children paraded through the streets chanting about martyrdom: "O mother, my religion has called me to jihad and self-sacrifice / O mother, I am marching toward immortality; I will never retreat / O mother, don't cry over me if I am shot down, laid out on the ground / For death is my path, martyrdom my desire."[6]

During the first intifada, Hamas targeted Israeli soldiers and Jewish settlements. These were not suicide bombings, although Hamas fedayeen were often killed at the scene of an attack or afterward in retaliatory raids by Israel. The Gulf War of 1991 briefly diverted the world's attention from the intifada, and the Palestinian resistance movement found the support of Arab states dwindling, in part because Arafat did not join them in condemning Saddam Hussein's invasion of Kuwait. With Scud missiles flying into Israel almost daily during the war, the Israeli government imposed a broad curfew in the Occupied Territories and prohibited Palestinians from entering Israel to work. The Palestinian economy collapsed along with the intifada.

The new hardships spread across the Occupied Territories but were felt most in the refugee camps. Anger and frustration grew, and militant groups had little trouble finding recruits for their campaign against Israel. The airlift to Israel of fifteen thousand Ethiopian Jews in May 1991 and the influx of more than half a million Jews from the former Soviet Union between 1990 and 1995 further angered many Palestinians. They correctly feared that many of the new immigrants would be settled in the West Bank and around the Old City of Jerusalem. Resentment boiled even as international diplomacy seemed to bring hope.

On September 13, 1993, millions watched as the historic Israeli–PLO peace accord was signed on the White House lawn. Israeli foreign minister Shimon Peres and then–PLO representative Mahmoud Abbas (who was elected president of the Palestinian Authority in 2005) completed the agreement after months of secret negotiations. The extraordinary event was capped when sworn enemies Yitzhak Rabin and Yasser Arafat shook hands in front of a smiling Bill Clinton. The agreement included a timetable for Israeli military withdrawal from and Palestinian self-governance of the West Bank and the Gaza Strip and a five-year transitional period during which negotiations for a permanent resolution of outstanding issues such as Jerusalem, Palestinian refugees, and Jewish settlements would begin.

The international community hailed the agreement—Arafat, Rabin, and Peres were awarded the Nobel Peace Prize—as did many hopeful Palestinians and Israelis. But others did not: Hamas called Arafat a traitor for recognizing Israel's right to exist, and Jewish zealots turned on Rabin for giving away the land of Israel. Hatred simmered on both sides. A spark could easily ignite a conflagration.

That spark came early on the morning of Friday, February 25, 1994, and is known to Palestinians as the Hebron Massacre. Almost a thousand Muslims were at prayers in the Ibrahimi Mosque inside the Tomb of the Patriarchs in the West Bank city of Hebron. A man dressed in Israeli army fatigues walked through two Israeli checkpoints before entering the mosque. Once inside, Dr. Baruch Goldstein threw a hand grenade and then began spraying bullets from an automatic rifle. Twenty-nine Muslims were killed and more than one hundred were wounded before Goldstein was overpowered and beaten to death by the enraged worshippers.

Goldstein was a Jewish-American physician and West Bank settler who was also an ardent follower of the assassinated orthodox rabbi Meir Kahane and his extremist Kach Party. Some writers subsequently claimed that Goldstein was trying to preempt a planned massacre of Jewish settlers by Hamas. The truth is unclear, but one thing is not: Goldstein's attack personified the militant fury of unbridled holy war. He would take down as many Muslims as he could, giving his own life in the process. Jewish extremists and settlers from the village of Kiryat Arba quickly called Goldstein a heroic martyr, and a special gravesite and monument were built to commemorate his sacrifice. The monument is periodically knocked down by the Israeli army, only to be quickly rebuilt.

The rage that had turned Goldstein the zealot into Goldstein the predatory martyr was matched on the Arab side and surfaced immediately in angry demonstrations. Hamas vowed revenge. The rage intensified when the Israeli government imposed a curfew on Palestinians in the West Bank but allowed armed Jewish settlers to move about freely. In April 1994, Hamas began using suicide bombers in its campaign against the Jews. The first attack took place at a bus stop in the center of Afula, a city in northern Israel famous for its falafel, a Middle Eastern snack made from chickpeas. A nineteen-year-old Hamas martyr named Ra'id Zarkana drove his booby-trapped car into an Israeli bus, killing seven people and wounding fifty more. Seven days later a second Hamas martyr blew himself up on an Israeli commuter bus in the town of Hadera, killing five and wounding thirty. These were but a preview of things to come. Early in 1996, a bus bombing in Jerusalem killed twenty-six and injured eighty, another soon after killed nineteen more, and the next day a suicide-bomber exploded an improvised explosive device (IED) in a Tel Aviv shopping center, killing twenty and wounding seventy-five. These attacks helped conservative Benjamin Netanyahu and his Likud Party coalition win the Israeli election in May 1996.

Fanned by dreams of victory for Islam—the Hamas slogan reads "Islam is the solution"—and the promised glories of martyrdom, predatory attacks continued off and on over the next five years. Some were claimed by Hamas, some by Islamic Jihad, and some by both groups. Neither wished to be upstaged in the holy war or in the competition for recruits. Mia Bloom writes in *Dying to Kill: The Allure of Suicide Terror,* "With the absence of monopoly over force, groups compete and outbid each other with more spectacular bombing operations and competition over claiming responsibility for them. At the same time, the operations whip up nationalist fervor and swell the ranks of the Islamic Jihad and Hamas, who use the bombings in conjunction with the provision of social services to win the hearts and minds of Palestinians."[7]

Negotiations on implementing the peace agreement between Israel and the PLO, now recognized as the Palestinian Authority, sputtered along despite continuing attacks on Israelis by Islamic militants and retaliation by Israel with aircraft, tanks, and bulldozers to level homes and businesses linked to the resistance. The burdens of poverty and corruption continued to weigh heavily on Palestinians, as did the daily round of humiliation and degradation endured by many in the West Bank and Gaza, now mostly under Palestinian control but entered at will by the Israeli military in response to attacks or for other security reasons. Loss of self-respect weighed heavily, too. Palestinian poet Mourid Barghouti writes,

> Occupation prevents you from managing your affairs in your own way. It interferes with every aspect of life and death; it interferes with longing and anger and desire and walking in the street. It interferes with going anywhere and coming back, with going to the market, the emergency hospital, the beach, the bedroom, or a distant capital.... Israel closes down any area it chooses whenever it wants. It prevents people from entering or leaving until the reason for the closure is over. There are always "reasons."[8]

If the dawning of the new millennium brought any hopes to Palestinians and Israelis, they were soon dashed; instead the conflict grew even more murderous, with a significant escalation in attacks by predatory martyrs. More than twenty successful suicide attacks were launched against Jewish targets in 2001. And the following two years saw even more. By then a third militant group had appeared, also adopting predatory martyrdom in its cause: the al-Aqsa Martyrs' Brigades. This group is linked to Fatah as an offshoot of its militant youth organization known as Tamzin. Arafat's public renunciation in 1993 of the use of suicide attacks and other acts of violence and his recognition of Israel's right to exist distanced him from the predatory attacks on Israeli citizens by the al-Aqsa Martyrs. Intelligence experts believe that early al-Aqsa missions were overseen by the popular West Bank secretary-general of Fatah, Marwan Barghouti. Barghouti is a former leader of Tamzin who is now serving five consecutive life terms in Israel for orchestrating killings of Israelis; he was captured in 2002, and his subsequent trial and conviction further elevated his status among Palestinians.

The predatory martyrs of the al-Aqsa Brigades burst on the scene with the coming of a second intifada, known as the Al-Aqsa Uprising. The spark was Likud Party leader Ariel Sharon's much-publicized visit on September 28, 2000, to the Temple Mount, known to Muslims as al-Haram as-Sharif, the "Noble Sanctuary," and site of the Al-Aqsa Mosque. Sharon, long hated by Palestinians for his association with the Sabra and Shatila massacres in Lebanon, arrived at al-Haram as-Sharif with an escort of one thousand Israeli police. Although Sharon had every right to be there and did not enter the Al-Aqsa Mosque itself, the spectacle was enough to enrage many Muslims. Thousands of stone-throwing Palestinians took to the streets in protest. Barghouti later asserted that an uprising had been in the making for months, spurred by Palestinian frustration over the failed peace process and the continued construction of Jewish settlements in the Occupied Territories. Sharon's visit was the perfect moment for unleashing the intifada.

Over the next three years, the al-Aqsa martyrs claimed responsibility for many suicide bombings, including some of the most deadly. Indeed, in 2002 they killed more Israeli civilians in predatory suicide attacks than Hamas or Islamic Jihad. The killings by al-Aqsa escalated in response to the targeted killing by Israeli forces of their West Bank leader, Raed Karmi, in January 2002. Two attacks by al-Aqsa predatory martyrs in Jerusalem during March of that year killed fourteen civilians and wounded more than fifty.

But it was in January 2003 that the al-Aqsa martyrs made global headlines. A two-person team carried out a predatory suicide attack in Tel Aviv, the ancient seaside metropolis known for its beaches, modern skyscrapers, and fancy shopping malls. Tel Aviv had been attacked before; who could forget the June 2001 suicide bombing of the Silent World beachfront discotheque that killed seventeen and wounded seventy? Islamic Jihad had claimed responsibility for that attack. The 2003 al-Aqsa attack in Tel Aviv was even more devastating: twenty-three killed, more than one hundred wounded.

In this attack, two al-Aqsa martyrs from the West Bank city of Nablus blew themselves up near a crowded shopping center near Tel Aviv's Old Central Bus Station. The first IED was detonated around 6:30 p.m., ripping away the facade of a nearby building and sending glass, bodies, and body parts flying down the street. Thirty seconds later, as panicked shoppers and pedestrians fled the scene, a second bomber detonated his IED near a bus stop on a parallel street, maximizing the carnage. The al-Aqsa Martyrs' Brigades issued a statement on its Web site claiming full responsibility for the attack and identifying the suicide bombers as Burak Rifat Abed El-Rahman Halifa and Samer Imad Muhammad Ibrahim El-Nuri. The statement praised the course of the holy jihad against Israel and promised that additional "suicide operations" would soon follow in Allah's name. In Saudi Arabia, a telethon raised over $100 million in support of the al-Aqsa intifada.

Although an offshoot of Fatah and Arafat's mainly secular struggle for Palestinian statehood, the al-Aqsa Martyrs' Brigades have adopted the rhetoric and practice of holy war. Like the martyrs of Hamas, Hezbollah, and Islamic Jihad, its fighters die "with hopeful heart, smiling, and happy."[9] Death is the beginning of life, and special honors await martyrs in Paradise. "Living people grow old but martyrs grow younger," writes poet Mourid Barghouti.[10]

The Islamic hadith narrated by al-Tirmidhi and Ibn Maajah says that a martyr has six bounties:

> He will be forgiven with the first drop of his blood that is spilt; He will see his place in Paradise (at the time of death); He will be saved from the "Great Horror" (on the Day of Judgment); A Crown of Dignity will be placed on his head, which contains many corundums, each one being more precious than this life and all that it contains; He will have seventy two Women of Paradise; And, he will be allowed to intercede for seventy of his family members (who would have otherwise gone to hell).[11]

But as the next chapter shows, some important issues in Islam had to be resolved before predatory martyrs could feel certain that the fruits of self-sacrifice would indeed be theirs.

It is pretty clear that the decades-old struggle for Palestinian independence and dignity had taken a new turn during the two popular uprisings. On one hand, the intifadas and Israel's response galvanized Palestinians even as their daily lives became more miserable; on the other, the willingness of growing numbers of people to blow themselves up to kill Israelis had increased the clout of militant groups and the appeal of Islamic fundamentalism. This, in turn, undermined Arafat's influence and the public's confidence in the secular Palestinian Authority. So the world looked on anxiously as the violence escalated, a cycle of destruction fueled by action and counteraction. For increasing numbers of Palestinians, especially the young, jihad was the only answer; far from dimming, the appeal of predatory martyrdom grew.

Chapter 10

Predatory Martyrs and the Rejection of Innocence

The West Bank town of Jenin is at least three thousand years old. The Bible refers to it as En-gannim, and the crusaders called it Le Grand Gerin. After the Six-Day War the city became a center of Palestinian resistance and militancy. During the second intifada locals gave Jenin a new name: City of Martyrs.

Depending on the source, Jenin has anywhere from thirty-five thousand to fifty thousand inhabitants today; around twenty thousand are crowded into a refugee camp occupying less than half a square mile. Extreme poverty, high unemployment, low educational standards, despair, and humiliation are common complaints throughout the West Bank and the Gaza Strip, but they are concentrated in the refugee camps. And conditions in the Jenin camp are among the worst. Few people enjoy regular employment outside the camp, and those who have jobs work mostly in Israel or in the now-declining agricultural sector, which for centuries had been the mainstay of the city's economy.

Commenting on the feelings of humiliation common in the camps, Palestinian psychologist Eyad Sarraj observes, "To survive under Israeli occupation you are given the chance to work in jobs that Israelis do not like, sweeping streets, building houses, collecting fruit or harvesting.... We are building their homes in our villages, and we clean their streets."[1] In a July 7, 2004, interview on Britain's BBC Two *Newsnight*, Egyptian-born Sheikh Yusuf al-Qaradawi asked rhetorically, "Do you know what it does to you when you have to be the slave of your enemy in order to survive?"

The second intifada made life worse for Palestinians. First, the Israeli army closed border crossings into Israel, cutting off many Jenin residents from their jobs. Then it attacked militant strongholds with F-16s and Apache helicopters, killing many civilians along the way. Troops, tanks, and bulldozers were sent in to ferret out militants and to demolish the homes of suicide bombers and others who had killed Israeli citizens. Attacks on Jews escalated, so Israel turned to targeted killings of high-ranking officers of Hamas and other Palestinian resistance groups.

Israel claimed that its military response to the second intifada was no more than a necessary defense against deadly attacks by Palestinian militants and suicide bombers. Yet the escalation in violence drew more Palestinians to the cause of martyrdom. Targeted killings, in particular, enraged many Palestinians, enabling militant groups like Hamas and Islamic Jihad to make convincing arguments for defensive counter-attacks using suicide bombers.

In April 2002, under Operation Defensive Shield, troops from the Israeli Defense Forces (IDF) attacked the Jenin refugee camp in a sustained assault lasting many days; the fighting killed more than fifty residents, including at least twenty-two civilians. Arab newspapers gave daily reports on the death toll. On April 10, for instance, the Egyptian daily *Al-Quds* reported that the "most violent attack by the Israeli army on Jenin Camp resulted in terrible human tragedies.... The bodies of martyrs are still lying in the streets and between the rubble of the demolished homes and in the alleys. Meanwhile, the families of Jenin Camp were dispersed to the neighboring towns and villages to the point that it can be described as a new forceful eviction and dispersion."

The 2003 Human Rights Watch (HRW) report on the Middle East and North Africa said that during Operation Defensive Shield

Israeli soldiers repeatedly used indiscriminate and excessive force, killed civilians willfully and unlawfully, and used Palestinian civilians as human shields. IDF troops also inflicted damage to homes, businesses, and government offices; looted and stole in the course of searches; coerced civilians to assist military operations; and detained at least 4,500 Palestinian men and boys, many of whom reported ill-treatment during arrest and interrogation.[2]

The 2004 HRW report found little improvement in the situation in Jenin and other refugee camps in the Occupied Territories. Reporter Kevin Toolis has described life in the Jenin refugee camp during the second intifada: "Inside, all the shops are shuttered and only a few skittish cars are driven by the brave or the foolhardy, who chance their lives on the streets defying the curfew. Violent death is an everyday occurrence and the city's walls are emblazoned with fading martyrdom posters of scores of Palestinian fighters."[3]

Among those profoundly affected by the escalating violence was a young Palestinian attorney from Jenin whose brother and a cousin had been killed by undercover Israeli soldiers. Around 7:30 a.m. on the morning of October 4, 2003, twenty-eight-year-old Hanadi Darajat left for work as usual. Her mother hardly noticed that she left without saying good-bye.

Darajat did not go to work; instead she passed through an Israeli checkpoint and made her way to the Israeli city of Haifa. Once there, she walked into Maxim's, a restaurant catering to both Arab and Jewish Israelis, and blew herself up. The ball-bearing-filled improvised explosive device (IED) killed nineteen and wounded over fifty more. Television coverage later showed Darajat's severed head amid the carnage. After the bombing, cards celebrating "the bride of the Haifa martyrdom operation" were passed around to schoolchildren in Gaza and the West Bank. Islamic Jihad claimed responsibility, and the Israelis blew up Darajat's family home in Jenin as punishment for her predatory self-sacrifice.

Darajat's martyrdom pointed to an emerging trend in the militant response to occupation: the use of women suicide bombers against targets in Israel. Darajat was the sixth woman to blow herself up and the second associated with the Palestinian Islamic

Jihad. Nineteen-year-old Hiba Azzam Daragme had been their first, four months earlier.

The al-Aqsa Martyrs' Brigades had started the trend of female suicide bombers in the Middle East, but they had not invented the strategy. The Tamil Tigers of Sri Lanka used dozens of women—most famously, Dhanu, who killed Indian prime minister Rajiv Gandhi—as did Shamil Basayev's separatists in Chechnya and the Kurdistan Workers Party (PKK) in southeast Turkey. There is no doubt that these groups were inspired in turn by women suicide bombers in Lebanon. The first known female suicide bomber was Sana'a Mehaydali. Mehaydali was a seventeen-year-old Lebanese girl who worked in a video store and was a member of the Syrian Socialist National Party (SSNP). In 1985 she blew herself up alongside an Israeli army unit patrolling southern Lebanon. The SSNP, a secular group, eventually conducted a dozen suicide operations, five involving women.

Wafa Idris is credited with being the first Palestinian *shahida* through suicide bombing, although her martyrdom was more accident than intention: On January 27, 2002, she was delivering a backpack full of pipe bombs to an al-Aqsa militant when it exploded. An Israeli civilian was killed, and more than one hundred wounded. While many Arabs in Palestine and around the world reacted in horror to the use of women on the front lines, others responded with approval. Students at Palestine's Birzeit University called for more women to participate.

Approval grew among Arabs after eighteen-year-old Ayat al-Akhras killed herself and three Israelis at a supermarket in Jerusalem on March 29, 2002. In a video made shortly before her mission, Ayat chastised Arab leaders: "Stop sleeping. Stop failing to fulfill your duty. Shame on the Arab armies who are sitting and watching the girls of Palestine fighting while they are asleep."[4] The Saudi ambassador to Britain, Ghazi Algosaibi, responded with a poem on the front page of London's Arabic newspaper *Al Hayat* titled, "You are the Martyrs": "Tell Ayat, O' bride of the Heavens! ... She kisses death with a smile While leaders flee away from death. Paradise opened its gates for you...."[5]

An editorialist in the Egyptian paper *Al-Shaab* wrote, "It is a woman who teaches you today a lesson in heroism, who teaches you the meaning of jihad, and the way to die a martyr's death.... It is a woman who blew herself up and with her exploded all the myths about women's weakness, submissiveness, and enslavement...."[6] Ayat's father later expressed both anguish and pride at her death. "Nobody should have to experience this kind of loss," he said. But he also taped a picture of his daughter with kaffiyeh—the Arabic headdress—and pistol on his windshield.[7]

In Palestinian communities, the initial shock and outrage at the use of women in martyr operations soon gave way to growing public support. In 2004, a Palestinian teacher told Kevin Toolis that female suicide bombings had become "immensely popular." "These girls are our rockets," he added.[8] Being first to use women in predatory suicide attacks on Israel had given the nationalist al-Aqsa Martyrs' Brigades a temporary advantage over their militant Islamic rivals on two fronts: military strategy and political influence.

As military strategy, the use of women in predatory martyr attacks made sense given the four well-known advantages of the IED: First, they are easy to manufacture and easy to transport. Second, the scope of their destruction is broad, from dozens of human victims and some property damage at the low end to hundreds of people and whole buildings at the high end. Third, the martyr can hide behind a mask of innocence or blend in with the target, enhancing the likelihood of a successful attack. With borders virtually closed to Palestinian men, women wearing IEDs—and feigning pregnancy—could more easily get through to targets in Israel. And the first three reasons help create the fourth: IED explosions create high levels of apprehension and fear in the target population.

Suicide bombings are a cheap method of attack relative to the damage they can wreak. One Arab observer has claimed that "the average harvest of each act of martyrdom is ten dead and fifty wounded. Thus, a thousand acts of martyrdom would leave the Zionists with at least ten thousand dead and fifty thousand wounded."[9] The pragmatics of lopsided battles, where one side's military resources are far superior to the other's, requires adaptation and innovation by the weaker side—even if this includes turning women into predatory martyrs.

On the political front, the new development drew a lot of media attention, much of it focusing on the despair resulting from occupation. Perhaps most important, it showed that the al-Aqsa Martyrs' Brigades were willing to challenge traditional Arab views of the innocence and vulnerability of women. Women must fight alongside men—winning the fight for statehood is that important. And so, Mia Bloom observes, the line between combatants and noncombatants is blurred and eventually erased. On a strictly emotional level, the use of women on the front lines stirred some Arab men's hearts by showing them up. The al-Aqsa shahidas thus helped Arafat and the Fatah leadership recoup some of the political losses suffered from years of corruption and failed promises. The al-Aqsa Brigades started a unit for women, and recruits included a university student named Dareen Abu Ish, who had been turned away by Hamas.

The initial reluctance of Hamas to use women in suicide missions was based on Islamic law and tradition and was not particularly controversial, even among militants. Somewhat tongue in cheek, Hamas cofounder and spiritual leader Sheikh Ahmed Yassin once said, "We will start using women when we run out of men."[10]

There were plenty of male recruits, but when Hamas found itself lagging behind its rivals, especially the Palestinian Islamic Jihad, Yassin changed his mind. Other important clerics changed their minds as well. The grand sheikh of Egypt's Al-Azhar University, Muhammad Sayyid Tantawi, declared, "Anybody blowing himself up in the face of the occupiers of his land is a martyr."[11] The head of the Religious Ruling Committee at the same university put it this way: "If the enemy has conquered and plundered a single inch of Muslim land, jihad becomes a personal duty of man, woman, slave, and master."[12] Interviewed on the Aljazeera television station, Sheikh Muhammad Hussein Fadlallah, the spiritual head of Hezbollah, said that women are permitted to participate in martyrdom operations when the "necessities of defensive war" demand it.[13]

There were other reasons to consider putting Islamic women on the same military footing as men. One Hamas leader reached back to the earliest days of Islam, noting that "the Prophet would draw lots among the women who wanted to go out to wage jihad with him. The Prophet always emphasized the woman's right to wage jihad."[14] It was not uncommon in those early days to see women on the battlefield, "collecting weapons, armor, and anything else of value to the moving Muslim force."[15] Women also gave the coup de grâce to wounded enemy soldiers.

If all this were not enough to justify turning women into predatory martyrs, leaders of the Izz al-Din al-Qassam Brigades, the military wing of Hamas, could also point to the opinions of Abdullah Yusuf Azzam, one of their heroes from the rebellion against the Soviet occupation of Afghanistan. Azzam had written in his will, "I believe that every Muslim who passes away without a gun in hand faces Allah with the sin of abandoning fighting. Now fighting (jihad) is compulsory on each and every Muslim on earth except those who are excused—the blind, the terminally ill, the lame and the oppressed, men, women, and children *who cannot get or find their way to the battlefield.*"[16]

Yassin spoke publicly of his support for female suicide missions only after Hamas claimed its first successful operation. He said the new development was a "significant evolution" for the al-Qassam Brigades and a necessary adjustment to the reality that male fighters faced many obstacles in carrying out suicide missions. He continued, "The holy war is an imperative for all Muslim men and women ... and will continue until the enemy is driven from our land."[17]

On January 14, 2004, a twenty-two-year-old mother of two became the first female suicide bomber sent by Hamas. Wearing a bomb belt around her waist, Reem Saleh al-Raiyshi was driven to the Erez checkpoint in Gaza by her husband. She told Israeli border guards that she had a metal splint in her leg that would set off the detector. She detonated an IED as she was being taken to a room for a personal search. Four Israelis died and seven others were wounded in the blast. "I heard the explosion," an Israeli bus driver told reporters. "Then I saw body parts everywhere."[18]

In her martyr video, al-Raiyshi said, "I always wanted to be the first woman to carry out a martyr attack, where parts of my body can fly all over. That is the only wish I can ask God for."[19] Her funeral was a gala affair attended by thousands. Citing Hamas leader Abdel Aziz al-Rantissi, the United Press International later reported that al-Raiyshi's family received a monthly allowance of $200, half that given to the families of male martyrs.

Like Hamas, al-Qaeda resisted using women in its predatory attacks, but it has now adopted them in its fight against the American occupation of Iraq. Wadad Jamil Jassem appeared on a martyr tape shown April 4, 2003, on Aljazeera television. She said, "I have devoted myself to jihad for the sake of God and against the American, British, and Israeli infidels and to defend the soil of our precious and dear country."[20]

It is not clear whether Jassem actually blew herself up. The first known successful predatory attack by a woman in Iraq occurred on September 28, 2005. The suicide bomber killed six people outside a police recruiting station in Tal Afar, a town in northwest Iraq not far from the Syrian border. The woman was disguised as a man. Al-Qaeda in Iraq claimed responsibility: "A blessed sister from Al-Baraa bin Malek martyrdom brigade carried out a heroic attack defending her faith and honor on a gathering of volunteers for the apostate forces at a center for recruiting apostates in Tal Afar. May God accept our sister among the martyrs."[21]

Finding Justification for Predatory Martyrdom

Just as Arab militant groups had reinterpreted Islamic conventions on the innocence of women to justify their use in martyrdom operations, they also had to address the Prophet's admonition against attacking women and children, the elderly and the infirm—to say nothing of fellow believers. By its very nature, predatory martyrdom leaves nobody safe.

The issue resonates just as strongly today. More than five hundred suicide attacks have occurred in Iraq since 2003, most of them killing Muslim noncombatants.[22] Elsewhere, the Arab world was stunned in 2005 by two large-scale attacks that killed or wounded many Muslims. In the first, three bombs went off almost simultaneously in the Red Sea resort town of Sharm el-Sheikh in July. In the second, in November, suicide bombers simultaneously attacked three hotels in Amman, Jordan. In one bombing, a married couple targeted a wedding reception; the woman survived because her IED failed to detonate. The toll in the first attack was nearly one hundred killed, with more than two hundred wounded; in the second, more than sixty died, and three hundred were wounded.

Muslims have also been killed by suicide attacks in Pakistan. One of the most recent occurred on April 12, 2006, during a Sunni prayer service attended by thousands in Karachi's Nishtar Park. The blast killed fifty-seven and wounded scores. Survivors and witnesses said that a bearded man blew himself up near the stage where leaders of Tehrik, a growing Sunni political movement, were assembled. No one claimed responsibility, and the bomber's head was later shown on television and in the newspapers to see if anyone would identify him. The prime minister of Pakistan claimed the attack was aimed at destabilizing the country. The information minister claimed the attack was part of a plot to eliminate Tehrik's leadership. There was speculation that Shiites had masterminded the attack in retaliation for a February suicide bombing in which forty died during a Shiite procession in the town of Hangu. Some people saw the imprint of al-Qaeda. But there seemed to be no doubt that this attack was yet another example of Muslim predatory martyrs killing other Muslims. Prime Minister Shaukat Aziz called the attackers "enemies of Pakistan as well as Islam."[23]

Responding to the Sharm el-Sheikh attack in Egypt, Grand Imam Sayyid Tantawi said that those who kill innocents "have no justification, ... and are liars, liars and charlatans, and Islam disavows them."[24] And Hezbollah condemned the attacks as an "evil phenomenon." Earlier, in February 2004, during a sermon on Mt. Arafat just outside Mecca, Sheikh Abdul Aziz al-Sheil asked two million Muslim pilgrims performing the hajj, "Is it holy war to shed Muslim blood?" "Islam," he reminded them, "forbids all forms of injustice, killing without just cause, treachery."[25]

But leaders of militant Islamic groups, and the would-be martyrs themselves, have redefined the rules so that their predatory actions are compatible with their understanding of Islam. They have done this with spiritual guidance from some prominent Islamic scholars and clerics.

Sheikh Yusuf al-Qaradawi, the Egyptian-born cleric held in high esteem by many Muslims, said after the 9/11 attacks on the World Trade Center and the Pentagon that "Islam never allows the Muslim to kill the innocent and the helpless."[26] But he does not consider the women of Israel innocent or helpless. He told the BBC in 2004 that "Israeli women are not like women in our society because Israeli women are militarized."[27]

Some go further, implicitly redefining Israeli children as justifiable targets because they will inevitably become *future* combatants: "For most Palestinians," Mia Bloom writes, "there is no civilian immunity due to the universal conscription of men and women. Any civilian is either a current, past, or future soldier."[28]

One imprisoned Palestinian would-be suicide bomber whose mission failed brought up another argument for killing innocents: There is no choice if the jihad is to continue. "The situation we are in leaves us with the choice of either ... continuing our activity without obeying every word in these matters, or not resisting the occupation and upholding the prohibition in full."[29]

When the victims of Muslim suicide bombers are also Muslims, the killers risk God's retribution. The Quran says, "If a man kills a Believer intentionally, his recompense is Hell, to abide therein (forever); and the wrath and the curse of Allah are upon him, and a dreadful penalty is prepared for him" (Surah 4:93). Centuries later, Muslims found themselves on both sides of the wars between the Mamluks and the Mongols. This led seventeenth-century Islamic theologian Ibn Taymiya to declare that it is permitted for believers to kill brothers who are directly involved in the conduct of a war. But this does not accommodate such events as the 9/11 attacks or the Sharm el-Sheikh bombings, where many innocent Muslims were killed.

Militant Islamic organizations have addressed the issue of Muslims killing Muslims in two ways: first, by redefining the Muslim victim as an apostate or heretic—and thus a fair target of jihad; and second, by making the Muslim victim part of the unfortunate but unavoidable collateral damage in modern warfare. Bin Laden's spiritual mentor, Abdullah Azzam, beloved by Hamas as the archetypal warrior-martyr, had made both arguments during the Soviet occupation of Afghanistan. Osama bin Laden accused Muslims killed on 9/11 of collaborating with the Western infidel and, therefore, against the interests of Islam. And the leader of al-Qaeda in Iraq, Jordanian Abu Musab al-Zarqawi, recently called Muslims in the Iraqi government "agents of the Jews and Christians," saying, "we have nothing for you but the sword." They are "the eyes, ears, and hands of the American occupiers," he said in a letter to bin Laden. In a statement aired on June 15, 2005, Zarqawi followed this up with: "Shiites helping the Jews and Christians is nothing new. It is in their blood."[30] Here Zarqawi was doubtless referring to the long-ago collaboration between the Shiite Assassins and the crusaders.

In adopting predatory self-sacrifice as a weapon of choice, al-Qaeda and the militant campaigns of resistance in Sri Lanka, Chechnya, Turkey, Palestine, and now Iraq have largely done away with the concept of innocence. But it seems only fair to point out that states went down that path long ago in the evolution of conventional warfare. In *Confronting War*,[31] Ron Glossop shows how invention took the world from clubs, spears, bows, and arrows capable of killing one person at a time, to exploding grenades capable of killing four or five people at once, to artillery shells and torpedoes that could kill ten to twenty people (at the end of World War I, a single shell from Germany's "Big Bertha" gun could kill forty), to the large bombs of World War II that killed sixty or seventy, and finally to nuclear weapons. When the United States dropped the first atomic bomb on Hiroshima, Japan, on August 6, 1945, from seventy-five thousand to one hundred thousand people were killed instantly, and thousands more died later on from radiation poisoning if not from other injuries. The dead were mostly women, children, the old, and the infirm.

Earlier in the war, British prime minister Winston Churchill had adopted the idea of an "absolutely devastating exterminating attack by very heavy bombers from this country upon the Nazi homeland." Arthur "Bomber" Harris, head of the RAF Bomber Command, eventually put the plan into action, directing thousand-bomber raids against German cities, among them Cologne, Hamburg, and Dresden. In Dresden alone, sixty thousand perished. Similar extermination tactics were used by the United States in the firebombing of Japanese cities in 1945. Tokyo was almost burned to the ground.

Massive propaganda campaigns helped turn German and Japanese civilians into justifiable targets. In *War without Mercy*,[32] John Dower has documented the use of propaganda by both sides in the Pacific theater of World War II. By the end of 1944, the Japanese people had been demonized as beasts, vermin, or devils; in other words, they had been rendered subhuman. There were no innocent Japanese. Admiral Halsey's famous slogan, "Kill Japs, kill Japs, kill more Japs," no longer raised eyebrows. After the war, official Japanese and American estimates put the number of civilian men, women, and children killed in U.S. bombing raids on Japan at nearly four hundred thousand. Almost all were killed in the five-month period from March to August 1945.

In the Occupied Territories of Gaza and the West Bank, militants commonly point out that they are engaged in a war against an evil, subhuman enemy. In a martyr video taped before he blew himself up, killing eighteen Israelis and wounding thirty-six, Salah Abed El Hamid Shaker said, "I am going to take revenge upon the sons of the monkeys and the pigs . . . the Zionist infidels and the enemies of humanity. . . ."[33]

The father of a young suicide bomber who had detonated explosives attached to the car he was driving told Kevin Toolis, "I am happy when I see the Jews crying every day. The Jews raped and occupied our land. They desecrated al-Aqsa. They deserve this."[34] A prisoner whose martyr mission had been thwarted by Israeli security forces told interviewer and fellow Palestinian inmate Walid Dakah, "I am convinced that Israel is not killing Palestinian civilians by mistake, but that its intention is to kill [them]. The reality is that they are killing elderly people, women and children. Therefore, I consider myself exempt from the duty not to kill civilians."[35] And so, the would-be predatory martyrs and their leaders have rationalized away any reservations about using women as suicide bombers, or killing innocent men, women, or children, by defining away innocence itself.

Chapter 11

The Martyr's Smile

Martyrs find pleasure in their self-sacrifice. That is the message seen time and again in stories of martyrdom. Remember Vibia Perpetua and her five companions? They entered the Roman arena "cheerful and bright of countenance; if they trembled at all, it was for joy, not for fear." And al-Hallaj, the martyred Sufi mystic? Burdened by heavy chains, he nevertheless "strode out proudly" to the gallows. He smiled when the executioner cut off his hands and feet. Then there was Banda Singh and his shackled followers. Abused and taunted, they "seemed happy and cheerful" and shouted out, "Kill us, kill us, why should we fear death?"

Just as martyr legends emphasize the joy expressed in acts of self-sacrifice, they also remind us that martyrdom has instrumental value as well. The stories say that good consequences flow from self-sacrifice for a cause; these may be enjoyed by the martyr or by others. Martyrdom helps create things of value—life, independence, honor, peace; martyrdom helps protect things of value—reputation, religion, family, community; and martyrdom helps end bad or evil things—persecution, oppression, occupation, humiliation, war.

As I have shown throughout this book, the instrumentality of martyrdom is expressed in many different ways. "The martyr smiles his way to death and death opens the door to paradise," writes M. J. Akbar in *The Shade of Swords*.[1] In the Maccabean legend, Eleazar "welcomed death with honor rather than life with pollution." "The good shepherd lays down his life for the sheep," said Jesus. "Please watch for the results of my meager effort," wrote one kamikaze pilot to his parents. "If they prove good, think kindly of me and consider it my good fortune to have done something that may be praiseworthy." "Our words remain dead until we die in their cause so they remain alive amongst the living,"[2] wrote Sayyid Qutb, a key philosopher of the modern Islamist movement.

It should come as no surprise that these themes are reiterated in the world of predatory martyrs. Yet it is not uncommon to find commentators, particularly Western observers, seemingly bewildered by the martyr's smile. How can the suicide bomber smile as he or she detonates an explosive device in a crowded market or coffee shop?

We are fortunate to have answers from recent studies of the attitudes and culture surrounding predatory martyrdom, some of which include personal testimonials from soon-to-be martyrs or from militants whose suicide operations failed. The most exhaustive information comes from two Americans who spent six years off and on in the Gaza Strip, the West Bank, and the Old City of Jerusalem during the first intifada. Anne Marie Oliver and Paul Steinberg created a massive portfolio of posters, photos of graffiti, martyr cards, martyr videos, interrogations of collaborators, and audiocassettes related to the intifada. The authors discuss some of this material in *The Road to Martyrs' Square: A Journey into the World of the Suicide Bomber.*

Other insights into the attitudes and culture of predatory martyrs are found in studies by Robert Pape, Farhad Khosrokhavar, and Mia Bloom,[3] and on the Internet. The organizations that claim modern martyrs have found the Internet to be an invaluable tool for disseminating their ideology and goals, as well as for recruitment. Web sites present events in real time and inspire sympathy, indignation, and solidarity. I have seen claims that there are more than four thousand Web sites supporting militant Islamic groups engaged in suicide attacks.[4]

As the last four chapters have shown, predatory martyrdom provides militant organizations with a weapon that is cheap, efficient, potentially very destructive, and symbolically very powerful. Leaders turn to it when other strategies fail to produce desired results. So an obvious question to ask is, Does it work? One way to answer this question is to look at the experiences of those groups that adopted suicide attacks in the past.

Suicide attacks certainly didn't work for Japan. Indeed, the idea backfired seriously because the Japanese proclivity for martyrdom was one of the reasons the atomic bomb was dropped on Hiroshima and Nagasaki. Japan would choose death before surrender, the Allies believed, costing the lives of thousands, perhaps millions of soldiers, should an Allied invasion of Japan prove necessary.

The kamikazes were not predatory martyrs, since they targeted only enemy soldiers. The LTTE's Black Tigers in Sri Lanka more closely approximated predatory martyrs, and so did the Kurdistan Workers Party (PKK) in southeast Turkey. These groups may not have achieved their ultimate goal—independence—but their use of suicide attacks that often killed civilians was one of the factors that encouraged their enemies to seek a negotiated solution. It remains to be seen whether the diplomatic strategy will produce a lasting peace.

In the Middle East there are currently no French, American, or Israeli troops stationed in Lebanon, and militant groups claimed that suicide attacks persuaded those forces to leave. President Ronald Reagan obviously agreed. He wrote in his memoirs, "The price we had to pay in Beirut was so great, the tragedy at the barracks was so enormous.... We had to pull out.... We couldn't stay there and run the risk of another suicide attack on the Marines."[5]

In Palestine, militant groups claimed credit for the withdrawal of Israeli Defense Forces (IDF) from the Gaza Strip in 1994 and again in 2005. In his chapter "Learning Terrorism Pays," Robert Pape cites newspaper interviews with leaders of Hamas and the Palestinian Islamic Jihad shortly after the first IDF withdrawal. A Hamas leader said, "Israel can beat all Arab armies. However, it can do nothing against a youth with a knife or an explosive charge on his body."[6] In a similar vein, Islamic Jihad leader Fathi al-Shaqaqi said, "It has become clear that the enemy can be defeated.... Martyrdom actions ... are a realistic option in confronting the unequal balance of power. If we are unable to effect a balance of power now, we can achieve a balance of horror."[7] After the 2005 IDF withdrawal, the *Los Angeles Times* reported this comment by Mohammad Deif, a senior Hamas leader and the mastermind behind many suicide attacks: "Without this jihad . . . we would not have achieved the liberation of the Gaza Strip."[8]

The leaders of the current insurgency in Iraq are claiming, rightly, that the American people and many of their leaders are tiring of the U.S.-led occupation. The U.S. State Department reported that by the end of 2005 more than five hundred suicide bombings had taken place in Iraq since the American invasion.[9] Citing U.S. officials in December 2005, *Time* magazine asserted that seventy insurgent attacks were occurring *each day*, though not all involved suicide bombings. Despite President Bush's insistence that he will stay the course, Abu Musab al-Zarqawi and other militant leaders believe that the occupation's days are numbered, and they point to a steady stream of recruits willing to die for their cause. "You love life, we love death," they tell Westerners. "Westerners want to go on living at all costs," writes Farhad Khosrokhavar. This is seen as "a weakness in the face of Muslims who are prepared to sacrifice their lives."[10]

After reviewing thirteen predatory martyr campaigns around the world since 1983, Pape shows that they produced significant political concessions from targeted states at least half the time. It is this instrumental element in predatory martyrdom that militant leaders fall back on time and again when justifying its use. When a Hamas leader was asked in 1994, "why not just plant a bomb and run?" he replied, "There are more fatalities in a suicide attack."[11] In a war against superior forces, fatalities are the practical measure of the underdog's tenacity and ingenuity, and they impress both supporters and enemies.

If militant leaders smile about the strategic benefits of suicide attacks, what about the predatory martyrs who actually carry out the attacks? I believe that people on a mission of suicidal murder smile because *they feel good about what they are about to do.* They feel good for a variety of reasons, some embedded in the act itself and some related to what they believe the act will accomplish—for themselves and/or for others. All forms of martyrdom are potentially both selfish and altruistic.

It is important to keep in mind that beliefs and opinions—even feelings—are learned. Most of this learning takes place in social contexts, that is, through our interactions with other people. We look at how others behave and react to understand ourselves, to learn what makes us happy or sad, calm or agitated, fearless or afraid. This is also the way we learn the relative value of different things, for others as well as for ourselves. The meaning of something we do or something that happens to us—including its value or worth—is socially constructed. This includes dying and killing.

Perhaps because real death occurs for each individual only once and ends human life (near-death experiences don't count), people have constructed many ideas about death, including its value relative to life. Most of the time life is valued over death. Think how people respond when they have escaped death: "I'm lucky to be alive," they might say; or if they've been badly injured they might declare, "I'm just happy to be alive." Everyone understands why they feel good: They cheated death. And the good feeling is reinforced because important people in their lives are happy for them.

In his 2005 commencement address to the graduating class at Stanford University, Steve Jobs, the cofounder of Apple computers, also mentioned the idea that life is valued over death: "No one wants to die," he told the class. "Even people who want to go to heaven don't want to die to go there."[12] Martyrs seemingly take the opposite view; they value death over life. Yet rather than being angry at them for turning convention on its head, society often nods approvingly at their self-sacrifice. It even maintains lists to commemorate their valued acts. The names of martyrs are passed across generations, and they are honored guests in believers' dreams and visions. During the current conflict in Iraq, some radical Islamic Web sites have been publishing the phone numbers of martyrs so that people can call their families to congratulate them.[13]

Even mothers sometimes encourage their sons to die for the cause. We saw this with Hannah and her youngest son in the story of the Maccabees, and again in the Christian legend of the forty martyrs of Sevastia. Although parents of Palestinian martyrs often have no idea their son or daughter is planning to carry out a suicide bombing, there are known to be some cases where mothers encouraged it. More often, they participate in a ritual that recognizes the contribution mothers make to the cause through their offspring. "When at last her son is martyred, she is said to be overjoyed to hear the news and emits a *zaghrada* (a high-pitched wailing sound made by women on happy occasions such as the entrance of a bride and groom at their wedding), sometimes also expressing the wish that all her sons will thus be taken."[14]

So predatory martyrs might be smiling because self-sacrifice for a cause is highly valued in itself by people that matter to them.

But predatory martyrs kill others as well. Where is the pleasure in murder? Surely only psychotics enjoy killing. But there is no evidence that predatory martyrs are psychotic, or even particularly different from anyone else. They come from all walks of life, all ages, and all social classes; some are single, some are married; some have children, some do not; some are highly religious, some only moderately so, and some not at all.

We know that predatory martyrs are generally linked with some group or organization. We also know that these groups applaud their self-sacrifice and may even have recruited them for it in the first place. Such recruitment occurred in Sri Lanka, in the refugee camps of the Occupied Territories of Palestine, and among militant Islamist groups across the world. There have been many walk-in volunteers as well, and only those turned away would presume that their intended martyrdom was disapproved of.

So predatory martyrs might be smiling because the killing they are about to commit through their sacrifice is pleasing to the group they represent, especially its leaders. Knowing that he was pleasing the emperor was reward enough to a kamikaze pilot. In Sri Lanka, the Black Tigers revered their charismatic leader Velupillai Prabhakaran, whose many speeches applauding their near-predatory sacrifices doubtless strengthened their pride and resolve.

None of this is particularly selfish. In Pape's words, "many suicide terrorists are killing themselves to advance what they see as the common good."[15] The pleasing thought that their suicide attack serves the public good is bolstered if there is broad community support for their actions. This, in turn, confers honor on the predatory martyrs and their families, and enhances their reputation throughout the community. "If suicide bombing does not resonate with the larger population the tactic will fail," writes Bloom. "If it is applauded it will flourish."[16]

During the height of the suicide attacks in Sri Lanka, public support among Tamils for armed resistance was strong. Special Heroes Day speeches and permanent memorials lauding Black Tigers and Tigresses left little doubt that they were heroes in the eyes of the public. However, Mia Bloom notes that there was little public support for killing innocent bystanders.[17] In Sri Lanka, the attack strategy of Black Tigers was to target specific individuals, usually politicians or other government officials. The civilians often killed in such attacks fell in the category of collateral damage—unfortunate but inescapable.

In the West Bank and Gaza, on the other hand, posters, songs, poems, graffiti, martyr cards, and well-attended burial processions all publicly acknowledge the heroism of Palestinian suicide bombers, whose targets are often civilians. The *Palestinian Opinion Pulse* published on the Internet by the Arabic Jerusalem Media and Communication Center shows that public support for suicide attacks on Israelis during the second intifada was consistently high, at between 60 and 76 percent of those polled from 2000 through July 2004. Not surprisingly, support was strongest in the refugee camps and among younger Palestinians.[18]

Some of the comments in interviews and martyr videos confirm the importance of honor and reputation in the thinking of suicide bombers. The late Hamas leader Abdel Aziz al-Rantissi said, "For Hamas, and Palestinian society in general, becoming a martyr is among the highest, if not *the highest* honor."[19] Khosrokhavar writes, "The more Israeli people and military men are killed as a consequence of their martyrdom, the more famous they [the suicide bombers] will become."[20] A Palestinian teacher in Gaza's Jabalya refugee camp told *Newsweek* reporter Christopher Dickey in April 2002, "They see the images on TV, the posters in the streets, the honor of martyrs' families, and they want that kind of honor for themselves, for their families."[21]

After Hamas cofounder Sheikh Ahmed Yassin was killed in an Israeli targeted assassination in March 2004, the *New*

York Times reported that more than two hundred thousand Palestinians joined the funeral procession. A Hamas spokesman vowed, "All of the Muslims in the world will be honored to join in on the retaliation for this crime."[22] After watching a martyr video of three Palestinian youths about to embark on their suicide mission, Oliver and Steinberg comment, "These guys knew they were going to die.... We get the feeling that life has never seemed better to them—so intense, so exuberant, so full of meaning. Perhaps that's why they keep on smiling—they just can't believe they're about to become Martyrs, about to take their place in the roster of great men. Who would ever have believed it? They must be thinking 'They've never gotten so much attention in their lives.'"[23]

Writing for the Middle East News Online, Mouin Rabbani, director of the Palestinian American Research Center in the West Bank town of Ramallah, describes how the community responded to the suicide attack by Diya Tawil, a student of engineering at Birzeit University: "Hundreds of Palestinians came to congratulate the Tawil family rather than mourn its son."[24] In a December 16, 2001, article in the *Sunday Observer,* Kevin Toolis observed, bluntly, "In life most suicide bombers are nobodies, but in death they rise and become shaheed, and their families rise with them."[25] "Violence has become *the* source of all honor among Palestinians," writes Bloom, and "the *shahids* gain increased social status as a result of suicide bombing operations."[26] Honor and pride ride high even as the occupation humiliates and degrades, and neither parents nor politicians seem capable of doing anything about the spiraling violence.

So predatory martyrs might be smiling about the honor and public recognition that will be bestowed on them and their families by the larger community.

During the second intifada, the families of predatory martyrs who attacked Israelis began receiving money and other financial support. The Associated Press reported in May 2000 that Hamas was offering $150 a month to the families of its members killed by Israelis or in suicide missions. This was later increased to $400 for suicide martyrs. The money came mainly from private sources in Saudi Arabia. As an incentive for Palestinians to attack Israel, Saddam Hussein very publicly offered $10,000 to the families of suicide bombers; in April

2002 he increased the amount to $25,000. The martyr's father might receive an envelope containing the money during the Hamas wake following a successful suicide attack.

An honorable reputation takes a family only so far in a declining economy with few opportunities, so prospective suicide bombers appreciate the reassurance that their families will be taken care of after their deaths. Perhaps this is why they are smiling on their way to murderous self-destruction.

Suicide attacks are rarely carried out on the spur of the moment; most involve some degree of planning. The al-Qaeda attacks on the World Trade Center and the Pentagon may be the extreme example—Mohamed Atta and some of his companions spent over two years getting ready for "The Planes Operation" as bin Laden called it. Once trained, the kamikaze pilots of World War II had at most a few weeks before they were called on for a sortie against enemy ships. A similar scenario appears to be the case for Palestinian suicide bombers. Volunteers receive a few days of training and are then kept on hold while military planners work out the specific details of an attack. As the day grows near, the recruits are kept away from their families and devote more time to religious study and spiritual preparation. They get their mission with usually no more than a day or two's advance notice, sometimes less. This is not much different from the situation facing kamikazes once they had been assigned to their units; if the weather cleared or enemy carriers were sighted unexpectedly, off they went.

In the Palestinian refugee camps, as in the stomping grounds of the Tamil Tigers in Sri Lanka, children are primed for violence at an early age. "Parents dressed their babies and toddlers as suicide bombers and had them photographed in local photography studios."[27] The culture of militant resistance ensures that children, boys especially, learn how to think and talk like fighters even if they are not directly recruited into the ranks of martyrs. In Palestine, the playground games and bravado of the young become the taunting, rock-throwing, curfew-violating resistance of the teenage *shabab*. Some of these boys will be killed in the conflict but not by their own design; nevertheless, they are still honored as shaheed.

Others will eventually join the ranks of the "living martyr" (*shahid al hay*), those young men who have pledged to die for

Palestinian independence or Islam, often both. Until his death, the living martyr enjoys the status of a TV or movie star, and poems are written in his honor. Kevin Toolis describes how in the streets of Gaza City, the stronghold of Hamas and also home of the Palestinian Authority, "Hamas militants shroud themselves in the white robes of the paradise-to-come, and strap dummy explosives to their waists to symbolize their willingness to sacrifice their lives."[28]

Oliver and Steinberg reprint a poster showing Mahmud az-Zaraini, former commander of Fatah's Black Panther group. On it are the words "Name: Martyr with a stay of execution. Occupation: Fida'i [self-sacrificer]."[29] There are reports that Hamas sometimes stages mock burials for its living martyrs so they can experience the so-called Torment of the Tomb, when the angels Munkar and Nakir interrogate the dead before they pass into the afterworld.

So martyrs may be smiling because the wait, at once uncertain, guarded, and thrilling, is finally over.

Fear wipes away most smiles, so it is worth asking what happens to the suicide bomber's fear of death. If any fear is "natural," this is probably it. Are would-be martyrs immune? Clearly, Hamas doesn't think so, which is one of the reasons behind the mock burial and other rituals would-be martyrs must endure to prove their mettle. By the time predatory martyrs are on their way to their targets, they have either come to terms with dying or the fear has been successfully suppressed.

One of the essential functions of the group, whether it is a unit of kamikaze pilots or an al-Qaeda cell, is helping would-be martyrs overcome their fear of death. Muslim militants are helped through prayer, reading the Quran, having a cleric mentor the candidate, and mixing with other would-be martyrs. Together, they form an "umma in death."[30] As part of the purification process preceding and implied in the death act itself, martyrs appeal for forgiveness from their families and ask them to take care of their debts and not to do anything that would tarnish their image in the eyes of God. If recruits begin to waver, mentors raise flagging spirits by emphasizing illustrious predecessors, from the Prophet's companions to the young Palestinian shuhada who have gone before. Different stories were used with the same effect among kamikaze units, and the carefully orchestrated cult of heroes did the same for Prabhakaran's Black Tigers.

Among Muslims, the fear of dying is also tempered by the Islamic idea that Allah has predetermined the moment of death. Khosrokhavar writes, "The martyr therefore complains that it is better to embrace a holy death than to die the cowardly inept death of those who die in their beds."[31]

Death can also be a welcome escape from the trials of living in this world. "Dear family and friends!" begins suicide bomber Abd-el-Rahman Hamed. "I write this will with tears in my eyes and sadness in my heart. I want to tell you that I am leaving and ask for your forgiveness because I decided to see Allah today and this meeting is by all means more important than staying alive on this earth."[32] The everyday life of many young Palestinian men is full of boredom, humiliation, and despair, with nothing to look forward to except more of the same. In testaments on martyr videos and in letters to family and friends, would-be martyrs often say they have had enough. This is a common complaint of many Muslim immigrants in Europe, whose hopes of fully enjoying the modern Western life were never fully realized. They have become marginalized instead. In an August 16, 2005, report, the *Los Angeles Times* described five would-be bombers, whose failed attack in London mimicked the July 7, 2005, London bombings that killed fifty-six and injured approximately seven hundred, as marginalized East Africans "who lived by their wits, dabbling in street crime and manipulating the immigration and welfare systems."

Self-sacrifice is not only a way out but also a way of demonstrating the ultimate control of one's destiny. Palestinian suicide bombers may thus say to themselves: Even with their tanks and helicopter gunships, the Israelis (for Iraq and al-Qaeda read Americans, for the Black Tigers read Sinhalese) cannot stop me from sacrificing my life. Cynthia Mahmood makes a similar observation about Sikh militants: "Sikhs perceive themselves as always in control of their destinies, even in the face of death, that one thing that overcomes any human attempt to control. A major task of a human being is then, in a way, to figure out how to die meaningfully. Sikhs are joyous about martyrdom because it represents the liberation of utter control over fate."[33] Control is demonstrated all the more powerfully if the self-sacrifice gets back at those considered responsible for the martyrs' torment. This is revenge, born of anger, hatred, and despair. Revenge is a human emotion that everyone seems to understand. Small wonder, then, that leaders of militant groups use the notion freely in their rhetoric of resistance. I've already mentioned the Hamas response to the targeted assassination of Ahmed Yassin: "All of the Muslims in the world will be honored to join in on the retaliation for this crime." In a videotaped speech to the American people aired on Aljazeera on October 29, 2004, Osama bin Laden said that the U.S.–Israeli military occupation of Lebanon "produced a great desire to punish you as you punished us . . . [so that the] U.S. gets a taste of its own medicine." And in a press release published on its Web site in January 2005, the al-Aqsa Martyrs' Brigades said, "We promise you, our nation, that we will avenge the blood of our brave martyrs and we promise that there will be more suicide operations. . . ."[34]

Even though the victimization and injustice that fuel revenge are collective, retaliation is often expressed as an individual right stemming from a personal grievance. Such claims are quite common among suicide bombers in Chechnya, Palestine, and Sri Lanka, especially among women. Female suicide fighters in Chechnya are known as Black Widows because most have lost spouses to the conflict with Russia. Likewise, in Sri Lanka, women volunteers for suicide missions are often victims of widowhood or sexual assault at the hands of Sinhalese soldiers. The women may feel they have little to lose, and retaliation through suicide attack at least gives them a meaningful way to respond. A failed suicide bomber interviewed by Nicole Argo said, "Pictures of dead kids had a major effect on me. Many were killed [right] before me, like my friend. . . ."[35]

And so some predatory martyrs may be smiling because they are about to demonstrate ultimate control: In death they will forever escape the earthly world of loss, despair, and injustice, and in killing they will take the ultimate revenge.

It is certainly plausible that some suicide bombers enjoy their moment of ultimate control, selfish as it is. But it is only a moment, a fleeting opportunity at control, and we have seen time and again that would-be martyrs are encouraged to think long-term. That is, something important and good is expected to happen *after* their suicide mission is completed. For those driven by religious zeal, this may be a blissful eternity in Paradise. For those driven by more altruistic motives, such as an end to occupation by foreign troops or victory in war, it is the expectation that others will someday enjoy the fruits of their sacrifice. Predatory martyrs driven by a combination of nationalism and religious zeal are clearly in a win-win situation. No wonder they smile.

It should therefore come as no surprise that we find al-Qaeda, Hamas, Islamic Jihad—and, yes, the al-Aqsa Martyrs' Brigades, a secular nationalist group made up mostly of Muslims—devoting most of their public testimony to the twin goals of expelling foreign occupiers *and* promoting or defending their religion. For example, an official spokesman of the al-Aqsa Martyrs' Brigades, Usama Al-Najjar, told the Hezbollah weekly *Al-Intiqad* on August 17, 2001, "The Al-Aqsa Martyrs' Brigades will continue as long as the reasons for the resistance exist, i.e. the occupation, the settlements, and the defiling of the holy places."[36] Recent al-Aqsa martyr videos shown on its Web site include this verse from the Quran (Surah 9:14): "Fight them, and Allah will Punish them by your hands, Cover them with shame, Help you (to victory) over them, Heal the breasts of Believers."

In his book *Knights under the Banner of the Prophet*, Ayman al-Zawahiri, al-Qaeda's second-in-command, speaks directly to the twin goals of the jihad. "The restoration of the caliphate and the dismissal of the invaders from the land of Islam ... must remain the basic objective of the Islamic jihad movement, regardless of the sacrifice and the time involved."[37] Osama bin Laden echoed these sentiments in his 1996 *Declaration of War against the Americans Occupying the Land of the Two Holy Places*. "It is a duty on every tribe in the Arab peninsula to fight, Jihad, in the cause of Allah and to cleanse the land from these occupiers."[38]

Oliver and Steinberg found "countless" slogans of the intifada promoting the "happy death" of Palestinian martyrs who fight for their land and for Islam. A common message on Hamas posters reads, "I will die smiling in order that my religion live."[39] Harking back to the martyr themes of antiquity, and reminiscent of Prabhakaran's speeches on Heroes' Day, poems and songs speak of intifada blood irrigating the land

and freeing it of the infidel. A Fatah verse says Palestine is "a green tree whose thirst can only be quenched with the blood of martyrs."[40] A similar sentiment is expressed among Shiite villagers in Iran. A young village merchant in Iran told sociologist Reinhold Loeffler, "the blood shed by Iranian martyrs is like the water of an irrigation canal which gives life to the crops. From it the religion will grow."[41]

A martyr video shown on a radical Islamic Web site and dated March 1, 2005, shows Abu Abdullah of Ansar al-Sunnah (Army of Sunni) before his suicide attack on the National Council in Iraq. Bracketed by two men, one wearing a kaffiyeh and one in a hooded sweatshirt, one with a rifle and one holding a piece of paper, the suicide bomber first recites Surah 5, verse 51: "O ye who believe! Take not the Jews And the Christians For your friends and protectors; They are but friends and protectors To each other. And he amongst you that turns to them (For friendship) is of them. Verily Allah guideth not A people unjust." Then the bomber says, "There have to be some sacrifices for us to succeed. Islam will only rise back up on the bodies of its fighters. This is not the path of cowards. We will destroy the nonbelievers with our bodies and our blood. God accept our blood that we offer you. God accept us as martyrs. God unite us in heaven with our prophet Muhammad. Allahu Akbar [God is great]." The bomber then hugs the men on each side of him.[42]

Death denies predatory martyrs—indeed, any martyr—the pleasure of seeing the earthly results of their self-sacrifice, but death is the gateway to many anticipated heavenly rewards for the religiously inspired. In his 1996 declaration of war against America, bin Laden pointed out that his young jihadists "have no intention except to enter paradise by killing you."

Allah's six bounties awaiting the martyrs of jihad must surely be on the minds of many suicide bombers as they carry out their predatory missions. The bounties were listed at the end of chapter 10, but here they are again. This version is from an article written by the grand mufti (Islamic scholar) of the Palestinian Police and was published by the Palestinian Authority in 1999: "From the moment his first drop of blood spills, he feels no pain, and he is absolved of all his sins; he sees his seat in heaven; he is spared the tortures of the grave [and] the horrors of Judgment Day; he is married to black-eyed virgins; he can vouch for seventy of his family members to enter paradise; he earns the crown of glory whose precious stone is worth all of this world."[43] It is impossible to know what successful suicide bombers think about as they approach the defining moment of their lives. We must therefore rely on comments from martyr videotapes and the occasional interview of aspiring or failed martyrs.

The 2003 jail interviews by Walid Dakah showed one would-be martyr gripped by a euphoric state of anticipation as he approached his target. He was asked, "What were your feelings when you were on the way to die? What did you think about?" His answer: "The feelings are that you are floating in the air, flying, not walking on the ground. You take your leave of everything around you, the material things. It is a farewell from the world. I thought about what lay in store for me as a reward for my action, I asked myself what it would be like in Paradise. I cruised a long way from here in my imagination."[44]

The Western press has made a lot of the seventy-two virgins awaiting martyrs. The comments are usually derisive and focus on sex in the afterlife. Among Muslims there has been debate as to whether the reference to "black-eyed virgins" or "chaste women" found in the Quran and hadith has anything to do with sex. In a comment on the *hur*, or female companions in Paradise, 'Abdullah Yūsuf 'Alī writes, "Lest grosser ideas of sex should intrude, it is made clear that these Companions for heavenly society will be of special creation—of virginal purity, grace, and beauty inspiring and inspired by love, with the question of time and age eliminated."[45]

It really doesn't matter what scholars decide about the issue; more relevant is what would-be martyrs think. One clue comes from the abundant references in posters and graffiti to martyr weddings or marriages. In one example from Oliver and Steinberg's book, Hamas graffiti at the entrance to a cemetery in Jenin proclaimed of a would-be martyr: "Wedding and exaltation await him in Paradise. The virgins of Paradise are in ecstasy, calling, O Omar/Glad Tidings, glad tidings: Paradise and eternity."[46]

Other sources indicate that the heavenly virgins are firmly on young men's minds. The will of one suicide bomber who killed twenty-three Israelis on June 1, 2001, read, "Call out in joy, oh my mother; distribute sweets, oh my father and brothers; a wedding with the 'black-eyed' awaits your son in Paradise."[47] A sixteen-year-old boy from a Gaza refugee camp told *USA Today*'s Jack Kelley that "most boys can't stop thinking about the virgins."[48]

Explaining the excitement of anticipation evident on his martyr video, would-be suicide bomber Salah Mustafa 'Uthman likened the feeling to a wedding night. "On the night before our operation, we had that feeling when you first get married, on the night of the wedding, so excited."[49] He also recalled that on the night before their suicide mission, he and his two companions, Hamza Abu-Surur and Muhammad al-Hindi, talked about what they would see in heaven. Hamza joked, "Seventy virgins are enough for me. I'll give you and Muhammad two."[50]

So some predatory martyrs may be smiling in anticipation of wedding the seventy-two virgins of Paradise. I doubt this bounty appeals to women suicide bombers, however. So their smiles may be prompted by the other bounties, including, for some, being reunited with their dead husbands.

The number of suicide attacks in Iraq has now overtaken that of any other militant campaign, though attacks continue periodically against Israelis. Some of the attacks in Iraq involve Muslims killing other Muslims, with Shiites more often killed at the hands of Sunni suicide bombers than the other way around. As noted earlier, the attackers justify their predatory martyrdom on the grounds that the victims are collaborating with the United States and its allies in the occupation. They are therefore committing apostasy, which the Quran punishes with death.

We have seen that religion legitimizes martyrdom throughout history, though there are secular exceptions such as the Japanese kamikazes and the Black Tigers of Sri Lanka. I believe that many predatory martyrs smile because they are fulfilling their understanding of an obligation or bargain that they have voluntarily accepted. It is, if you like, the ultimate moment of truth that few of us ever get—or choose—to meet in this life. And the martyr now sees that he or she is up to the task! Those martyrs who die while killing in the name of Islam (as they understand it), or who die killing for independence while armed with verses from the Quran, surely fall into this category.

The verse that is considered by many to be *the* justification for suicide attacks is this one, from *Al-Tawbah*, the "repentance" surah. Even though it does not mention martyrdom (*shahadat*) or martyr (*shahid*), Khosrokhavar avers that "it is, in theory, the justification for martyrdom in Islam."[51] Sometimes referred to as the "noble" verse, we first encountered it in chapter 3: "Allah hath purchased of the Believers Their persons and their goods; For theirs (in return) is the Garden (of Paradise); They fight in His Cause, And slay and are slain: A promise binding on Him In Truth, through the Law, The Gospel, and the Quran; And who is more faithful To his covenant than Allah? Then rejoice in the bargain Which ye have concluded: That is the achievement supreme."

Oliver and Steinberg asked Salah Mustafa 'Uthman what he meant when he said on the martyr video that he wanted to fight on the path of God and to be martyred on the path of God. 'Uthman replied that this verse was the "push" that sent him on his road to martyrdom.

The noble verse exhorting Muslims to die and kill in a bargain with Allah is Surah 9, verse 111. Written in the conventional American numerology of the yearly calendar, the reference is 9/11/1. This could mean the ninth month and the eleventh day of the first year following the dawn of the new millennium. Is this a bizarre coincidence, or could this be the reason Mohamed Atta chose September 11, 2001, as the day to attack America? To my knowledge, no one has mentioned the possibility of a connection between 9/11 and this key verse in the Quran. But Atta and his companions in predatory martyrdom would certainly know the verse, and its connection to the date of their attack on American soil might well have given them reason to smile while fulfilling their bargain with God.

Chapter 12

Some Thoughts on the Future of Martyrdom

This book grew out of my desire to better understand the suicide attacks of 9/11, which killed thousands of people, most of them civilians. I now see those attacks as a case of predatory martyrdom, a phenomenon that emerged only recently but whose evolution took three thousand years.

Martyrdom originated in antiquity. It was the extraordinary last gift of inspired individuals who willingly sacrificed themselves in active submission to persecution, oppression, and exploitation. From there, martyrdom evolved along two paths, each illustrating and refining the expressive and instrumental values associated with self-sacrifice for a sacred cause.

On the path of active submission, individuals, and sometimes entire groups, chose death (and often torture) rather than abjure their faith or change their ways. As Christianity developed and spread, cults of martyrdom appeared from time to time, stimulated by the writings or oratory of religious leaders and the effects of contagion. Spontaneous outbreaks of martyrdom occurred as well, sudden eruptions of commitment and resistance that ruling authorities felt obliged to put down harshly. The willing self-sacrifice of a few members reminded the group in general of the need for recommitment and the rewards awaiting the faithful. Though monks often led these outbreaks, women also participated, perhaps drawn to martyrdom by the promise of eternity in the embrace of the True Bridegroom.[1]

The second path of martyrdom emerged with the rise of Islam and the attempts of the Prophet Muhammad to protect the fledgling community of believers, the umma, from extinction. Along this path, martyrdom attracted warriors, not pacifists. Resistance was no longer passive; warriors fought back, and sometimes they attacked first. When they sacrificed themselves in battle, they achieved the honor of martyrdom. The medieval Shiite Assassins introduced a new practice: sending warriors on murder missions that were almost certain to be suicidal; these suicide commandos would reappear seven centuries later. In the meantime, the religiously inspired martyrdom of Muslims and Christians during the Crusades became a defining trait and obligation of the Khalsa Sikhs in the Indian Punjab. These warrior-martyrs happily sacrificed themselves in defense of faith, community, and justice. So instinctive was their self-sacrifice in battle that enemies admired them as fearless, in the mold of Sikh hero and martyr Baba Deep Singh.

When the Japanese introduced the kamikaze suicide squads into the Pacific theater of World War II, they turned warrior-martyrs into martyr-warriors; martyrdom had become an organized strategy of warfare, with fighters specially recruited and trained to sacrifice themselves in airborne attacks on the advancing Allied navy. The kamikazes targeted soldiers, not civilians. This last-ditch effort by the Japanese High Command gained worldwide condemnation but also spurred the emergence of the modern predatory martyr. Exemplified by the suicide bomber, predatory martyrdom is a group-supported strategy adopted by the weaker side in seriously lopsided conflicts; the resister's last gift is self-sacrifice through the act of indiscriminate murder.

This brief treatment of a complex historical issue is surely inadequate. I hope that readers will be spurred to learn more about martyrdom in general, and predatory martyrdom in particular. Discussions about the current situation should certainly stimulate this question: Where is martyrdom headed in the future? Here are some of my speculations as to what the answer might be.

First, there is no reason to believe that martyrdom will ever disappear. History has laid the groundwork too well: The idea of martyrdom is a firmly established concept; some people are willing to die for their beliefs, practices, or community, and others are willing to kill them because of those beliefs and practices. Most important, the perceived individual and group benefits of willing self-sacrifice for the cause are so compelling that it is highly unlikely that oppressed, persecuted, or exploited groups will stop recognizing those who die for the cause as martyrs.

As for predatory martyrdom itself, I do not believe this will be a short-lived phenomenon. This is partly because the underlying conditions that spawn it are unlikely to disappear anytime soon and partly because the perceived benefits associated with suicide attacks will remain compelling for desperate people locked in seriously uneven conflicts over a sacred cause, be it their independence, their religion, or, more generally, their rights and freedoms.

At the group level, more powerful nations and groups will continue to impose their will on weaker ones, and occupation of enemy territory will be a strategic option for the stronger side; independence movements, with or without outside help, will continue to adopt militant strategies of resistance, and when the chips are down, predatory martyrdom may be appealing as a last resort. Religious schisms with long histories will continue to spawn conflicts that turn ugly when one side uses its influence and power to oppress or exploit the other.

There is no better example of all these conditions at work than in Iraq today. Since early 2004, predatory martyrdom has become a routine feature of everyday life. Suicide attacks against the U.S.-led occupation force, characterized by al-Qaeda as a modern-day iteration of the medieval Crusades, and in the bitter Sunni–Shiite conflict that occupation has unleashed, are continuing unabated. Some of the latest attacks have produced large numbers of casualties; for example, on April 7, 2006, suicide bombers dressed as women attacked a Shiite mosque, killing seventy-nine and wounding hundreds more. And it looks increasingly unlikely that suicide attacks will cease if, and when, occupying forces withdraw: Instead, the country could very well plunge into civil war. Before his death on June 7, 2006, in a targeted U.S. air strike, Abu Musab al-Zarqawi had warned that any government made up of "hated Shiites" or formed under the auspices of Western powers will be unacceptable. Since predatory martyrdom is now an established military strategy for both "insurgents" and independence movements in the Middle East, it is likely to play a continuing role as the struggles in Iraq play out.

Even if the situation in Iraq calms down, with occupation by foreigners ended and sectarian conflicts replaced by cooperation, the growing international conflict over the nuclear ambitions of Iran could easily resurrect the fertile conditions for predatory martyrdom. For if this brewing conflict turns physical, there will undoubtedly be a unified and militant Shiite resistance against those nations that threaten their interests. In the event of an attack or occupation by the "infidel" United States and its allies or possibly even a sustained economic and political embargo, the world should expect to see fedayeen warriors reaching deep inside enemy territory on suicidal missions. Unfortunately, as of June 2006, the prospects of defusing this conflict look bleak: Iran continues to assert its right to produce nuclear energy, in defiance of the United States, much of Europe, and, of course, Israel.

This thought points to another possible future for predatory martyrdom: It will become state-sponsored, like the martyrdom of the kamikaze pilots in World War II. To a degree, this is already the case in the Israeli–Palestinian conflict, inasmuch as the suicide campaign against Israel has received direct support from foreign governments, Iran among them. Of course, the Iranian situation regarding nuclear technology may be solved peaceably, diplomacy overruling force. But the possibility of state sponsorship of predatory martyrdom remains very strong in the continuing Israeli–Palestinian conflict, because Hamas now leads the Palestinian Authority, having won 74 of 132 available seats in the January 2006 parliamentary elections. Neither Israel nor Hamas appears likely to soften its hostile stance toward the other any time soon. In widely reported speeches, leaders of both sides continue to employ the rhetoric of hate and distrust. Worse, their actions have backed up the rhetoric. Thus, in a move with severe economic consequences for Palestinians, Israel refused to recognize the

Hamas-led government and stopped the transfer of taxes due to the Palestinian Authority. And Hamas officials refused to delete references to the destruction of Israel in its charter and have not ruled out the resumption of suicide attacks against Israeli citizens.

Indeed, as of June 2006, violence and predatory martyrdom continue in the conflict. On March 30, a suicide bomber attacked a Jewish settlement in the West Bank, killing four Israelis; on April 18, suicide bomber Sami Hammed killed nine in Tel Aviv on behalf of Islamic Jihad. The Israeli army struck back on both occasions, continuing the cycle of attack and counterattack. Hamas has not been directly implicated in these martyrdom operations, but a spokesman described the Tel Aviv bombing as "self-defense."[2] In the meantime, the competition among militant groups has not disappeared, and Hamas continues to fight Fatah, the party of President Mahmoud Abbas, for control of Palestinian security forces. That battle took a violent turn on April 24, with a shoot-out at the Palestinian health ministry in Gaza.

Watching all this from the sidelines is Iranian president Mahmoud Ahmadinejad, whose country has financed predatory martyrdom operations throughout the Middle East. In April 2006, Iran gave $50 million to the Hamas-led Palestinian Authority, a helping hand, certainly, but Palestinians need this much and more *every* month to have any hope of economic and social recovery from the decades of conflict with Israel. In the doubtful event that Hamas changes its charter and recognizes Israel's right to exist, its benefactor will not be happy: When a suicide bomber killed five Israelis in October 2005 in retaliation for an earlier targeted killing by Israel, Ahmadinejad had called for more suicide attacks on Israel so it could be "wiped off the map." He went on, "Anybody who recognizes Israel will burn in the fire of the Islamic nation's fury."[3] No matter its history, Hamas is surely caught between the proverbial rock and a hard place.

At the individual level, the lure of martyrdom will continue to thrive because its perceived benefits—the reason martyrs smile—outweigh the pains of living under occupation, oppression, or exploitation. Some martyrs will doubtless die in active submission, their last gift an expression of commitment and love; others will kill themselves fighting back, confident that in doing so they achieve glory for themselves and their cause, material benefits for their family or community, and perhaps also the pleasure of revenge.

Because predatory martyrs kill indiscriminately, the use of suicide attacks in the future will be contingent on a continuing relocation of the boundaries of innocence. When the medieval Shiite Assassins attacked their Muslim political enemies during Friday prayers, the heresy was no doubt muted by expediency and the anticipated benefits. When Muslim suicide bombers attack fellow believers today in their mosques, at work, or during celebrations and processions, the victims are redefined as heretics and apostates or lumped in with other civilians as part of the regrettable collateral damage that occurs during war. There is no reason to believe that such moral accommodations will disappear in the future.

History has shown that martyrdom spreads through contagion. We saw this during the early centuries of Christendom, and again among Christians in Córdoba during the ninth century. In *Salvation at Stake*, Brad Gregory shows that contagion also played a major role during the resurgence of Christian martyrdom in western Europe during the sixteenth century.[4] Contagion also accounts for the spread of suicide attacks around the world during the past twenty-five years—a sort of globalization of predatory martyrdom. In this case, militant resistance groups from around the world shared knowledge, training, imagery, and ideology in their quest for more effective techniques and strategies. In the West Bank and the Gaza Strip, competition among militant groups contributed to an escalation in suicide bombings against Israel, another way contagion fuels predatory martyrdom.[5] I have no reason to believe that contagion effects will diminish in the future; in fact, it is more likely that they will increase, at least in the short term, due to the wide and powerful reach of the Internet and the growing perception among militant groups that suicide attacks work.[6]

If this picture seems gloomy, remember that from the vantage point of martyrs, their self-sacrifice is a positive thing, and they approach it with excitement and passion. The future looks brighter *because of* their actions. In all its versions, martyrs die for the Good. In a world where there is no oppression, persecution, or exploitation of weaker groups by stronger ones, or where differences are settled by a redress of grievances rather than by the powerful claiming to know what's best for others and imposing it by force, perhaps there will be no martyrdom. The politics of power makes such accommodations unlikely, but perhaps they are not impossible. Yet in the future, even under the best of imaginable circumstances, there will be interests that are considered to be worth dying for, and people prepared to sacrifice themselves. Whenever the two come together, the possibility of martyrdom exists. Its occurrence awaits only the approval of the group whose interests are threatened. Without approval there can be no martyrdom, for it will have no social value. And social value is the source of rewards for all behavior that affects other people.

Notes

Introduction

1. Cynthia Keppley Mahmood, *Fighting for Faith and Nation: Dialogues with Sikh Militants* (Philadelphia: University of Pennsylvania Press, 1996), 201.

2. Steve Tamari, "Americans Need to Know Palestinian History," *St. Louis Post-Dispatch*, April 10, 2002, B7.

3. CE denotes the Common Era (sometimes called the Christian Era); BCE is Before the Common Era. For readers unfamiliar with these terms, 200 CE is the same as 200 AD. I use the more neutral terms out of respect for readers who do not share in the Christian faith.

Part I

1. Lacey Baldwin Smith, *Fools, Martyrs, Traitors: The Story of Martyrdom in the Western World* (New York: Knopf, 1997).

2. This quote is from Plato's *Apology*; the description of Socrates' death and the other quotes are from Plato's *Phaedo*. Both are available on-line at the MIT's Internet Classics Archive, www.classics. mit.edu/Plato/.

Chapter 1

1. Unless otherwise noted, biblical quotations throughout this book are from the *New International Version of the Holy Bible*

(Grand Rapids, Mich.: Zondervan, for the International Bible Society, 1984).

2. Thomas Cahill, *Desire of the Everlasting Hills* (New York: Anchor Books, 1999), 35.

3. "Glad to suffer" and "share in the Greek way" in the next paragraph are quotations from *The Third and Fourth Books of Maccabees*, trans. and ed. Moses Hadas (New York: Harper, 1953).

4. Cited in Cahill, *Desire of the Everlasting Hills*, 47

5. Arthur J. Droge and James D. Tabor, *A Noble Death* (New York: HarperSanFrancisco, 1992).

6. Sidney Goldstein, *Suicide in Rabbinic Literature* (Hoboken, N.J.: KTAV, 1989), 56; cited in Droge and Tabor, *A Noble Death*, 98.

7. The following quotations from Eleazar's speech are from Flavius Josephus, *War of the Jews*, book 7, chapter 8, sections 6–7. The translation of Josephus is by William Whiston; it is available on numerous Web sites; try Christian Classics Ethereal Library at www.ccel.org/j/josephus/JOSEPHUS.HTM.

8. Droge and Tabor, *A Noble Death*, 106.

9. "All my life I was troubled ..." and the next quotation are from the Babylonian Talmud and are cited in Daniel Boyarin, *Dying for God: Martyrdom and the Making of Christianity and Judaism* (Stanford, Calif.: Stanford University Press, 1999), 106.

Chapter 2

1. Translation by Rodolphe Kasser, Marvin Meyer, and Gregor Wurst, in collaboration with François Gaudard, copyright © 2006 by the National Geographic Society. Available on-line at www.nationalgeographic.com/lostgospel/.

2. The works of early Christian writers can be found on many Web sites; the quotes from Justin Martyr, Clement, and Origen used here are found in David W. Bercot, *A Dictionary of Early Christian Beliefs* (Amberson, Pa.: Scroll Publishing, 1998).

3. This is one of the last sentences of Tertullian's great defense of the Christians, *The Apology* [Apologeticum], from a translation by the Rev. S. Thelwall, late scholar of Christ's College, Cambridge University. The entire work is on-line at http://www.ccel.org/fathers2/ANF-03/anf03-05.htm#P253_53158.

4. Ross Shepard Kraemer, *Her Share of the Blessings* (New York: Oxford University Press, 1992).

5. The story and related quotes are from W. H. Shewring, trans., *The Passion of Perpetua and Felicity* (London: n.p., 1931). This

translation is available on the Internet Medieval Sourcebook Web site maintained by Fordham University Center for Medieval Studies at http://www.fordham.edu/halsall/sbook.html.

6. Reference to Nero's and Valerian's methods of execution is from John Fox's *Book of Martyrs: A History of the Lives, Sufferings and Triumphant Deaths of the Early Christian and the Protestant Martyrs,* first published in 1563 and available on-line at http://www.sacredtexts.com/chr/martyrs/begin.htm.

7. From *The Shows* [De Spectaculis], trans. the Rev. S. Thelwall, www.ccel.org (the Christian Classics Ethereal Web site). Here, Tertullian called upon Christians to cease attending public games, circuses, chariot races, and gladiatorial combat because they were idolatrous, Devil-inspired pleasures.

8. "The spoil of life eternal" and "therefore we conquer in dying" are from *The Apology,* trans. the Rev. S. Thelwall, chapter 50.

9. See Fox, *Book of Martyrs.*

10. Cited in the *Catholic Encyclopedia* at http://www.newadvent.org/cathen/04295c.htm.

11. *Catholic Encyclopedia,* on-line at www.newadvent.org.

12. Cited in Bercot, *A Dictionary of Early Christian Beliefs,* 435.

13. The quotations in my recounting of the story of the Forty Martyrs of Sevastia are from "The Holy Great Forty Martyrs of Sevastia," from the official Web site of the Greek Orthodox Archdiocese of America, www.goarch.org/access/calendar/march/march_9.html.

14. Cited by Arthur J. Droge and James D. Tabor, *A Noble Death* (New York: HarperSanFrancisco, 1992), 138.

15. Fox, *Book of Martyrs.*

16. See the discussion in Brad S. Gregory, *Salvation at Stake: Christian Martyrdom in Early Modern Europe* (Cambridge, Mass.: Harvard University Press, 1999), 104–5.

17. Cited in Lina Eckenstein, *Woman under Monasticism* (New York: Russell & Russell, 1963 [1896]), 339–40. Available on-line at www.yale.edu/adhoc/etexts/Eckstn1.htm.

Part II

1. M. J. Akbar, *The Shade of Swords: Jihad and the Conflict between Islam and Christianity* (London: Routledge, 2002), 21.

2. Akbar, *The Shade of Swords,* 106.

3. Akbar, *The Shade of Swords,* 107.

4. Farid al-Din Attar, *Muslim Saints and Mystics: Episodes from the Tadhkirat al-Auliya'* (Memorial of the Saints), trans. A. J. Arberry

(Chicago: University of Chicago Press, 1966). Quotations in the following paragraphs are from pages 268–70.

Chapter 3

1. There are many accounts of Muhammad's life, including anecdotes that originated with the earliest followers of Muhammad and eventually formed the hadith, or sayings of the Prophet Muhammad. One of the earliest and best-known biographies is *The Life of Muhammad* by Ibn Ishaq, trans. and ed. Alfred Guillaume (Oxford, U.K.: Oxford University Press, 1955). Two recent and accessible books on the more general topic of Islam written for Western readers are Andrew Rippin, *Muslims: Their Religious Beliefs and Practices* (London: Routledge, 2001), and Karen Armstrong, *Islam: A Short History* (New York: Modern Library, 2002). Both of these books include extensive bibliographies. Though harder to find, a wonderful illustrated book on Muhammad and the early years of Islam is *Mecca the Blessed, Madinah the Radiant* by Emel Esin (New York: Crown, 1963). There are also many Internet sources that readers can explore using the outstanding Web site maintained by Alan Godlas at the University of Georgia, www.arches.uga.edu/~godlas/.

2. Esin, *Mecca the Blessed, Madinah the Radiant*, 82.

3. All excerpts and verses from the Quran are from the English translation by the late 'Abdullah Yūsuf 'Alī, *The Meaning of the Holy Qurân*, rev. ed. (Beltsville, Md.: Amana Corporation, 1989). This translation of the Quran is considered "moderate" when compared to the "radical" Wahhabi translation published by scholars at Saudi Arabia's Islamic University in Medina. Note also that parenthetic words throughout the cited verses are the translator's clarification. Capitalized letters usually indicate the start of a new line within the original verse.

4. Cited in Anne Marie Oliver and Paul F. Steinberg, *The Road to Martyrs' Square: A Journey into the World of the Suicide Bomber* (New York: Oxford University Press, 2005), 70.

5. Akbar, *The Shade of Swords*, 9.

6. Cited by ninth-century Arab historian Ahmad Ibn-Jahir al-Baladhuri. See "Al-Baladhuri on Early Muslim Conquests," in *The Crusades: A Reader*, ed. S. J. Allen and Emilie Amt (Guelph, Ontario: Broadview Press, 2003), 15–16.

7. Farhad Khosrokhavar, *Suicide Bombers: Allah's New Martyrs* (London: Pluto Press, 2005), 12.

8. From the hadith *Sahih Al-Bukhari,* cited in Jamilah Kolocontronis, *Islamic Jihad in Historical Perspective* (Indianapolis: American Trust Publications, 1990), 31.

9. Amin Maalouf, *The Crusades through Arab Eyes* (New York: Schocken Books, 1984), 81.

10. Alan D. Corré, introduction to the *Synagoga Judaica* [Judenschül, or "Jews' School"] written in the early seventeenth century by Johannes Buxdorf, at http://www.uwm.edu/~corre/buxdorf/myintro.html.

11. Quoted in Kenneth Baxter Wolf, *Christian Martyrs in Muslim Spain* (Cambridge, U.K.: Cambridge University Press, 1988), 97.

Chapter 4

1. M. J. Akbar, *The Shade of Swords: Jihad and the Conflict between Islam and Christianity* (London: Routledge, 2002), 63.

2. *The Song of Roland,* line 1934, from a 1919 translation by Charles Scott Moncrief, reprinted by the Online Medieval and Classical Library at the University of California, Berkeley (http://sunsite.berkeley.edu/OMACL/Roland/).

3. *Song of Roland,* lines 1134–35.

4. This and other quotations from Urban's speech are from accounts by Robert the Monk, Fulcher of Chartres, and Baldric of Dol. Excerpts can be found in S. J. Allen and Emilie Amt, eds., *The Crusades: A Reader* (Guelph, Ontario: Broadview Press, 2003). They can also be found in the Internet Medieval Sourcebook on-line at http://www.fordham.edu/halsall/sbook.html.

5. James Reston Jr., *Warriors of God* (New York: Anchor Books, 2002), xiii.

6. Karen Anderson, *Holy War,* 2nd ed. (New York: Anchor Books, 2001), 374.

7. Solomon bar Samson, "The Crusaders in Mainz, 1096," reproduced in the Internet Medieval Sourcebook (http://www.fordham.edu/halsall/sbook.html). A portion of this account is also contained in Allen and Amt, *The Crusades,* 54–56.

8. Anderson, *Holy War,* 190.

9. Bernard of Clairvaux, cited by Piers Paul Read, *The Templars* (Cambridge, Mass.: Da Capo Press, 2001), 106.

10. Bernard of Clairvaux, from an excerpt cited in Allen and Amt, *The Crusades,* 197.

11. From "Letter of Stephen of Blois," in Allen and Amt, *The Crusades,* 66.

12. Ibn al-Qalanisi, cited in Allen and Amt, *The Crusades*, 132.

13. John L. Esposito, *Unholy War: Terror in the Name of Islam* (Oxford, U.K.: Oxford University Press, 2002), 74–75.

14. Cited by Maalouf, *The Crusades through Arab Eyes* (New York: Schocken Books, 1984), 148.

15. Anderson, *Holy War*, 179.

16. From the account of Raymond of Aguilers reproduced in Allen and Amt, *The Crusades*, 77.

17. See Charlotte Edwards, "Historians Say Film 'Distorts' Crusades," *London Sunday Telegraph*, January 18, 2004.

18. Cited in Maalouf, *The Crusades through Arab Eyes*, 255.

19. Cited in Allen and Amt, *The Crusades*, 146.

20. Farhad Khosrokhavar, *Suicide Bombers: Allah's New Martyrs* (London: Pluto Press, 2005), 43.

21. Maalouf, *The Crusades through Arab Eyes*, 44.

22. James Wasserman, *The Templars and the Assassins: The Militia of Heaven* (Rochester, Vt.: Inner Traditions International, 2001), 109.

23. Maalouf, *The Crusades through Arab Eyes*, 103.

24. From *The Itinerary of Benjamin of Tudela: Critical Text, Translation, and Commentary* (New York: Philipp Feldheim, 1907); cited in Allen and Amt, *The Crusades*, 117.

25. Barnard Lewis, *The Assassins: A Radical Sect in Islam* (London: Phoenix, 1967), 47.

26. Wasserman, *The Templars and the Assassins*, 110.

Chapter 5

1. From the writings of Guru Nanak, *Raga Asa*, p. 360 of the *Guru Granth Sahib*, the compilation of teachings of the Sikh gurus also known as the *Adi Granth*. English translation by Dr. Sant Singh, available at www.sikhs.org/english/frame.html.

2. Gurmit Singh, *Guru Nanak's Relationship with the Lodis and Mughuls* (New Delhi: Atlantic Publishers, 1987), 42.

3. Jagjit Singh, *The Sikh Revolution* (New Delhi: Kendri Singh Sabha, 1984), 160.

4. Cited in Singh, *The Sikh Revolution*, 162.

5. From the *Bachittar Natak* by Guru Gobind Singh.

6. J. S. Grewal, *Sikh Ideology, Polity, and Social Order* (New Delhi: Monohar, 1996), 51.

7. Patwant Singh, *The Sikhs* (New York: Doubleday, 2000), 53.

8. Surjit Singh Gandhi, *Struggle of the Sikhs for Sovereignty* (Delhi: GDK Publications, 1980), 460.

9. Cynthia Keppley Mahmood, *Fighting for Faith and Nation: Dialogues with Sikh Militants* (Philadelphia: University of Pennsylvania Press, 1996), 146.

10. Singh, *The Sikh Revolution,* 198–99.

11. Gandhi, *Struggle of the Sikhs for Sovereignty,* 458.

12. Guru Nanak, *Guru Granth Sahib,* 1412, cited in Jaswant Singh, "Martyrdom in Sikhism," *Sikh Studies* (January 2002), available at www.sikhstudies.org.

13. Cited in Mahmood, *Fighting for Faith and Nation,* 191.

14. Khafi Khan, cited in Singh, *The Sikhs,* 70.

15. These accounts were translated by William Irvine in the nineteenth century and are cited in Singh, *The Sikh Revolution,* 197, and also in Gandhi, *Struggle of the Sikhs for Sovereignty,* 460–61.

16. Singh, *The Sikh Revolution,* 200.

17. Cited in M. J. Akbar, *The Shade of Swords: Jihad and the Conflict between Islam and Christianity* (London: Routledge, 2002), 127.

18. Singh, *The Sikhs,* 168.

19. Singh, *The Sikhs,* 170.

20. Quoted in Gandhi, *Struggle of the Sikhs for Sovereignty,* 469.

21. Singh, *The Sikhs,* 191.

22. Singh, *The Sikhs,* 197.

23. Ramka Naragan Kumar, *The Sikh Unrest and the Indian States* (Delhi: Ajanta Publications, 1997), 163.

24. Mahmood, *Fighting for Faith and Nation,* 40.

25. Cited in Mahmood, *Fighting for Faith and Nation,* 91–92.

26. Sharda Jain, *Politics of Terrorism in India* (New Delhi: Deep and Deep Publications, 1995), 208–9.

27. Singh, *The Sikhs,* 228.

28. Mahmood, *Fighting for Faith and Nation,* 201.

29. Mahmood, *Fighting for Faith and Nation,* 202.

30. Mahmood, *Fighting for Faith and Nation,* 132.

31. Mahmood, *Fighting for Faith and Nation,* 205.

Chapter 6

1. The personnel and equipment figures cited in the opening paragraph are from Edward J. Drea, *In the Service of the Emperor* (Lincoln: University of Nebraska Press, 1998), 39, 51. Drea took them from official U.S. and Japanese publications.

2. Boye De Mente, "Introduction," in Hatsubo Naito, *Thunder Gods: The Kamikaze Pilots Tell Their Story,* trans. Mayumi Ichikawa (New York: Kodansha International, 1989), 20.

3. Maurice Pinguet, *Voluntary Death in Japan,* trans. Rosemary Morris (Cambridge, U.K.: Polity Press, n.d.), 217.

4. Cited by De Mente, "Introduction," 20.

5. Quoted in Drea, *In the Service of the Emperor,* 107–8.

6. Cited in Masanori Ito with Roger Pineau, *The End of the Imperial Japanese Navy* (New York: Norton, 1962), 192.

7. Quoted by Rikihei Inoguchi and Tadashi Nakajima in *The Divine Wind: Japan's Kamikaze Force in World War II* (Westport, Conn.: Greenwood Press, 1978), 28. Inoguchi and Nakajima served under Admiral Onishi.

8. Drea, *In the Service of the Emperor,* 12.

9. Pinguet, *Voluntary Death in Japan,* 63.

10. In later analysis of the action at Leyte Gulf, U.S. naval experts claimed that while Admiral Arima certainly died, he was shot down and never got near the carrier. See Samuel Eliot Morison, *Leyte: June 1944–January 1945* (Boston: Little, Brown, 1958), 101.

11. Quoted by Inoguchi and Nakajima, *The Divine Wind,* 56.

12. Morison, *Leyte,* 302.

13. The account referred to here is Denis Warner, Peggy Warner, and Sadao Seno, *The Sacred Warriors: Japan's Suicide Legions* (Cincinatti: Van Nostrand Reinhold, 1982), 106–7.

14. Loss figures for the battle of Leyte Gulf are official estimates from Drea, *In the Service of the Emperor,* 135.

15. George A. Tusa, ed., "Sonarman First Class Jack Gebhardt," reproduced and adapted by the Naval Historical Foundation Oral History Program, Navy Historical Center, Department of the Navy, Washington, D.C. Oral histories of naval operations in the Pacific theater of World War II can be found on-line at http://www.history.navy.mil/.

16. Quoted in Morison, *Leyte,* 303.

17. The sinking of the *Yamato* is described in Russell Spurr, *A Glorious Way to Die: The Kamikaze Mission of the Battleship Yamato, April 1945* (New York: Newmarket Press, 1981).

18. Toshiyuki Yokoi, "Kamikazes in the Okinawa Campaign," in *The Japanese Navy in World War II* (Annapolis, Md.: U.S. Naval Institute, 1969), 131. Emphasis added.

19. Ryuji Nagatsuka, *I Was a Kamikaze* (New York: Macmillan, 1974), 192.

20. Quoted in Nagatsuka, *I Was a Kamikaze,* 196.

21. Admiral Ugaki's message is quoted in Inoguchi and Nakajima, *The Divine Wind,* 160.

22. Onishi's suicide note is quoted in Inoguchi and Nakajima, *The Divine Wind*, 162.

23. Pinguet, *Voluntary Death in Japan*, 226.

24. Nagatsuka, *I Was a Kamikaze*, 180.

25. Inoguchi and Nakajima, *The Divine Wind*, 18.

26. Quoted in Inoguchi and Nakajima, *The Divine Wind*, 181.

27. Quoted in Inoguchi and Nakajima, *The Divine Wind*, 184.

28. Cited in Richard O'Neill, *Suicide Squads: Axis and Allied Special Attack Squads of World War II: Their Development and Missions* (London: Salamander Books, 1999), 197.

29. Yokoi, "Kamikazes in the Okinawa Campaign," 134.

30. Pinguet, *Voluntary Death in Japan*, 227.

31. Use of propaganda by all sides in the Pacific war is explored in detail in John Dower, *War without Mercy: Race and Power in the Pacific War* (New York: Pantheon Books, 1986).

32. Ito, *The End of the Imperial Japanese Navy*, 195.

33. Pinguet, *Voluntary Death in Japan*, 91.

Part IV

1. From the spiritual handbook for the suicide attack on the World Trade Center, titled "The Sky Smiles, My Young Son," reprinted in *Inside 9-11*, by the reporters, writers, and editors of *Der Spiegel* magazine (New York: St. Martin's Press, 2002), 308–14.

2. From the statement of Dr. Magnus Ranstorp to the National Commission on Terrorist Attacks upon the United States [hereafter, 9/11 Commission], March 31, 2003, www.9-11commission.gov/hearings.

3. Osama bin Laden in a videotaped conversation translated by the U.S. government and reprinted in *Inside 9-11*, 314–22.

Chapter 7

1. Reprinted at http://www.tamilnation.org/ltte/vp/interviews/8608newsweek.htm.

2. Yoram Schweitzer, "Suicide Terrorism: Development and Characteristics," paper presented to the International Conference on Countering Suicide Terrorism at the Institute for Counter-Terrorism, Herzeliya, Israel, February 21, 2000.

3. Reported at www.tamiltigers.net/fallencomrades/fallen_comrades.html.

4. Robert Pape, *Dying to Win: The Strategic Logic of Suicide Terrorism* (New York: Random House, 2005), 146.

5. This and most of the other quotes in this paragraph are from Prabhakaran speeches reported at the Tamil Web sites www.eelamweb.com. and www.tamiltigers.net/fallencomrades/fallen_comrades.html.

6. From "Batticaloa Marks 'Black Tiger' Day," www.tamilnet.com, July 6, 1999.

7. From the Interim Report of the Jain Commission of Inquiry on the Assassination of Shri Rajiv Gandhi, Former Prime Minister of India, on 21st May, 1991. The entire report is available at http://india-today.com/jain/.

8. The comment of Mangalika Silva, Tamil researcher and coordinator of Women for Peace in Colombo, quoted by Ana Cutter in "Tamil Tigresses: Hindu Martyrs," *Slant,* the magazine of Columbia University School of International and Public Affairs (Spring 1998), available at www.columbia.edu/cu/sipa/PUBS/SLANT/SPRING98/article5.htm.

9. Mia Bloom, *Dying to Kill: The Allure of Suicide Terror* (New York: Columbia University Press, 2005), 159.

10. This quote and the statistics on suicide attacks by women are from Yoram Schweitzer, "Suicide Terrorism: Development and Characteristics."

11. From "Sri Lanka: Former Tamil Tiger Child Soldiers Remain at Risk," *Human Rights News,* April 27, 2004, at www.hrw.org.

12. "Sri Lanka: Living with Terror," PBS *Frontline World* feature, May 2002, available at http://www.pbs.org/frontlineworld/stories/srilanka/feature.html.

13. "Sri Lanka: Former Tamil Tiger Child Soldiers Remain at Risk."

14. Human Rights Watch, "Asia Watch: Sri Lanka," http://www.hrw.org/reports/1990/WR90/ASIA.BOU-11.htm#P718_161127.

15. From an interview conducted in 1985 titled "We Are Prepared to Pay for Freedom with Our Lives," at http://eelam.com/interviews/leader_sept_85.html.

16. See Tamil Eelam homepage at http://eelam.com.

17. From a speech by E. Kousalyan, May 3, 2004, reported at www.tamilnet.com.

18. The entire speech is available at www.ealamweb.com.

19. ABC's *The World Today,* at http://www.abc.net.au/worldtoday/content/2006/s1624290.htm.

20. For more on this, see Ed Maloney, *A Secret History of the IRA* (New York: Norton, 2002), 347–49.

21. Pape, *Dying to Win,* appendix 1, 259.

22. Sebastian Smith, *Allah's Mountains: The Battle for Chechnya* (London: I. B. Tauris, 2001), xxvi.

23. Smith, *Allah's Mountains,* 79–80.

24. Bloom, *Dying to Kill,* 131.

25. Bloom, *Dying to Kill,* 27.

Chapter 8

1. From a manifesto of Arab Nationalists published in Cairo around the start of World War I and reprinted in Sylvia Haim, *Arab Nationalism* (Berkeley: University of California Press, 1964), 83.

2. The entire Palestinian Mandate is available on-line through the Avalon Project at Yale University Law School at http://www.yale.edu/lawweb/avalon/mideast/palmanda.htm.

3. These two quotes are from the 1939 White Paper on Palestine. Excerpts cited in Ian J. Bickerton and Carla L. Klausner, *A Concise History of the Arab-Israeli Conflict,* 4th ed. (Upper Saddle River, N.J.: Prentice-Hall, 2002), 66–67.

4. This and other survivor accounts can be read at the Deir Yassin Remembered Web site, www.deiryassin.org. See especially Matthew Hogan, "The 1948 Massacre at Deir Yassin Revisited," available on the same Web site.

5. From an interview with Meir Pail conducted October 1, 1998, by Ami Isseroff at the Yad Tabenkin Institute of the United Kibbutz Movement Seminar in Ramat Efal, Israel. The entire interview can be found at http://www.ariga.com/peacewatch/dy/dypail.htm.

6. The first Rabin quote is from Dan Kurzman, *Soldier of Peace: The Life of Yitzhak Rabin* (New York: HarperCollins, 1998), 142; the second is from David K. Shipler, "Israel Bars Rabin from Relating '48 Eviction of Arabs," *New York Times,* October 23, 1979, A1.

7. Mourid Barghouti, *I Saw Ramallah,* trans. Ahdaf Soueif (New York: Anchor Books, 2000), 3.

8. From Resolution 3 of the Khartoum Resolutions signed by eight Arab heads of state on September 1, 1967. The full text of the resolutions is widely available on the Internet.

9. From the 1981 Party Platform of the Likud Party; excerpts reprinted in Bickerton and Klausner, *A Concise History of the Arab–Israeli Conflict,* 207.

10. The full interview is contained in *The Martyr's Smile,* a Channel 4 Television (U.K.) film in the series "Beirut to Bosnia: Muslims and the West."

Chapter 9

1. Ian J. Bickerton and Carla L. Klausner, *A Concise History of the Arab-Israeli Conflict,* 4th ed. (Upper Saddle River, N.J.: Prentice-Hall, 2002), 232.

2. Anne Marie Oliver and Paul F. Steinberg, *The Road to Martyrs' Square: A Journey into the World of the Suicide Bomber* (New York: Oxford University Press, 2005), 7.

3. Oliver and Steinberg, *The Road to Martyrs' Square,* 11.

4. This and the other Hamas quotes in this paragraph are from "The Charter of the Hamas" at www.hamasonline.com. Since I wrote this chapter, this Web site has disappeared. However, the Hamas Charter can be found on-line using a search engine like Google.

5. From a 1996 interview given by Mahmoud Zahar; quoted in John L. Esposito, *Unholy War: Terror in the Name of Islam* (New York: Oxford University Press, 2002), 97.

6. Quoted in Oliver and Steinberg, *The Road to Martyrs' Square,* 60.

7. Mia Bloom, *Dying to Kill: The Allure of Suicide Terror* (New York: Columbia University Press, 2005), 27.

8. Mourid Barghouti, *I Saw Ramallah,* trans. Ahdaf Soueif (New York: Anchor Books, 2001), 48. Returning to Ramallah after a thirty-year exile, poet Barghouti gives a personal account of his journey home.

9. This depiction of the martyr is by Hezbollah leader Sheikh Hassan Nasrallah from a 1994 interview with Robert Fisk of the *Independent* newspaper. The full interview can be seen in *The Martyr's Smile,* a Channel 4 Television Corporation film in the series "Beirut to Bosnia: Muslims and the West."

10. Barghouti, *I Saw Ramallah,* 37.

11. See http://www.ummah.com/forum/showthread.php?t=348.

Chapter 10

1. Eyad Sarraj, "Why We Have Become Suicide Bombers," available at the Mission Islam Web site, www.missionislam.com.

2. Human Rights Watch, *World Report 2003: Israel, the Occupied West Bank and Gaza Strip, and Palestinian Authority Territories,* available at http://www.hrw.org/wr2k3/mideast5.html. For a special HRW report on Operation Defensive Shield, see "Jenin: IDF Military Operations," at http://hrw.org/reports/2002/israel3/.

3. Kevin Toolis, "Walls of Death," *Observer,* November 23, 2003.

4. Joshua Hammer, "Special Report: Suicide Mission," *Newsweek,* April 15, 2002, 24.

5. The complete poem can be found at http://www.islamonline. net/English/Views/2002/04/article17.shtml. Translation by Zafarul-Islam Khan.

6. Cited in Mia Bloom, *Dying to Kill: The Allure of Suicide Terror* (New York: Columbia University Press, 2005), 148.

7. Hammer, "Special Report," 25.

8. Kevin Toolis, "The Revenger's Tragedy: Why Women Turn to Suicide Bombing," *Observer,* October 12, 2003.

9. Amru Nasif in a May 2001 article published originally in Egypt and rereleased by the Middle East Media Research Institute at www. memri.org.

10. Yassin's well-known comment is cited in Hammer, "Special Report," and many other places.

11. Cited in Bloom, *Dying to Kill,* 151.

12. Bloom, *Dying to Kill,* 151.

13. Cited in Bloom, *Dying to Kill,* 151.

14. Cited in Bloom, *Dying to Kill,* 149.

15. Youssef H. Aboul-Enein and Sherifa Zuhur, "Islamic Rulings on Warfare," publication of the Strategic Studies Institute of the U.S. Army War College, October 2004, 26; available at http://www. strategicstudiesinstitute.army.mil/pubs/.

16. Excerpts from the will of Abdullah Yusuf Azzam are available at www.IslamicAwakening.com. Italics added.

17. Cited in Bloom, *Dying to Kill,* 151.

18. Reported by the Associated Press, January 15, 2004.

19. Associated Press, January 15, 2004.

20. Cited in Bloom, *Dying to Kill,* 153.

21. Reported by Thomas Wagner, Associated Press, September 28, 2005.

22. See U.S. State Department, *Country Reports on Terrorism* 2005, 131; on-line at http://www.state.gov/s/ct/rls/crt/c17689.htm.

23. *Daily Times* [Pakistan], April 30, 2006. On-line at www.dailytimes. com.pk/.

24. Quoted by the Associated Press, July 3, 2005.

25. Quoted by the Associated Press, February 1, 2004.

26. Speech given September 12, 2001, reported at www.islamonline. com.

27. In BBC2, *Newsnight* interview, July 7, 2004.

28. Bloom, *Dying to Kill,* 40.

29. Amira Hass, "Confessions of a Dangerous Mind," *Haaretz,* April 12, 2003. From an interview of fellow inmates by imprisoned Palestinian Walid Dakah.

30. Statement issued by al-Qaeda in Iraq, June 15, 2005, at www. siteinstitute.com.

31. Ron Glossop, *Confronting War,* 3rd ed. (Jefferson, N.C.: Mc-Farland, 1994).

32. John Dower, *War without Mercy* (New York: Pantheon Books, 1986).

33. Quoted in Boaz Ganor, "Suicide Terrorism: An Overview," Paper presented to the Institute for Counter-Terrorism, Israel, February 15, 2000.

34. Kevin Toolis, *Sunday Observer,* December 16, 2001.

35. Hass, "Confessions of a Dangerous Mind."

Chapter 11

1. M. J. Akbar, *The Shade of Swords* (London: Routledge, 2002), xv.

2. Cited in Anne Marie Oliver and Paul Steinberg, *The Road to Martyrs' Square: A Journey into the World of the Suicide Bomber* (New York: Oxford University Press, 2005), xxii.

3. Robert Pape, *Dying to Win: The Strategic Logic of Suicide Terrorism* (New York: Random House, 2005); Farhad Khosrokhavar, *Suicide Bombers: Allah's New Martyrs,* trans. David Macy (London: Pluto Press, 2005); and Mia Bloom, *Dying to Kill: The Allure of Suicide Terror* (New York: Columbia University Press, 2005).

4. Needless to say, such Web sites come and go, and many are in Arabic. As of fall 2005, three accessible Web sites were www. qudsway.com, www.katebaqsa.org, and www.qal3ah.org.

5. Cited in Pape, *Dying to Win,* 65.

6. Cited in Pape, *Dying to Win,* 70.

7. Cited in Pape, *Dying to Win,* 71.

8. *Los Angeles Times,* August 28, 2005.

9. U.S. Department of State, *Country Reports on Terrorism 2005,* 131; on-line at http://www.state.gov/s/ct/rls/crt/c17689.htm.

10. Khosrokhavar, *Suicide Bombers,* 161.

11. Cited in Pape, *Dying to Win,* 192.

12. *Stanford Report,* June 14, 2005, at http://news-service. stanford.edu/news/2005/june15/jobs-061505.html.

13. Susan B. Glasser, "'Martyrs' in Iraq Mostly Saudis," *Washington Post,* May 16, 2005.

14. Oliver and Steinberg, *The Road to Martyrs' Square,* 100.

15. Pape, *Dying to Win,*180.

16. Bloom, *Dying to Kill,* 78.

17. Bloom, *Dying to Kill,* 68.

18. At http://www.jmcc.org/publicpoll/opinion.html.

19. Bloom, *Dying to Kill,* 30.

20. Khosrokhavar, *Suicide Bombers,* 137.

21. Christopher Dickey, "Special Report: Inside Suicide, Inc.," *Newsweek,* April 15, 2002.

22. *New York Times,* March 23, 2004.

23. Oliver and Steinberg, *The Road to Martyrs' Square,* 118.

24. Mouin Rabbani, "Suicide Attacks in the Middle East Are Fueled by Alienation and Futility," Middle East News Online, at www.middleeastwire.com.

25. Kevin Toolis, "Where Suicide Is a Cult," *Observer,* December 16, 2001.

26. Bloom, *Dying to Kill,* 29, 30.

27. Oliver and Steinberg, *The Road to Martyrs' Square,* xxii.

28. Toolis, "Where Suicide Is a Cult."

29. Oliver and Steinberg, *The Road to Martyrs' Square,* caption to photo 18.

30. Khosrokhavar, *Suicide Bombers,* 65.

31. Khosrokhavar, *Suicide Bombers,* 64.

32. Cited by Boaz Ganor, "Suicide Terrorism: An Overview," February 15, 2000. Presentation to the Institute for Counterterrorism, Tel Aviv, Israel.

33. Cynthia Keppley Mahmood, *Fighting for Faith and Nation: Dialogues with Sikh Militants* (Philadelphia: University of Pennsylvania Press, 1996), 191.

34. At www.qal3ah.org. (since disappeared). Readers who speak Arabic may find links at www.kataebaqsa.org, the "Alaqsa Martyrs Troops" Web site.

35. Cited in Bloom, *Dying to Kill,* 86.

36. "Statements by Heads of Fateh Sections," Special Dispatch No. 260, at www.memri.org.

37. Quoted in Pape, *Dying to Win,* 122.

38. Quoted in Pape, *Dying to Win,* 124.

39. Oliver and Steinberg, *The Road to Martyrs' Square,* 122.

40. Oliver and Steinberg, *The Road to Martyrs' Square,* 92.

41. Reinhold Loeffler, *Islam in Practice: Religious Beliefs in a Persian Village* (New York: State University of New York Press, 1988), 230.

42. This video was on the Web site www.maktabal-jihad.com, which has disappeared since I watched the video.

43. Oliver and Steinberg, *The Road to Martyrs' Square,* 196, note 12.

44. Amira Hass, "Confessions of a Dangerous Mind" *Haaretz,* April 12, 2003. Prison interviews conducted by Walid Dakah.

45. 'Abdullah Yūsuf 'Alī, *The Meaning of the Holy Quran,* rev. ed. (Beltsville, Md.: Amana Corporation, 1989), 1411, note 5240.

46. Oliver and Steinberg, *The Road to Martyrs' Square,* 76.

47. Yotam Feldner, "72 Black-Eyed Virgins: A Muslim Debate on the Rewards of Martyrs," Inquiry and Analysis #74, Jihad and Terrorism Studies, October 30, 2001, at www.memri.org.

48. Jack Kelley, "Devotion, Desire Drive Youths to Martyrdom," *USA Today,* July 5, 2001.

49. Oliver and Steinberg, *The Road to Martyrs' Square,* 136.

50. Oliver and Steinberg, *The Road to Martyrs' Square,* 137.

51. Khosrokhavar, *Suicide Bombers,* 12.

Chapter 12

1. See, for example, Lina Eckenstein, *Woman under Monasticism* (New York: Russell & Russell, 1963).

2. Associated Press, April 18, 2006.

3. Associated Press, October 27, 2005.

4. Brad S. Gregory, *Salvation at Stake: Christian Martyrdom in Early Modern Europe* (Cambridge, Mass.: Harvard University Press, 1999).

5. For more on contagion and suicide bombing, see Mia Bloom, *Dying to Kill: The Allure of Suicide Terror* (New York: Columbia University Press, 2005), esp. chap. 6.

6. On the belief that suicide attacks work, see Robert A. Pape, *Dying to Win: The Strategic Logic of Suicide Terrorism* (New York: Random House, 2005), esp. chap. 5.

Suggested Readings

This list includes some of the more accessible books that readers may wish to consult for further information on the topics discussed in this book. The books are organized according to subject matter.

On Martyrdom in Antiquity

Boyarin, Daniel. *Dying for God: Martyrdom and the Making of Christianity and Judaism.* Stanford, Calif.: Stanford University Press, 1999.

Cahill, Thomas. *Desire of the Everlasting Hills.* New York: Anchor Books, 1999.

Droge, Arthur J., and James D. Tabor. *A Noble Death.* New York: HarperSanFrancisco, 1992.

On Warrior-Martyrs: Muslims, Christians, Assassins, and Sikhs

Akbar, M. J. *The Shade of Swords: Jihad and the Conflict between Islam and Christianity.* London: Routledge, 2002.

Anderson, Karen. *Holy War.* 2nd ed. New York: Anchor Books, 2001.

Maalouf, Amin. *The Crusades through Arab Eyes.* New York: Schocken, 1984.

Mahmood, Cynthia Keppley. *Fighting for Faith and Nation: Dialogues with Sikh Militants.* Philadelphia: University of Pennsylvania Press, 1996.

Read, Piers Paul. *The Templars.* Cambridge, Mass.: Da Capo Press, 2001.
Reston, James, Jr. *Warriors of God.* New York: Anchor Books, 2002.
Singh, Patwant. *The Sikhs.* New York: Doubleday, 2000.
Wasserman, James. *The Templars and the Assassins: The Militia of Heaven.* Rochester, Vt.: Inner Traditions International, 2001.

On Martyr-Warriors: The Kamikazes

Dower, John. *War without Mercy: Race and Power in the Pacific War.* New York: Pantheon, 1986.
Naito, Hatsubo. *Thunder Gods: The Kamikaze Pilots Tell Their Story.* Translated by Mayumi Ichikawa. New York: Kodansha International, 1989.
O'Neill, Richard. *Suicide Squads: Axis and Allied Special Attack Squads of World War II: Their Development and Missions.* London: Salamander, 1999.

On Predatory Martyrs

Bloom, Mia. *Dying to Kill: The Allure of Suicide Terror.* New York: Columbia University Press, 2005.
Esposito, John L. *Unholy War: Terror in the Name of Islam.* Oxford, U.K.: Oxford University Press, 2002.
Khosrokhavar, Farhad. *Suicide Bombers: Allah's New Martyrs.* London: Pluto, 2005.
Oliver, Anne Marie, and Paul F. Steinberg. *The Road to Martyrs' Square: A Journey into the World of the Suicide Bomber.* New York: Oxford University Press, 2005.
Pape, Robert A. *Dying to Win: The Strategic Logic of Suicide Terrorism.* New York: Random House, 2005.
Smith, Sebastian. *Allah's Mountains: The Battle for Chechnya.* London: I. B. Tauris, 2001.

Index

About the Author

Hugh Barlow was born and raised in Birmingham, England. After graduating from the University of Southampton, he earned his Ph.D. in sociology at the University of Texas, Austin. He became a U.S. resident and has taught for more than thirty years at Southern Illinois University, Edwardsville. He is currently professor emeritus and director of criminal justice studies. He has written extensively on crime and criminal justice; this is his fifth book. In 1993 he received the Herbert Bloch Award of the American Society of Criminology for outstanding service to the society and profession. Though he has always had a love for history, *Dead for Good* is a departure from his usual subject matter and audience.